Hired Hands or Human Resources?

Hired Hands *or* Human Resources?

CASE STUDIES OF HRM PROGRAMS AND

PRACTICES IN EARLY AMERICAN INDUSTRY

Bruce E. Kaufman

ILR Press

AN IMPRINT OF

Cornell University Press *Ithaca and London*

First published 2010 by Cornell University Press

Printed in the United States of America

Library of Congress Cataloging-in-Publication Data

Kaufman, Bruce E.
   Hired hands or human resources? : case studies of HRM programs
and practices in early American industry / Bruce E. Kaufman.
       p.   cm.
   Companion volume to: Managing the human factor.
   Includes bibliographical references and index.
   ISBN 978-0-8014-4830-0 (cloth : alk. paper)
   1. Personnel management—United States—History—19th
century—Case studies.   2. Personnel management—United States—
 History—20th century—Case studies.   I. Kaufman, Bruce E.
 Managing the human factor.   II. Title.
   HF5549.2.U5K375 2010
   658.300973—dc22   2009023927

Cornell University Press strives to use environmentally responsible suppliers and materials to the fullest extent possible in the publishing of its books. Such materials include vegetable-based, low-VOC inks and acid-free papers that are recycled, totally chlorine-free, or partly composed of nonwood fibers. For further information, visit our website at www.cornellpress .cornell.edu.

Cloth printing   10 9 8 7 6 5 4 3 2 1

Dedicated to Clarence J. Hicks,
the "Dean of Industrial Relations Men"
and
Chairman of the Board, Industrial Relations Counselors, Inc.

Contents

Preface

This is the second book of a two-volume set on the early history of human resource management (HRM) in American industry. The time frame starts in the mid-1870s and extends to the very early 1930s—the beginning of industrialization and an emergent *labor problem* in the former case and onset of the Great Depression and collapse of the welfare capitalism movement in the latter.

Volume 1, published by Cornell University Press in 2008, is titled *Managing the Human Factor*.[1] It presents an in-depth and wide-ranging review of the major people, ideas, trends, and developments that led to the emergence of human resource management in these years as a formally recognized and constituted area of management practice in business firms and field of study in universities. During this historical era, however, people did not use the HRM label to describe the activity of labor management, but two others: *personnel management* (PM) and *industrial relations* (IR). *Managing the Human Factor* gives the "big picture" view of the early development of PM/IR (hereafter abbreviated PIR). Identified and described there are the fourteen roots of PIR (among them, for example, the industrial welfare, scientific management, and industrial democracy movements), a detailed description of the pioneering people who helped create PIR shortly after World War I, and a lengthy examination of the development of PIR in the welfare capitalism era of the 1920s and its implosion in the early years of the Great Depression.

This second volume complements and extends the first with a detailed set of fifteen case studies of HRM over the same time period. The volume is broken into two parts. Part 1 covers the years up to the formal birth of PIR in the World War I period; part 2 covers the period during the 1920s. Together, these case studies provide what is, to the best of my knowledge, the most extensive and detailed portrait of the organization, practice, policies and methods of HRM before the New Deal.

Part 1 includes nine case studies. Seven cover individual firms, one primarily focuses on a particular firm (the Burlington Railroad) but includes several other firms in the industry, and one—due to absence of firm-level data—covers an entire industry (coal mining). These case studies are assembled from a wide variety of books, dissertations, archival records, academic journal articles, government reports, and magazine and newspaper accounts published both then and now. All are in the public domain, but none have heretofore been used to create tightly focused case studies of HRM. Together, they provide an unparalleled look at what I call the "traditional" or "hired-hand" approach to labor management and employee relations.

Part 2 includes six firm-level case studies, with the first staring in 1923 and the last ending in 1930. The 1920s is the era of welfare capitalism—the period when PIR became consolidated after its birth in the World War I years and developed into a formidable operation in leading corporations. The heart of the new HRM model of the 1920s was a shift from the traditional hired-hand approach to labor management to a new "human resource" approach. However, only two of the six firms in our case studies (an oil firm and steel firm) extensively adopted this new model and occupied a position in the first tier of welfare capitalist firms. A third firm occupied a middle ground, while three others practiced labor management and employee relations in largely traditional ways. The result is a highly diverse but instructive contrast.

The six case studies of part 2 come from confidential consulting reports obtained from the archives of Industrial Relations Counselors Inc. (IRC). IRC is located in New York City, was incorporated in 1926 as a nonprofit research, training, and consulting organization, and was created and largely funded by John D. Rockefeller Jr. Three of the reports used in this book were prepared by the industrial relations staff of IRC's predecessor organization, the law firm of Curtis, Fosdick, and Belknap. As described in chapter 7, IRC was widely regarded in the pre–World War II era as the nation's foremost HRM consulting firm, as well as a leader in HRM research (primarily pensions, benefits, and wage-payment systems) and managerial training. The consulting reports, heretofore unavailable to any researcher, undoubtedly provide the most detailed portrait in existence of what HRM programs at American companies looked like in the 1920s.

In the concluding chapter of this book I synthesize from these case studies six "insights and lessons learned" regarding the development of early HRM in American industry. The most important of these is that labor is human and not a commodity—a lesson and insight that was more than any other the foundation stone for PIR as both an intellectual research area and vocational area of business practice.

In closing, I wish to make several acknowledgments and expressions of gratitude. First and foremost my thanks go to Industrial Relations Counselors, Inc. and, in particular, Robert Freedman, president and chief executive officer of Organization Resources Counselors (ORC) Worldwide; Richard Beaumont, former chairman of ORC and IRC research director, and Roy Helfgott, former IRC president. Without their cooperation and trust this volume would not have been possible. More than that, if I had not developed the relationship with IRC that I have had over the last decade I never would have fully discovered and appreciated the immense contribution that John D. Rockefeller Jr. and his associates such as Clarence J. Hicks made to the field and practice of industrial relations and human resource management.

I also wish to thank Joy Correge at ORC Worldwide for reviewing the manuscript and offering very useful counsel, and to Sharon Lombardo at ORC Worldwide for her much appreciated archival and library guidance.

Thanks are also due to my colleague Barry Hirsch, holder of the W. J. Usery Chair of the American Workplace at Georgia State University, for a generous financial contribution that made acquisition and printing of the photographs in this book possible.

A thank you also goes to Fran Benson at Cornell University Press for agreeing to take on yet another one of my projects and for helping guide it to a successful outcome. Also appreciated are Brian Bendlin, Susan Specter, and Emily Zoss for helping in all phases of manuscript preparation, and George Whipple for expertly putting together the photo section.

I end with a thank you to my wife Diane and children Lauren and Andrew for sharing our time together so I can work on my other life's love—exploring the world of economics, industrial relations, and human resource management and writing up what I discover in books.

Hired Hands or Human Resources?

1

Early Human Resource Management

Context and History

This book is the second volume of a two-volume set on the roots, birth, and early development of the human resource management (HRM) function in American industry. The story starts in the mid-1870s with the emergence of large-scale industry, an urban-based wage-earning workforce, and a growing *labor problem*, heralded by the Great Railway Strike of 1877; it ends in 1932 at the nadir of the Great Depression when the nonunion welfare capitalism movement of the 1920s is in tatters and its New Deal union replacement lies just over the horizon. Between these two end points lies a remarkable half-century evolution in human resource management philosophy and practice that in cumulative form and effect can only be described as a transformation.

The first volume, *Managing the Human Factor: The Early History of Human Resource Management in American Industry* (2008),[1] presents the "big picture" side of the story with a broad historical account of the people, events, and ideas that together led a small band of innovative, pioneering companies to transform the way they managed their employees. Parading through these pages are the main forces and actors that revolutionized labor management a century ago.[2] Counted in the former, for example, are the welfare, safety, and scientific management movements; the rise of trade unionism and labor law; World War I and the industrial democracy movement, and the invention of the assembly line and mass production; counted among the latter are such "big names" as Henry Towne, George Patterson, Frederick Taylor, Samuel Gompers, John D. Rockefeller Jr., Meyer Bloomfield, Walter Dill Scott, John Commons, Henry Ford, and Clarence Hicks. At the height of the HRM transformation in the late 1920s, labor management at leading companies in the United States had much greater similarity to what was to follow a half century later (in the 1980s) than to what had already passed a half century earlier (in the 1880s).

This volume complements the first by filling in and rounding out the story with a set of fifteen detailed case studies of early HRM programs and practices in individual companies and industries. The time span is exactly the same as the first volume—the mid-1870s to the early 1930s—but is broken into two distinct parts. Part 1 is devoted to nine case studies that extend through the World War I years, and the six case studies of part 2 cover the 1920s and early 1930s.

This division reflects both historical developments and data availability. Regarding the former, the World War I years effectively separate two alternative regimes of labor management. Prior to the war, nearly all firms utilized the traditional HRM model that relied on a decentralized, informalized, and externalized approach to labor management and frequently treated labor as a "hired hand"; after the war an influential minority of firms pioneered a new and distinctly modern HRM model and transitioned to a "human resource" view of labor.[3] The modern model of labor management featured a centralized personnel management or industrial relations (PM/IR, hereafter abbreviated PIR) department, formal PIR policies and procedures administered by specialized middle managers and staff, and significant replacement of the external labor market forces of supply and demand with bureaucratic administration in an internal labor market. Although the shift from traditional to modern HRM in reality stretched over a number of years, and at many companies never took place at all even by the end of the 1920s, the World War I dividing line nonetheless captures the reality that here occurred a major inflection point in labor management philosophy and practice.

Practical issues of data availability also mandate this two-part division. The nine case studies in part 1 are drawn from diverse sources in the public domain, including books, articles, and government reports written a century ago about labor management practices at these companies and also numerous more contemporary academic works, including unpublished doctoral dissertations and a rather far-flung, cross-disciplinary journal literature. Although all of this material is publicly available and much has been previously published by scholars in bits and pieces, it is nonetheless for the first time drawn together here to form the in-depth case studies you are about to read. The objective with these case studies is to provide a detailed view of how firms—sometimes very large firms with thousands of employees—were able in the late nineteenth and early twentieth centuries to manage their workforces with no organized or formalized HRM system and, indeed, why they thought such a system was "best practice" in light of the conditions and constraints they faced. Also an objective is to examine the strengths and weaknesses of the traditional system, why firms adopted different strategic versions of the traditional model, and why some began to innovate with more modern management methods.

The six case studies in part 2 are of an entirely different character. They are drawn from confidential consulting reports prepared for corporate clients by the industrial relations staff of the New York City law firm Curtis, Fosdick, and Belknap (CFB), which in 1926 was spun off and incorporated as the nonprofit consulting firm Industrial Relations Counselors, Inc. (IRC). Both the CFB labor section and the IRC were closely connected to and financially supported by John D. Rockefeller Jr., who a decade earlier had become greatly interested and involved with promoting more progressive labor management practices.

The consulting reports prepared by IRC were the product of a multiperson investigative team that spent several months doing on-site interviews and fact finding. The completed reports, often of two hundred or more pages and resembling a PhD dissertation, provide an A-to-Z overview and description of each client company's personnel and industrial relations system. Each report starts with a description of the company's labor policy (in certain respects, that era's equivalent of an HRM strategy statement), outlines the organization and structure of the labor management function, and then reviews each area of PIR practice. For this volume I condense each report into a fifteen- to thirty-page summary. These consulting reports, heretofore unavailable to any researcher, provide an unmatched data source on how HRM was practiced at companies both on the leading and trailing edge of labor management in the 1920s.

Case study evidence on the organization and practice of HRM at different companies before the 1930s is rare but available. The largest comparative study of PIR practices across firms is provided by Walter Licht in *Getting Work: Philadelphia, 1840–1950*.[4] Licht uses company archival records from a dozen or more Philadelphia companies to sketch a portrait of the diverse personnel programs and practices that existed among these firms, often with information going back to 1900 and even before. Also notable is Sanford Jacoby's *Modern Manors: Welfare Capitalism Since the New Deal*. Although the bulk of analysis is for the 1930s and afterward, Jacoby's case studies of PIR policies and practices at Kodak, Sears, and TRW begin in the 1920s and provide illuminating insight on the era of welfare capitalism.[5] Then, of course, there are also a number of individual firms' case studies, although often written as part of a larger corporate history or analysis of the unionization and/or deunionization of a company or industry.[6] I draw on many of these for this volume.

With due recognition to what has come before, I think it is nonetheless accurate to say that the case studies of parts 1 and 2 in this volume provide what is to now the most comprehensive and in-depth portrait of HRM practices at American companies during this particular historical era. Besides being of considerable interest in their own right, these case studies provide real life "data points" to illustrate the broader trends and developments highlighted in *Managing the Human Factor*.

The Case Studies in Historical Context

The full value of these case studies only emerges if they are first grounded in a larger historical context, thus helping to situate them in terms of the broader flow of labor management events and developments. The simplest way to proceed would be to tell readers, "See the first volume, *Managing the Human Factor*." But this book is over three hundred pages in length and may not be available or of interest to all readers. So, before proceeding further I provide here a very brief and stylized thumbnail sketch of the key parts of the story.[7]

The latter part of the nineteenth century saw the emergence and growth of the modern corporation; large-scale capital-intensive railroads, factories, and mills; and a large urban-based wage-earning blue-collar workforce. Some industrial plants had over 5,000 employees at one site, while megamergers such as the one forming United States Steel brought together under one corporate roof 100,000 or more wage earners.

At first, employers tried to manage their new operations in traditional ways. This meant a highly externalized, informalized and decentralized system of labor management—externalized in that the firm relied mostly on external labor markets and the competitive forces of supply and demand to provide, price, and motivate labor; informalized in that labor management was conducted without benefit of any written policy, formal practices, or professional staff; and decentralized in that top company managers, after establishing the central elements of the labor policy, delegated most operational aspects to plant superintendents, foremen, and gang bosses. Sometimes companies took a paternalistic interest in their employees and treated them with some degree of consideration and respect, sensing that this was not only the ethical but also the profitable thing to do. Most often, however, companies took an autocratic, hard-fisted and "buy low/sell high" approach to labor in which they paid as little as possible, gave minimal attention to working conditions and employees' needs, used threats and harsh language to extract maximum work effort, and administered all aspect of labor management with unilateral and unquestioned authority. Appropriately enough, this method of managing employees was called the "drive system," and closely resembled the way cowboys in the latter 1800s drove a herd of cattle to market. Of course, workers are not cattle, but employers could more or less treat them as such because of the huge inflow of unskilled and often illiterate immigrant labor from southern and eastern Europe, frequent periods of recession with large-scale unemployment and crowds of desperate job seekers before the plant gates, and an indifferent public attitude toward the plight of the less fortunate. Personnel and industrial relations departments had no role in this model and, accordingly, could not be found in any American company beyond a one-room hiring office.

Part of the power of case studies is that they help give real world context and feel to the subject under discussion. Toward this end I point the reader to the three "mini" case studies provided in the accompanying boxed examples. They graphically illustrate the generalizations made above regarding the dominating role of supply and demand, the primitive and harsh management of labor, and the stark dangers and inhumanity of work life facing most employees before World War I.

The first, written by economists John Commons and William Leiserson, describes the labor market in Pittsburgh around 1908. Here is a close approximation to the economist's model of pure competition—a world ruled by supply and demand, where labor is bought and sold in highly competitive conditions, workers have extraordinarily high rates of turnover and mobility, and wages and employment ride the up-and-down escalators of the business cycle.

Demand and Supply Rule the Pittsburgh Labor Market

There is everywhere the great ocean of common labor—unprivileged, competitive, equalized—making up from two-fifths to one-half the total. Above this expanse, here and there for a time, appear like waves and wavelets those whom skill, physique, talent, trade unionism, or municipal favoritism lift above the fluid mass. Restless, unstable, up, down, and on, like the ocean, so is the labor of Pittsburgh. From the employment bureau of a huge machine works we learned that in a single year of continued prosperity, 1906, they hired 12,000 men and women to keep up a force of 10,000. And this restless "go and come" is only slightly less with the skilled than with the unskilled, for the foreman of the tool room in the same establishment estimated that to keep up his required force of 100 men possessing the highest grades of mechanical skill, he hired 100 men during the year. The superintendent of a mining property, lacking, however, the exact records of our machine-shop bureau, insisted on the amazing figure of 5,000 hired during the year to maintain a force of 1,000. The largest operator of the District thought this was too high, but said that hiring 2,000 in a year to fill 1,000 permanent positions was not an exaggerated index of labor's mobility in the Pittsburgh District.

What are we to infer? By minute specialization of jobs, by army-like organization, by keeping together a staff of highly paid regulars at the top, the industries of Pittsburgh are independent of the rank and file. Two-thirds of the steel workers are unskilled immigrants, and thousands of them in their ignorance of English are as uncomprehending as horses, if we may judge by the kind of Gee! Whoa! and gesture commands that suffice for directing them. Specialization, elimination of skill, payment by the piece or premium, speeding up—these are inherently the aims of the Pittsburgh business men, and the methods that turn out tons of shapes for the skilful workers of other cities to put into finished products. Without its marvelous framework of organization, eliminating dependence on personality in the masses and thereby rendering personality more indispensable in the captains, it would be impossible for Pittsburgh to convert its stream of labor into the most productive labor power known in modern industry. Large rewards for brains—to overseers, managers, foremen, bosses, "pushers," and gang leaders in descending scale; heavy pressure toward equality of wages among the restless, changing, competitive rank and file—these are the principles which Pittsburgh applies to the distribution of wealth in the production of which she holds supremacy.

These contrasts in the economic scale are scarcely more violent than the ups and downs in the common fortunes of the District. Andrew Carnegie has said of the iron and steel industry that it is a case of either Prince or Pauper. Certainly no staple manufactured article responds so violently to the prosperity and depression of the country as pig iron. So it is with all the industries of Pittsburgh that follow in the train of King Iron. When the Pittsburgh Survey began its work in September, 1907, the Prince was on his throne—full years of prosperity and glorious optimism had been his. Long before September, 1908, Carnegie's Pauper walked the streets. From every type and class of labor came the report of a year with only half, or three-fourths, or even one-third of the time employed. Hardly another city in the country was hit as hard or stunned as long by the panic as was Pittsburgh. The overwork in 1907 was the out-of-work in 1908.

Excerpted from John R. Commons and William Leiserson, "Wage Earners of Pittsburgh," in *Wage Earning Pittsburgh: The Pittsburgh Survey* (New York: Survey Associates, 1914), 116–18.

The second and third mini case studies transition from the external labor market to the "internal" labor market—that is, the management and treatment of labor inside the firm. Here we come face-to-face with horrendous working conditions, callous and arbitrary treatment of labor, and tremendous waste and inefficiency. These case studies are from autobiographies written by two HRM pioneers, Cyrus Ching and Don Lescohier, and recount their experiences and impressions when they entered the blue-collar work world as young men around 1900. (Note that Ching and Lescohier had above-average education and good English skills and thus started a notch or two above the position of unskilled immigrant labor.) Ching and Lescohier went on to become two well-recognized names in the personnel and industrial relations movement of the 1920s—Ching as head of industrial relations at the U.S. Rubber Company and Lescohier as one of the first professors to teach personnel management at an American university, the University of Wisconsin. The three case studies together give a dramatic if depressing sense for what HRM and employment were like in the period before World War I.

Recollections of Cyrus Ching and Don Lescohier on Work and Labor Management before World War I

CHING

It is hard now to tell people what things were like when I arrived in Boston in 1900 without my being accused of dreaming. There were no labor-management relations as we know them. A Socialist, Eugene V. Debs, was, in the language of the industrial leaders, still "trying to stir up trouble". The most respected man in the union ranks was Samuel Gompers. But even Mr. Gompers divided labor into two classes, the skilled and the unskilled. And, outside of Mr. Gompers' own cigar-makers, some on the railroads, in the coal mines, the printing and building trades, there were comparatively few union members.

It was a period when the law of supply and demand governed labor relations. And the supply of labor, at least around Boston, ran ahead of demand, with the still heavy flow of Europeans and Canadians into the country. Most of these immigrants were accustomed to little or nothing and they were willing to work for just that. They were handicapped by differences in language and customs. I was one of the "immigrants", but I was fortunate in having more of a community of interest with Americans than, for example, even some of my fellow Canadians, who spoke only French.

It wasn't long before I landed a job as a motorman with the Boston Elevated. The hours were long. The pay was something short of handsome. I was on the so-called "extra list", and my average pay for the first few months was $7 per week.

My experience in the early 1900's with the working man and management was, of course, limited to the situation on the Boston Elevated Railroad. But I have learned since that conditions of employment on the Elevated were little different from those in most big companies of the country, regardless of the type of business in which they were engaged. The history of employee-employer relations of the company for which I worked was typical of national relations between management and the workers.

The working man, at the time my story begins, and for years afterward, was subjected to long hours, a bare subsistence wage, and terribly bad and hazardous working conditions. The average employer regarded his employees, particularly in the lower ranks, with a sort of callous indifference to their plight which today almost defies comprehension. This was especially true of the larger companies. There were exceptions in the smaller outfits where the employers and their workers grew up together and enjoyed a closer relationship. The individual employee of the larger companies didn't count for much. Those were the days before the United States Supreme Court ruled that a worker was not a commodity, but a human being and must be treated as such. The worker was looked upon as just part of the machinery which kept the company operating and he was treated like that.

If he were injured or totally incapacitated, even in line of duty, he was cast aside and replaced like a broken piece of equipment. There was no workmen's compensation to tide him over. And rare was the employer who gave a tinker's damn what happened to him. If a man was injured on the job, the only remedy he had at that time was recourse to the common law, and when such action was taken, it was met by the "contributory negligence" defense. This defense was, in most cases, very effective in preventing any very large awards being made.

The main objectives of management in those days were to keep the surplus of manpower high and wages low. Even worse conditions in many foreign countries, coupled with an immigration policy in the United States which placed virtually no restriction on entry into the country, permitted managements to realize their objectives. There was a steady flow of manpower for the mills, factories and railroads from other countries. Most people today do not realize that these conditions existed in this country; they were so much superior to the conditions existing in many of the countries from which immigrants came that most people were happy and well satisfied with their changed status in the new country.

Employers and politicians alike didn't have the concept then of the worker and the consumer being identical. They didn't realize, as most of us do now, that if you improve the lot of the working people, you increase the business of the country and improve the lot of all people. In 1914, when Henry Ford established the $5-a-day minimum wage, it was considered by most people to be extreme radicalism, but it was the first time that the idea of the worker as a consumer began to take hold. There was no recognition or practice of the social sciences as we know them. The immigrants were brought in and dumped. Nothing was done to Americanize them, and many who spoke foreign tongues never learned English. They lived apart from old-line Americans, most of whom were on management's side. This situation prevailed in most New England communities, and also in many other parts of the country.

The social awakening began only after this country became involved in World War I. And it resulted from an economic situation, rather than an improvement of conscience of employers. The war stopped importation of labor and quickened the wheels of American industry. The demand for labor increased. Soon the demand exceeded the supply. In order to retain their workers, employers were forced to raise wages, reduce hours and improve working conditions. This period really marked the beginning of the development of labor relations as we know the subject.

LESCOHIER

Working in factories during the 1890's, or indeed, up to the time of the first World War, was very different from working in factories today. In the first place, the method of hiring the unorganized was for foremen to come to the front gate of the plant around 7 a.m., look over the gang of men congregated outside the gate, pick out men he knew or thought he wanted, or motion to this man or that, without interviewing, to come through the plant gate. It was a good deal like a butcher picking out particular animals from a herd.

When he got as many as he wanted he led them to his department, assigned them their work, with perhaps momentary interviews to find out whether they had any experience in the kinds of work in his department. Ordinarily a man hired in this process did not know what his pay would be until he got his wages on payday. If you asked the foreman that question when you were hired you would, ordinarily, be shown the gate. Complete submission of unorganized workers to the company was the expectation of the Detroit Stove Works. Like hundreds of other common laborers I had heard the foreman say to me: "Put on your coat," which meant that you were fired. You did as he said.

In the basement of the building where I worked at that time was a grinding room. The noise was terrific and the grinding room got its full share of dust. The grinding room was partly below the ground level. It had a row of windows in the outside wall but they had not been cleaned within the memory of man. The only artificial light was old fashioned gas lights, one above and between each pair of grinding wheels. It was in almost complete darkness—say dark twilight—since the gas flames gave so little light. You had to walk slowly and keep a hand out in front of you to avoid falling over a truck handle or other obstruction. One man, I remember, broke his leg by falling over a truck handle in that dark passage.

The employees in that place were all old men, not strong enough any more to do the harder work of most common laborers. They got $1.25 for ten hours' work in that department.

The stock room where I worked when I was sixteen was a corner partitioned off from the metal polishing department. On the side toward the polishing room were large removable windows which allowed light to come through the stock room to the polishers—who were skilled, union men. The windows also let in the south and southwest summer breezes. The polishers asked to have the windows opened each day during the summer so they could feel those breezes. The company refused. They said some one might climb through and steal things out of the stock room. The polishers went out on strike to force the company to remove the windows. When one union struck, they all did. So a plant with 2500 employees was tied up for three days over this simple grievance. But striking was the only grievance procedure the men had and only the union men had that [700–800 of the skilled workers were in unions; the remainder were unrepresented].

Another case: the only drinking water the company furnished was in large, hexagonal barrels elevated above the floor. Into the barrel they put two or three cakes of river ice from a river receiving the sewage of the quarter of a million people living in Detroit. They attached a couple of tin cups, on chains, to the barrel. At the barrel nearest the stock room the cups got rusty. The polishers asked for some new cups—price 5c each at retail. The company refused. Another three day strike, over a 10c capital investment. Such strikes occurred again and again throughout the year.

There were a lot of accidents in the stove works—no fatal ones that I know of. But there were emery wheel burns, bad cuts often three or four inches long from the edges of sheets of steel, burns from hot iron in the foundry, loss of fingers or toes. At sixteen years of age one of my duties was first aid for the injured. No one gave me any instructions and the medical supplies consisted of a bottle of oil, some unsterilized waste, and some unsterilized cotton bandage cloth, kept in an ordinary cupboard. I wrapped many bad injuries, such as a loss of a finger, bad cuts, and burns. So for $7.50 a week I was the medical department of the company in addition to my other duties.

There were no flush toilets in the shops at all—at least none for the shop workmen. The arrangements provided were so primitive that I am not going to describe them.

Excerpted from Cyrus S. Ching, *Review and Reflection: A Half-Century of Labor Relations* (Garden City, New York: B. C. Forbes and Sons, 1953), 3–7; and Don Lescohier, *Don Divance Lescohier: My Story for the First Seventy-Five Years* (Madison, WI: Art Brush Creations, 1960), 32–34.

As described in *Managing the Human Factor*, the traditional system of labor management had distinct benefits and costs. On the benefit side, for example, it was easy and familiar to implement, entailed very low direct and overhead cost to operate, kept the administration of HRM flexible and in the hands of the managers closest to production, and preserved maximum employer control and power over the workforce. It also seemed to have good strategic fit with the conditions of the time, such as the flood of unskilled immigrant labor, the ongoing shift from skilled craft-type jobs to unskilled or semiskilled machine and assembly jobs, and the freedom enjoyed by most firms from the constraints imposed by unions and labor laws. But there were also downsides. Lack of standards, policies, and administrative staff meant HRM at the shop floor level was often ineptly or haphazardly performed, gave rise to large and not-very-rational differences among workers in basics such as pay rates, work assignments, promotions and terminations, and often contained a pronounced element of arbitrariness and favoritism. Further, the traditional labor management system tended to create a dispirited, low skill, uncooperative, and sometimes rebellious workforce that frequently quit, slacked on the job whenever possible, and looked to unions for protection and advancement.

From these conditions was born a new approach to managing employees. This approach did not appear overnight but took roughly four decades to evolve and only emerged in full form in the decade after World War I. The two most common names given to this new approach were *personnel*

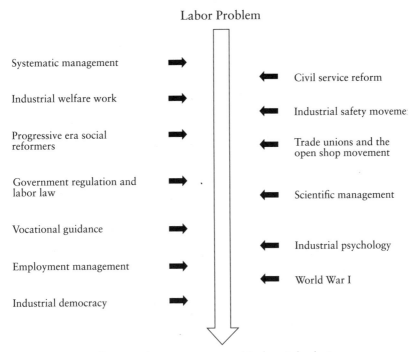

Labor Problem

Systematic management ➡

              ⬅ Civil service reform

Industrial welfare work ➡

              ⬅ Industrial safety moveme:

Progressive era social reformers ➡

              ⬅ Trade unions and the open shop movement

Government regulation and labor law ➡

              ⬅ Scientific management

Vocational guidance ➡

              ⬅ Industrial psychology

Employment management ➡

              ⬅ World War I

Industrial democracy ➡

Personnel management and industrial relations

Fig. 1. Events and ideas contributing to the birth of PIR.

management and *industrial relations.* Figure 1, taken from *Managing the Human Factor,* depicts the numerous different events, ideas, and developments spanning the 1880–1920 period that led to the creation of the new PIR function in American industry.

The beginning point of the story is the *Labor Problem,* denoted at that time with uppercase letters. Given the management methods and work conditions described above, the last two decades of the nineteenth century witnessed growing production problems on the shop floor and rise of tensions and hostilities between the bosses and bossed. The rise in workplace tensions was accompanied by the emergence of violent strikes, an aggressive trade union movement, and a plethora of radical political parties bent on overthrow of capitalism and the wage system. The marked deterioration of management-labor relations and rise of anticapitalist agitation became so threatening that many people at the turn of the century viewed the Labor Problem as the number one domestic challenge facing American society.

Companies, workers, governments and interest groups of that period adopted different strategies to the challenge of improving the management of labor and containing the Labor Problem. The thirteen most important streams of development are depicted in figure 1. Many companies chose to stay with the traditional model and deal with their problems with tried-and-true methods, such as closer supervision and harsher discipline. A number of others, however, began to experiment and innovate—sometimes motivated by the attraction of greater efficiency and profit or a deep-felt sense of moral responsibility and other times pressured by the threat of unions, government legislation, adverse public opinion, and a tight labor market. For example, the systematic management movement—and later the scientific management movement—sought to improve efficiency and gain workers' cooperation through new forms of incentive pay and gain sharing, while socially minded employers adopted new welfare programs and, later, employee representation plans. Also of significance were other developments, such as the safety movement, introduction of civil service reforms in government, and development of industrial psychology. Pushing employers to do better in the way they treated workers were other forces, such as an expanding trade union movement, agitation for laws to protect workers (e.g., child labor, overtime hours, minimum wages, accident insurance), the disturbing evidence presented to the public by social reform investigators and muckraking journalists, and the labor shortages caused by the World War I boom economy.

The companies that chose to stay with some variant of the traditional model continued to view labor as *hired hands*. In this model, labor is a commodity-like factor input that yields profit by utilizing it to get the maximum output for the least amount of pay the market allows. Further, labor is treated as a short-run expense and variable cost to be discharged when no longer needed; given no special consideration or position in the organization; pressured by economic insecurity, administrative control devices (e.g., time clocks), and tough bossing to perform; and instructed to follow orders and work hard while managers take care of running the business and thinking about the future. On the other end of the spectrum, the leading edge of innovative and progressive employers were in the process of developing a largely new and transformative approach that viewed labor as a *human resource*. In this model, labor is regarded as a distinctly human input that yields greater productivity and profit when treated with fairness and respect, as a longer-term member or even "junior partner" in the enterprise, and a valuable "human capital" asset on the firm's balance sheet. Instead of a "buy low/sell high" approach to labor, the firm seeks greater cooperation and improved citizenship behavior from workers by offering good conditions, reasonable security, and opportunities for advancement; making significant investments in selection, training, and workforce governance; providing opportunities for participation and promotion; and tying pay and benefit rewards to good performance and organizational objectives.

Leading up to World War I, the new "human resource" labor management system developed incrementally and in a somewhat ad hoc and piecemeal fashion among a number of diverse companies. These firms were innovative along a number of lines: some started industrial safety programs, while others created employee welfare departments, industrial training programs, and shop councils; likewise, some adopted gain-sharing and profit-sharing plans while others created labor hiring offices and implemented the first rudimentary employee testing and selection programs. It was only in the years 1917–19, during the height of the World War I–induced economic boom, union surge, and Bolshevist hysteria, that these disparate elements were for the first time brought together in an integrated whole, adopted by leading companies, and given an official name and place in the management hierarchy. The new HRM strategy went under different names but, as noted earlier, the most common were *personnel management* and *industrial relations*. Exemplifying this new approach, in turn, was the creation of new functional PIR departments in firms to organize and administer the management of labor. The organizational details and responsibilities varied from company to company, but typically these new personnel/industrial relations departments put under centralized management control areas such as hiring/recruitment, training, benefits, payroll, safety and health, employee representation, employee magazines, and a plethora of other labor-related matters. Many used these PIR departments to help implement only one or several elements of the human resource approach to labor; a few pioneers, however, endeavored to put in place a relatively integrated and fully developed version.

The coming of age of the new management philosophy and practice of PIR was formally marked by the founding of the Industrial Relations Association of America in 1920 (IRAA), itself formed from the National Employment Managers Association created in 1918. The IRAA had over 2,000 members, most of who were in some way involved in company-level labor management, and the association published a monthly magazine titled *Personnel*. Also in 1920, the University of Wisconsin, under the leadership of economist John Commons, started the first academic program (a "concentration") in industrial relations, while business consultants and teachers Ordway Tead and Henry Metcalf published the first college PIR textbook, *Personnel Administration: Its Principles and Practice*.[8]

When the crisis years of World War I passed, so did a significant part of the short-term impetus that had propelled hundreds of companies to create PIR departments and give labor and labor management more careful handling and attention. The PIR movement, which in full-fledged form had extended to perhaps 10 percent of the industrial workforce in the war years, suffered significant retrenchment in the next few years, particularly under the weight of the short but severe business depression of 1920–21. Once prosperity returned, however, so did the growth in PIR in terms of both the firms adopting it and the breadth and depth of programs and practices put in place. By the late 1920s, one-third or more of the largest-size plants had a centralized personnel or industrial relations department, while 10–15 percent of the entire nonagricultural workforce was employed in facilities with up-and-running PIR programs.[9] Many other firms adopted individual PIR practices, such as various employee benefits or a training program, although they stopped short of a centralized PIR function.

As these statistics suggest, most small- to medium-size companies in the 1920s, and a surprising number of large-size firms as well, remained largely outside the PIR movement and, accordingly, continued to manage employees with some variant of the traditional informal, decentralized, and externalized labor management system. A relatively small but highly visible group of American companies, on the other hand, pushed forward in the development of the PIR management model and by the end of the decade had put in place a truly different system from what had existed three and four decades earlier. Some of these companies used the *personnel* term while others used the *industrial relations* term. Although to some extent these labels were at the time employed interchangeably, the *industrial relations* term was nonetheless widely regarded as signifying a broader, more strategic, and liberal approach to labor management, with particular emphasis on joint employer-employee relations and some form of collective employee voice (generally of a nonunion variety), while the *personnel* term gave greater emphasis to management as the principal actor and connoted a more individualistic philosophy and sociopsychological approach to dealing with employees.[10]

The leading PIR companies in the 1920s formed the core of what is now known as the welfare capitalism movement.[11] Well-known examples include AT&T, DuPont, General Electric, Goodyear, International Harvester, Leeds and Northrup, Standard Oil of New Jersey (SONJ), U.S. Rubber, and Westinghouse. The epicenter of the welfare capitalism/PIR movement were the companies in the Rockefeller-connected and financed Special Conference Committee (SCC), including many of those companies just named. The flagship company of the Welfare Capitalism movement, in turn, was SONJ, and the executive in charge of the industrial relations function there, Clarence Hicks, was arguably the most influential PIR executive in the country. Illustrative of his position, Hicks served as the head of the SCC; he also later served as chairman of the board of IRC.[12]

The welfare capitalist companies made a strategic decision to obtain competitive advantage through a high-road, mutual-gain, cooperative and nonunion model of labor management. Employees were no longer commodities to be regularly hired and fired but human resources to be cultivated and developed for a long-term employment relationship. The end product was the partial to substantial replacement of the external labor market with a management-created and operated internal labor market where supply and demand, informalism, and decentralization were replaced with an administrative bureaucracy, formal employment policies and practices, and centralized management control. In this model, the PIR function comes to play a very important role and, indeed, in some cases played a strategic influence in company business plans and operations. As documented later in this book, the PIR programs and policies established in the leading welfare capitalist firms of the 1920s entailed large costs to create and operate, but nonetheless these companies calculated that the extra revenue from cost savings from reduced turnover and training and productivity gains from greater cooperation and higher employee morale more than made up the difference.

Although it is useful to generalize about "traditional" and "modern" labor management firms in the 1920s, the reality is more complex and nuanced. Firms of this period were not actually bunched into two distinct and largely separate groups, one traditional and the other modern, but were instead arrayed along a more or less bell-shaped frequency distribution of HRM practices, but with a notably skewed right-hand tail. At the bottom end of the distribution were numerous small- and medium-size firms that not only had no PIR department but also a near-complete lack of any type of formalized or systematized HRM practice. The largest clustering of firms in the distribution also had no PIR department but did use one or several HRM tools, such as a hiring office, written individual employment records, company safety program, or employee lunchroom. From this point the HRM frequency distribution rapidly declined (thinned out), reflecting the fact that only 20–30 percent of medium- to large-size firms had any kind of centralized PIR function, let alone the full panoply of HRM practices associated with the large welfare capitalist firms. Toward the end of the right-hand tail of the HRM distribution in the 1920s were the 50 to 100 or so firms that implemented something close to the full welfare capitalism HRM model, exemplified by the SCC companies.

In the 1920s hundreds of foreign businessmen, government officials, academics, and trade unionists traveled to America to see firsthand the economic miracle and gushing of prosperity unleashed by Taylorism, Fordism, and welfare capitalism. This same scene was repeated in the 1980s when planeloads of Americans and Europeans traveled to Japan to see that country's economic renaissance. What did the visitors to America see, and what did they return home thinking? One answer is provided in Hugh Adam's short book *An Australian Looks at America* (1928). Adam was associate editor of the *Herald* newspaper in Melbourne, Australia, and along with a large delegation of other Australians visited over ninety industrial facilities in the United States. Here as another mini case study are several excerpts from his book that provide a glimpse of the high end of the HRM frequency distribution:

An Australian's Evaluation of American Industry and Welfare Capitalism

It is impossible to study American industry without being impressed above everything else by the enthusiasm and genius of its management. Management has become a definite profession, almost an exact science, taught in the great universities just as thoroughly as the professions of medicine or law. . . . In America, the efficiency, the smooth running of every factor in industry, is regarded as a responsibility of hired management. This is best illustrated by the attitude of management towards the efficiency of labor. . . . If the workers in an American factory are inefficient, if their production per head is lower than that of workers in other factories, no one dreams of putting the blame on the workers. It is the management that must be at fault. . . .

In the American mass-production industries there is no unionism. There are never any strikes. Wages are good and almost everything that a worker needs to be done for him is done for him. How has this happy situation been reached? An essential condition of mass production is that each individual worker shall place himself unreservedly in the hands of the management, The controllers of these great industries recognize . . . that when once unskilled labor becomes organized . . . their days of trouble begin . . . So they have deliberately gone out of their way to do part of the work of the unions. I give them all credit for the strategy. . . . With good grace they have given these advantages to their workers, and also others that are new. . . . Labour leaders frankly admit they cannot organize these workers.

I found conditions in the Chicago plant of the Western Electric Company that were so much above the general run of factory conditions. . . . There, surely, was the highest development of American industry on the lines of factory organization, mass production, piece-work, and care of the welfare of the employees. I could not help being deeply impressed by the beauty, the orderliness, and the smoothness of modern industry conducted on a scale unimagined in Australia, and by the comfort and well-being of the workers in a place where the management was genuinely concerned for their welfare. . . . I heard how the management looked after their employees when they fell sick, how it ran cost-price stores, a school, a home-building society, recreation clubs, and athletic fields.

It is quite impossible to say what results these experiments would have under ordinary industrial conditions, because they are undertaken only by successful corporations after they have become successful. The industry that is still at the struggling stage is not experimenting—it is still buying labor at the lowest market-price and getting all it can out of it. When, therefore, you read that American employers provide insurance schemes, housing schemes, medical attendance and recreation clubs for their employees, do not forget that these conditions are found only in the comparatively few big plants controlled by manufacturing trusts that are enormously prosperous. They do not apply to the workers throughout industry in general.

Excerpts from Hugh Adam, *An Australian Looks at America* (London: Allen and Unwin, 1928), 24–26, 63–64, 99, 103.

When the Great Depression arrived in late 1929, and then cumulatively deepened in the early 1930s, the entire frequency distribution of firms

shifted sharply leftward, indicating the widespread curtailment and aban-
donment of HRM programs and practices during this period as firms relentlessly cut costs and pared payrolls in an effort to avoid bankruptcy. One
casualty was the welfare capitalist movement, for even the largest and most
progressive employers were forced to buckle under the weight of depression; another casualty were American workers, who in millions of instances
had their lives impoverished and their dreams shattered. This tragic end of
the story, covered in the last part of *Managing the Human Factor*, is largely
absent in the present volume since our case studies here go no farther then
late 1930.

The Historical Context: A Statistical Portrait

Words and eyewitness accounts are two ways to convey the evolution of
early labor management programs and practices; charts and numbers are
another. Presented below are several examples.

The function of HRM in American firms before 1900 was almost wholly
lacking any kind of formal policy, program or practice, even though some of
these firms employed many thousands of employees. An indication of this
situation is provided by the data in table 1, which shows the percentage of
railroad companies adopting six different HRM practices in the year 1892.

Business historian Alfred Chandler documents how modern management
in America first emerged in the 1870s and 1880s on the railroads.[13] The railroads were the first truly large-scale, capital intensive industrial concerns to
emerge after the Civil War and, as a consequence, the owners and top executives of the railroads were the first to pioneer modern management techniques, such as cost accounting, creation of line and staff organization, and
functional areas of management.

By the end of the nineteenth century the railroads had established a large
management bureaucracy, including cascading levels of management descending from president to vice presidents to divisional managers to the
foreman at the local roundhouse and the gang boss of the track section

Table 1. Adoption of HRM Practices at Railroads, 1892

	Percent
Aid for injured employees (e.g., alternative job, pay allowance)	36
Room for employee reading/rest	22
Relief/insurance fund for accidents, illness, death	17
Eating/lodging facility and/or reduced prices for employees	15
Provision for technical education	14
Old-age fund/pension	4

Source: *Sixth Annual Report of the Interstate Commerce Commission*
(Washington, DC: Government Printing Office, 1892), 324.

crew. They had also carved out separate functional departments to handle finance, accounting, sales, and purchasing. The handling of HRM, however, badly lagged behind in this management revolution. As will be described in chapter 2, not a single railroad before 1900 had established any kind of centralized labor management function; further, few of the railroads had introduced more than a handful of rudimentary and quite simple individual HRM practices, such as a written statement of employment policy and paying workers with checks instead of cash.

The data in table 1 illustrate this situation. They come from what is to the best of my knowledge the first survey of HRM practices done for a cross-section of American companies. The survey was distributed in 1892 by the Interstate Commerce Commission (ICC) to 350 independent railroad companies, who were asked about their adoption of six separate HRM practices.

Two aspects of these data are notable. The first is the extremely limited, bare-bones nature of the HRM programs at the railroads of this period. Only six separate HRM practices were included in the survey, presumably reflecting the paucity of such practices existing at this time, and several—for example, reading rooms/places—are from today's perspective quite modest in scope and expenditure. If we think in terms of a frequency distribution of HRM practices (described earlier), the one for 1892 would have had a peak very close to the vertical axis and an equally small variance ("spread") even for these firms that had the most developed management systems in the country. The second feature of table 1 is that the mean rate of adoption of the individual HRM practice was also relatively low. The lowest adoption rate was for pensions (4%) and the highest was for job transfers for disabled workers (36%). Also worth noting is that many of the railroads that provided pensions and job transfers did so on an individualized, case-by-case basis without general written policy, guidelines, or methods for review and appeal.

Fast-forward now a quarter century to the data presented in table 2. This table shows, for the year 1927, cross-section data on selected PIR practices for 1,600 large-size (250+ employees) industrial enterprises (plants) collected by the National Industrial Conference Board (NCIB). What a difference thirty-five years makes!

The breadth and depth of HRM practices is greatly expanded. Observe, for example, that the complete survey table 2 is drawn from included questions on nearly eighty separate HRM practices, compared to six for the railroads. Further, many of the HRM practices in table 2 are of far greater scope and expenditure. For example, whereas in the early 1890s personnel departments were unknown to even the largest firms, by 1927 one-third of large industrial plants had one. The breadth and depth of other PIR practices, including welfare benefits, also expanded dramatically. While only 4 percent and 17 percent, respectively, of railroads in 1892 provided pensions and accident/illness funds, in 1927 those proportions had increased to 26 percent and 33 percent, respectively, among large employers. Not only were

Table 2. Large Plants Adopting Selected HRM Practices, 1927 (%)

	Percent		*Percent*
Employment Management		*Safety and Health*	
Personnel department	34	Organized first aid	61
Centralized employment	42	Company hospital	24
Labor records	50	Initial physical exam	31
Exit interviews	36	Plant physician	34
Promotion/transfer system	24	Plant nurse	48
Rating system	14	Safety committee	67
Benefits/Welfare		*Training*	
Company housing	14	Apprentice training	30
Company store	7	Training for unskilled/semiskilled	20
Cafeteria	41	Foreman training	19
Savings plan	20	Americanization	10
Paid vacation (wage earners)	26	Company schools	9
Pension	26		
Group life insurance	33	*Joint Relations/Voice*	
Group health insurance	16	Works council	8
Unemployment insurance	1	Group meetings	15
Stock purchase	17	Foremen's committee	21
Profit Sharing	15	Trade union agreement	6
Athletic teams	43	Bulletin board	52
Restrooms (women)	56	Employee magazine	18
Shower baths	42	Suggestion system	23

Source: NICB, *Industrial Relations Programs in Small Plants* (New York: NICB, 1929), tables 3-9.

the rates of adoption many times higher but new HRM practices such as pensions and accident/illness funds were now often highly formalized and professionally developed plans, with the help of actuarial and compensation consultants such as those from the IRC. Numerous other PIR activities listed in table 2, such as works councils, promotion/transfer systems, and company-run cafeterias, also did not exist before the turn of the century.

We move next to figure 2. The data here come from a survey of seventy-four firms done in the year 1924. These firms are not a representative sample, but were selected by the researcher from among companies known to be active in PIR work. In 1900, none of the firms had a PIR department; by 1922, 86 percent had one. The diagram shows the years of establishment for these PIR departments. We see up to the World War I period a slow and somewhat sporadic adoption rate, followed by a burst of adoptions straddling the World War I years, and then a marked decline in the last three years. Were the sample of firms to be expanded and carried forward to the end of the 1920s, the adoption line would turn up again in 1923 or so and show a distinct rising trend over the remainder of the decade.

These events and trends are the historical context within which the individual case studies presented here are embedded. As will be seen, underneath the broad trends exists a great diversity among companies in their

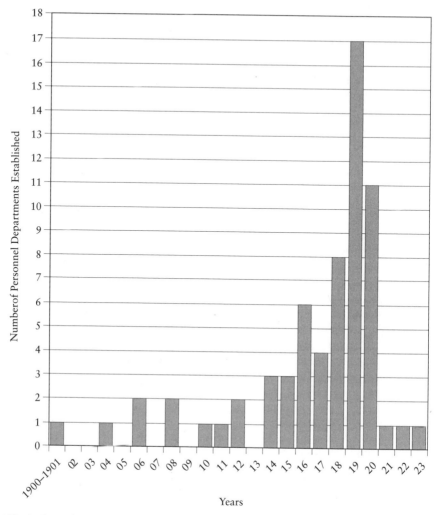

Fig. 2. Date of establishment of personnel departments, 1900–1922.
Source: Robert Lovett, "Present Tendencies in Personnel Practice," *Industrial Management* 65 (June 1923): 330.

particular HRM philosophies, strategies, and practices. The case studies reveal what was claimed in *Managing the Human Factor*—that part of this diversity flows from differences in the external environment to the firms, such as degree of product market competition, state of the business cycle, and union and government pressure, and part from differences in each firm's internal environment, such as quality of leadership's managerial philosophy and ability, company size, technology of production, profitability, and nature of the workforce. All of these factors work together in complex and shifting ways and reveal that there exists, contra to Frederick Taylor's theory of scientific management, no one "best way" in HRM practice.[14] The only metric in a capitalist economy for establishing long-run "best practice" is profit, and these case studies reveal that sometimes best practices mean treating labor as a hired hand and other times as a human resource. To the degree that we attach independent importance to the interests and work life experience of workers, clearly the human resource strategy is preferable and, fortunately, that was the slow but cumulatively significant direction of change up to the late 1920s. The Great Depression brought this progress to an end, however, and as a result American employers lost considerable status, credibility, and control over labor management—as appears to be happening again in the recession or depression of 2008–2009. But this phase of the story has been well treated by others and lies outside the bounds of the present study. So, let us turn to the case studies.

Part I

THE PRACTICE OF HUMAN RESOURCE MANAGEMENT, 1875–1920

2

HRM at the Beginning

The Chicago, Burlington, and Quincy Railroad

The modern practice of human resource management (HRM) has its roots in the rise of large-scale capital intensive enterprises spawned by the Industrial Revolution. Although rudiments of HRM as practiced today can be found in the textile mills of New England and Great Britain of the early 1800s, it was not until after the Civil War, when national markets and large limited liability corporations emerged, that employers had to come to grips with management of hundreds and thousands of employees.

This process first began in earnest in the railroad industry.[1] For this reason, our case studies of early HRM start here. The focal point of this case study is the Chicago, Burlington, and Quincy Railroad, commonly known as "the Burlington."[2] At times, however, supporting material from other railroad companies will also be introduced herein. This case study spans the last part of the nineteenth century and provides a good example of the informal, decentralized, and externalized practice of HRM as it existed at nearly all companies in this time period.

The railroads were the pioneers of the corporate form of business. They were also the first businesses to develop a formal management hierarchy, replace the owner/entrepreneur with salaried executives, adopt a functionalized organizational structure, and use systematic administrative procedures. As Alfred Chandler notes, "the men who managed these enterprises were the first group of modern business administrators in the United States."[3]

The Burlington was a medium sized railroad in the late nineteenth century. In 1880 it had 2,600 miles of track and 16,000 employees. Two decades later the company had more than doubled to 6,500 miles of track and 33,000 employees. The main line of the Burlington Road connected Chicago and Denver, with subsidiary lines spread through Illinois, Iowa, Nebraska, Colorado, and Wyoming.

The management of labor on the railroads before the Civil War was not much different than in many other small businesses.[4] Most railroads of the period spanned less than a hundred miles and had at most a few hundred employees. The relatively small scale of the enterprise allowed the small team of top executives to do most HRM tasks. For example, not only was labor policy set by the board of directors and the president of the company but these executives also typically conducted job interviews in the central office, set each person's pay rate, and approved discipline and termination. The business was small enough that they could also exercise significant day-to-day supervision of labor by traveling up and down the rail line.

A half century later, however, this type of personal involvement of top executives and centralized control in a railroad the size and expanse of the Burlington was impossible. Hence, under the direction of George Perkins, president of the Burlington in the 1880s and '90s and widely regarded as one of the industry's most able executives, the company adopted a two-tier system of labor management.[5]

As much as possible labor management for blue-collar workers was pushed down to the local level. Perkins described this as a system of "local self-government."[6] Formal authority over hiring, employment, pay setting, employee relations, and discipline and discharge was delegated to the various division superintendents. Each division superintendent maintained a separate payroll (the "train service" payroll, the "telegraph" payroll, etc.) that recorded all the employees working in his division, their rate of pay, the date of hiring, and so on. Although these superintendents had formal authority over labor management, in practice most of the decision making was actually done at the local level by the terminal agent, the master mechanic in charge of the train service roundhouse, the track section foreman, and so on.

These men (the railroad had only a few dozen women in its employ) had a great deal of autonomous authority to determine who was hired, the pay for each person, and discipline and discharge. Local self-government of labor by bottom-level line managers had both benefits and costs. On the benefit side, it minimized bureaucracy and overhead cost; promoted flexibility and local adaptation; allowed a "personal touch" and individual treatment; and invested authority in the managers most familiar with the volume of work that needed to be done, the nature of the job tasks, and the performance of the individual employees. This last consideration was particularly important because units of labor were much less uniform or standardized than other commodities and material inputs bought by the railroad and thus needed closer personal inspection and grading; the work effort of employees was highly variable and discretionary and thus required close supervision and specialized handling; and on-the-spot control and supervision of labor was needed in order to adapt to a highly variable and uncertain set of business contingencies (e.g., unforeseen train delays or equipment breakdowns).

The highly decentralized form of labor management used by the Burlington also had costs and shortcomings. A concomitant of local control and adaptation, for example, was lack of uniformity in company labor policy and its administration. Sometimes workers would be fired by one local manager and would then get hired the same week by another manager down the line. In other cases hiring decisions were made that clearly compromised customer safety and service, such as widespread hiring of conductors and engineers who could not read or write or were only sixteen or seventeen years old.[7]

Another serious problem was lack of uniformity in pay practices. Pay rates showed a marked dispersion within and across divisions of the railroad even for relatively standardized jobs. Monthly pay for freight brakeman and conductors in the mid-1870s, for example, ranged in the first case from $25 to $45 and in the second from $50 to $75.[8] Some of this variation reflected compensating differences in seniority, workload and local labor market conditions. But also important were noncompensating factors arising from the interplay of favoritism, opportunism, arbitrariness, and ignorance. A perennial source of employee complaint, for example, was that supervisors and foremen hired their family members, friends, and "pets," paid them more than other workers, and shielded them from discipline and layoff.[9] In other cases, foremen and supervisors paid higher rates to attract or keep mobile workers but left rates the same for long-service workers who for reasons of age, loyalty, or some other friction were not likely to depart. Also contributing to pay dispersion was the simple fact that most local managers had little or no idea what other managers in different towns and divisions were paying.

Also bedeviling the company was the penchant of local-level managers and first-line supervisors to make personnel decisions in ways that benefited their interests at the expense of the company. This form of principal-agent problem arose in a number of ways. For example, many first-line managers and supervisors operated their area as a miniature "spoils" system and used their power to hire favorites and extract gifts, bribes and other favors. Illustratively, a train engineer recalled that promotion depended on two to fifteen years of service, along with "gold watch chains, rocking chairs, bottles of wine, poultry, quails and cigars."[10] These managers, in order to avoid conflict with employees or as a form of tacit collusion, also often overlooked or tolerated employee practices that contravened company policy, such as when conductors skimmed a portion of the ticket receipts, engineers drank alcohol while operating their trains, and mechanics took tools and materials home for personal use. Another practice was the tendency of first-line managers to overstaff as a form of insurance policy, partly because it allowed them to always get the work out and thus avoid attracting the negative attention of higher management and partly because when orders for a reduction in workforce came in times of financial stringency they had some surplus labor that could be sacrificed. A final example was the practice of front-line managers to hide local problems or mistakes from upper management by firing or threatening to fire employees who complained or spoke up.

The strategy of the railroad's executives was to maximize the benefits of decentralization and minimize the costs. To promote the latter objective, they added at the top of the management hierarchy a second tier of labor control and coordination by the president and those who reported directly to him.

At the Burlington, the company president each month personally reviewed the payrolls of each division and subdivision and looked for increases in employment and compensation that appeared out of line.[11] This was done in two ways: by comparing changes from month to month and year to year for each division and subdivision, and by comparing head count and pay in each division and subdivision against others. If a particular division appeared as the high-cost unit of the company, the superintendent or local manager would be instructed to cut employment or salaries and wages. The Burlington also issued a railroad rule book to all employees that outlined in great detail the company's operational and administrative policies and procedures. Another stratagem was to have the president or one of the vice presidents take periodic road trips where they would personally visit a part of the railroad's operations, interview local managers and workers, and get a feel for whether the property was being well managed. Of a similar nature but less visible, the Burlington also employed undercover investigators and detectives who rode the trains and visited local stations and repair facilities looking for lax management, theft, and other violations of company policy. Finally, top executives also served as an informal grievance and appeals forum for dissatisfied employees, particularly since workers were often afraid to confront their immediate superiors and had no personnel department to go to. The company president, in particular, received numerous letters from individual employees, their families, or local committees of workers seeking his intervention to raise wages (or forestall a wage cut), reverse a local manager's termination or disciplinary action, or grant compensation for a work-related injury or death.

Given this two-tier nature of labor management, several other aspects of railroad personnel practices can now be examined. The first concerns the degree of influence of external labor markets. Through the early 1870s it appears that the terms and conditions of employment on the railroads were quite sensitive to product and labor market conditions and that turnover rates and mobility in the labor market were extremely high.[12] During recessions and depressions companies routinely cut wages, while in boom periods wages quickly rose. Illustratively, the Panic of 1873 began in mid-September of that year and within six weeks the falloff of traffic caused the Illinois Central Railroad to order a wage cut of 10 percent for all workers.[13]

The job attachment between company and worker was also quite weak and short-term in this early period. On the Hartford and New Haven Railroad, for example, upwards of 50 percent of the men hired by the company in the 1850s and '60s remained with it for no more than six months and only about 25 percent were still employed there after two years.[14] Illustrative of conditions is this observation of employment practices on the Illinois Central by David Lightner, who writes,

> The most striking aspect of labor policy . . . is the total lack of job security for laborers on the railroad. Work gangs were assembled, enlarged, reduced, and abolished with astonishing frequency. If there was some ditching to be done, a gang was hastily assembled and put to work, and whenever the job was finished the men were instantly dismissed. Even regular section crews were enlarged or reduced almost on the spur of the moment.[15]

This high degree of turnover reflected several factors, including the penchant of the men to readily move from job to job in search of better pay and conditions, the movement of men between agricultural jobs (most plentiful in the spring and fall) and industrial jobs (much railroad repair work was done in the summer), and the large instability in employment imparted by the marked seasonal variation in railroad business (tied to the agricultural production cycle) and the expansion and shrinkage of employment over the pronounced pattern of cyclical boom and bust in the economy.

Starting in the 1870s, however, railroad companies took the first steps to shift from an externalized form of employment to an internalized one. Along with this they also adopted the first rudimentary personnel practices in compensation and recruitment. The most significant step toward an internal labor market was the decision to promote from within. The general manager of the Lake Shore and Southern Railroad, for example, stated that the company " 'as a rule rewards faithful service by promoting its employees in each distinct Department and selects its best men to fill places of responsibility and trust.' "[16] In a similar spirit, an executive of the Burlington said, " 'We like to have young men enter the service at the foot of the ladder and then take great pleasure in *encouraging* them to climb.' "[17] An adjunct of the promote-from-within policy was a formal understanding among the railroad companies that none tried to pirate labor from the others.

A number of reasons were given for the adoption of a promote-from-within policy. One was that it brought higher morale and esprit de corps, as noted in one comment of Burlington's Perkins: " 'In that way, and in that way only can you get the zeal and esprit so essential to economy and efficiency.' "[18] Another was that it infused loyalty and reduced turnover. Also present was the fact that by binding employees to the company the company could pay lower wages (a form of monopsonistic exploitation), per the remark of a Burlington superintendent: " 'The fact that we do not displace competent men in the line of promotion enables us to hold men and get good service at less than other roads pay.' "[19] Promotion from within served a valuable training function and allowed railroads to end formal apprenticeship programs; it provided an effective way to weed out less competent employees; and it also helped create employee loyalty and made workers less interested in joining unions and more reluctant to go out on strike. For the favored "insiders" the promote-from-within policy was a distinct gain, but for "outsiders" the downside was that the companies became increasingly reluctant to hire people who were past their twenties. At the Burlington, notes Paul Black, "If a man had not entered the operating branch by his twenty-fifth birthday, he was too old."[20]

While a general policy, in practice promotion from within was applied more extensively for the higher-skilled groups of workers. Track men, for example, were often drawn from common laborers and were often laid off at the approach of the winter season when the work had to be curtailed. On the other hand, employees in skilled positions, such as conductors and locomotive engineers, had distinct lines of progression.[21] Locomotive drivers, for example, were typically hired in their teens or early twenties as shop or enginehouse hands. They would then get promoted to fireman and work this position four or five years before getting promoted to driver. Their first assignment as drivers would be freight locomotives, which they would serve for upward of ten years. If they performed well and impressed their superiors, they would get promoted to the most coveted driver's job—passenger locomotives. The cream of that job, in turn, was driving the fast inter-city passenger trains.

The most advanced form of internal labor market was developed for the executive team at the railroad companies. Experienced and competent management talent was in the shortest supply and railroad companies by the early 1880s had in place formal policies to develop and promote executive talent. The Burlington created a school for managers;[22] promising young men were systematically recruited as trainees, rotated through key positions to gain experience, and assigned to higher-level managers who served as mentors. Further, their superiors were required to provide the president detailed written performance assessments each year. At the top level, executives were given bonuses and stock as a reward for their services.

Walter Licht concludes that every two years one in six railroad employees advanced through the ranks.[23] This upward progression was a very visible and potent source of reward and loyalty. It also appears to have at least somewhat cut down the otherwise sky-high rates of employee turnover. But turnover apparently remained high. At the Burlington, even among executives, turnover was heavy. Of the fourteen general managers, between 1880 and 1901 only four stayed with the company; among superintendents the record was somewhat better—twenty-nine of thirty-nine remained.[24]

Railroads not only started to construct internal labor markets at an early time but made the first move away from purely market-determined rates of pay to institute the first formal programs of labor recruitment, hiring tests, and a centralized payroll.

The clearest indication that pay rates were starting to become unhinged from short-run market pressures was the decision of the companies not to cut wages during recessions and depressions. As noted earlier, in the depression of the mid-1870s railroad companies reduced wages quickly and repeatedly. The next major depression began in 1893, lasted four years, and was the most severe business downturn of the last half of the nineteenth century. Although under great pressure to reduce cost, this time railroads such as the Burlington and Illinois Central held the line on wages and instead cut cost through layoffs, hours reductions, and other economy measures.

The decision of the railroad companies to partially insulate their workforce from the external labor market seems to have been influenced by two considerations. The first arose largely from internal assessments of organizational efficiency and, in particular, the relationship between wages, treatment, and worker productivity. Notably, this issue also generated a strong debate over two alternative human resource management strategies and which one best served the overall business strategy of the railroads.

The historical record indicates that railroad executives were very profit conscious and, in general, managed the businesses to maximize shareholder returns.[25] This profit consciousness arose from the highly competitive nature of the industry, the large demand for cash flow to pay for expansions to plant and equipment, the unremitting pressure exerted by high fixed costs, and the executives' desire to preserve and advance their high-paying and prestigious jobs. Because of these factors, and the commodity nature of much of the product (freight haulage), the dominant business strategy was to minimize operating cost and build volume through low prices. Said a member of the board of directors for the Illinois Central, "'Our object is to carry freight and passengers at a cheaper rate than our rivals.'"[26] Given this business strategy, what human resource strategy best serves it? Here two factions emerged among railroad executives.

The "traditionalists" believed that the best human resource strategy was to take a market approach to labor which meant, in effect, treating labor like a commodity and buying it the cheapest rate possible, getting the most out of it possible, and then getting rid of it. Workers were, of course, people, but this meant only that exact and stern discipline was required. This strategic approach to labor was espoused by Perkins, president of the Burlington. His philosophy is indicated by these remarks: "'We must not spend a cent from good nature or for doubtful things. The knife must be put in without any feeling—the only consideration being the net result to the company.'"[27] Regarding treatment and compensation of labor, he argued, "'There are no obligations growing out of the relations of employer and employee beyond what are expressed in the agreement between them.'"[28] Regarding wages, he argued that they "'are solely dependent upon the law of supply and demand'" and in belief of this dictum he ordered that wages on the Burlington be held at the minimum rate paid by any competitor.[29] In this he was supported by a vice president who said, "'We must look at the cold side and pay for labor whatever it demands in the market, that is to say, we must get it as cheap as we can.'"[30] Perkins was also a committed antipaternalist and opposed nearly all special favors or welfare measures for workers. After a 10 percent wage cut, for example, workers in one division of the Burlington went on strike. Perkins refused all efforts at conciliation and instead shut down the line and starved the men into submission, proudly commenting, "'We made no concession of any kind. Anything like vacillation and unsteadiness in dealing with these men is fatal.'"[31] He also opposed company welfare measures on the grounds that "'The minute a large employer turns himself into an eleemosynary he has got to keep on doing more and more'" and that American workers found corporate welfare "'demoralizing and degrading.'"[32] He also opposed welfare measures on larger political grounds, worrying that they portended a more general trend toward greater union and government involvement in the affairs of business. As Perkins noted, for example, "'The spirit of the age is communistic. Perhaps the progress of civilization has developed more rapidly than it has *disciplined* the sympathies of people.'"[33]

A second, much smaller group of railroad executives counseled a more humanistic and—from today's perspective—progressive strategy toward labor management. Being smaller in number and ahead of their time, they usually lost the battle. Their critics called these managers "sentimentalists" and "paternalists," but in their own eyes they were simply pragmatic businessmen who recognized that one achieved greater productivity, less turnover, greater loyalty, and less union trouble by extending to workers a modicum of generosity, security, and fair dealing. In particular, they argued that a company got lower production cost by paying high wages rather than low wages. This philosophy was enunciated by Charles Adams Jr., a general manager of one of the Burlington divisions. In an anonymous editorial in *The Nation* magazine, he wrote,

> "If the Boston owners of railroads in the West would give some attention to advancing the personal welfare of . . . employees, it would pay them quickly and handsomely. . . . [The workers] would give our owners a more zealous and earnest service, would foster . . . a higher *esprit de corps*, would breed a strong attachment to the line and its owner, would remove the possibility of strikes and riots, and would lead to the securing of a better grade of men."[34]

The same point of view was expressed by Sidney Webster, a member of the board of directors of the Illinois Central, who commented,

> If we can really improve our own condition, and elevate our reputation, by conciliating those who are in our employ, or by conciliating labor organizations, I certainly would do it. . . . If, therefore, a policy of conciliation, and even a higher rate of wages than other railway companies pay, will bring us a more efficient, and therefore in the end a cheaper service, it does seem to me that good policy would prompt that line of action.[35]

Adams's and Webster's progressive points of view were supported by others at the Burlington and other railroads. Robert Harris, vice president of the Burlington, for example, thought the traditionalist's approach was shortsighted and sacrificed temporary gains for long-run costs. Commenting on the company's policy of paying the minimum wage rates in the market, he said in an internal memorandum, "'If we try to obtain labor at the lowest possible price at which it can be got, and thus half pauperize it, we should expect and most certainly will get the result of pauperized labor.'"[36] In this vein, another Burlington general manager noted, "'We had last year the poorest quality of labor on the C.B. & Q. Road that I have ever seen,'" in part because able-bodied men refused to take jobs with the railroad and it thus could only get "'boys or men too old to be efficient.'"[37] The result was that labor costs per unit were actually higher at substandard wage rates. Using similar logic, an executive at the Illinois Central advocated a liberal pay policy on the grounds that it led to "'the most contented, effective, and therefore the cheapest labor.'"[38] At the Burlington, Harris also recommended that certain privileges be extended to the employees, such as free passes on the trains and coal provided at cost, arguing that such practices would "'cultivate among employees a feeling of sympathy with the Road.'" He also counseled a less draconian and more case-by-case approach to discipline, arguing, "'This practice begets a feeling on the part of the employees from which we gain very much more we would by a rigid rule.'"[39] In a similar spirit, Harris voluntarily paid severely injured workers three to four weeks' wages and established a Burlington company hospital, arguing that this was not bleeding-heart sentimentality but good business since it fostered employee loyalty, prevented court suits, kept the government out of business affairs, and gave the workers less cause to seek out unions.

A second, more externally oriented, force also caused railroad managers to take the first formative steps toward development of internal labor markets and cyclical wage stability: the threat of trade unionism and strikes. Trade unions in the railroad industry were in their infancy in the 1870s, and few workers belonged to them. Yet in 1877 the greatest strike of the late nineteenth century, and the harbinger of the other great "labor wars" of the period such as those at the Homestead Pennsylvania mill of the Carnegie Steel Company and the Pullman Palace Car Company factory in Pullman, Illinois, erupted and swept over much of the nation. The cause of the strikes and the damage done to the profits and property of the companies was indelibly etched in the memory of the railroad executives and caused them to slowly but perceptibly move away from a pure commodity model of labor.

The depression that began in 1873 set the stage for the strike. After instituting several wage cuts, hours reductions, and large layoffs, the Baltimore and Ohio railroad ordered another wage cut in mid-1877 that was the spark that ignited a large and deep set of resentments and grievances among the employees.[40] A small protest strike by workers in Camden Junction, Maryland, quickly spread up and down the B&O and then to most of the other rail lines east of the Mississippi River. A particular cause of anger was that many of the railroads that were cutting wages at the same time maintained the rate of dividend payout to shareholders; the New York Central, for example, could have chosen to maintain wages and generate the same cost saving by cutting the dividend rate from 8 percent to 6 percent.[41] At the height of the strike much of the nation's rail system was shut down, mobs of rioters stormed the rail yards and put to the torch anything they could find, over one hundred people were killed, and President Grover Cleveland had to call in federal troops to restore law and order. As labor historian Joseph Raybeck has observed of the strike, "Not since the slaveholders had ceased to be haunted by dreams of a slave uprising had the propertied elements been so terrified," while an anonymous author in the *Locomotive Engineer's Journal* wrote, "'The uprising was the natural result of premeditated, preconcerted causes— the result of arbitrary rules and unjust discrimination allowed officers and operations, a culmination of stupid mismanagement and the fruits of unwise policies, and explosion was as unexpected as would be a thunderbolt from a cloudless sky.'"[42]

The result of this calamitous event made the railroad companies far more hesitant to reduce wages even in periods of extreme financial exigency. Throughout the 1880s, wages in the rail industry remained stable despite a continued fall in the domestic price level. The big test occurred, however, in the depression of 1893–97. Part way through this depression an Illinois Central executive wrote in an internal memorandum, "'We are, of course, all of the same mind that wages should be reduced,'" but then qualified it with the observation, "'but how to do it and whether we can get co-operation, is a question I think we should seriously consider.'"[43] With the events of 1877 in mind, supplemented by the fresh outbreak of nationwide strike violence associated with the Pullman strike of 1894 and the much stronger union presence among the employees, the Illinois Central executives finally decided the risks of a wage cut were simply too great and they left wage rates intact throughout the depression. Lightner concludes that "the strikes of 1877 tended to put a floor under the wages of American workingmen so that the earnings of the industrial labor force displayed a remarkable stability throughout the remainder of the nineteenth century."[44] Unable to reduce labor cost through wage cuts, companies used the alternative method of layoffs and pared employment to the bone. Workers and their unions, in effect, chose to concentrate the "pain" of cost reduction among a minority who ended up with no jobs at all rather than spread the pain more evenly by imposing a wage cut. That the reluctance of the workers and their unions to accept reduced wage rates came at the cost of fewer jobs (suggesting a downward sloping demand curve for labor) is indicated in the remark of an Illinois Central executive that "'it would have been better for the men, if it had been possible for us, by reducing the scale of wages a little, to have employed more men or to give them more work on full time.'"[45]

In addition to avoiding wage cuts where possible and instituting promotion from within, the railroads of the late nineteenth century also pioneered several other rudimentary personnel practices. Starting in the early 1880s, for example, they began to institute hiring and promotion tests.[46] People applying for the position of locomotive engineer, for example, had to pass an eye exam, a reading test, and a written test of technical and operational questions. The companies also made use of external labor recruiters and employment agencies during periods of labor shortage. Another personnel practice used in the recruitment of labor, although shrouded in secrecy, was a blacklist of employees who were not to be hired because they were union members or deemed as troublemakers.[47] The companies also centralized pay disbursement by appointing one person in each division to serve as divisional paymaster. On the Illinois Central the paymaster traveled over the lines in a special car and paid the employees once a month in coin and currency. In the early 1890s the company made another innovation in payroll management and paid the employees by bank check.[48]

Although the subject of trade unions and strikes has already been touched upon, additional aspects of this subject regarding the development of railway labor management are important to note. Into the mid-1880s the railroads were relatively free of any organized influence from trade unions and could thus unilaterally set their labor policy and manage the men. Gradually, however, trade unions began to form, first among the skilled operating employees such as engineers and conductors and then later among shop workers (e.g., machinists and blacksmiths) and later still among clerks and signalmen. At first the companies stoutly resisted the unions and refused to recognize them or negotiate contracts. An Illinois Central executive called them "'These damned infernal organizations'" and said that they "'were destined to give all RRs [railroads] trouble in the future.'"[49] By the late 1880s, however, attitudes and practices began to soften and another Illinois Central executive wrote his union counterpart and proclaimed "'I want the family feeling to prevail in this service, and both officers and men to realize that all are working in a common interest, and for the same employer, and that justice and right must be the basis of all relations.'"[50] This shift in attitudes arose from several factors, including the relatively conservative and responsible behavior of several of the rail craft unions (particularly the early formed and powerful Brotherhood of Locomotive Engineers), the growing presence and power of the unions forced the companies to come to some accommodation, and because the unions spread to nearly all railroads and thus none were placed at a competitive disadvantage. The first collective bargaining contracts appeared in the railroad industry in the mid-1870s; by the 1890s written trade union agreements were common.

The most important aspect of the unions was that they represented an alternative form of labor management and workforce governance. With the advent of collective bargaining the companies began to transition from a largely unilateral, informal, decentralized and market-oriented employment system to one that was more bilateral, formal and bureaucratized, and inter- and intraorganizationally oriented. Particularly with the strongly organized groups such as the engineers, railroad executives took care to consult with representatives of the unions before making policy changes and, as collective bargaining developed in the 1890s, labor policy changes increasingly became the subject of formal negotiation. Company managers also met with union representatives to discuss grievances and demands for changes in wages, hours, and other employment conditions. In his study of the Burlington, for example, Black estimates that while the skilled operating crafts represented only about 18 percent of company employment the company's executives nonetheless devoted more time and attention in labor management to this group than any other.[51]

The unions were, of course, interested in improving wages and shortening hours (the workweek was typically ten hours per day, six days per week). But just as often they concerned themselves with a myriad of work rules that in the absence of collective bargaining were unilaterally determined by the company and almost always structured to promote its interests. In this respect the unions provided workers with collective voice on working conditions and helped fill in, or restructure, the incomplete nature of the employment agreement.

Several examples will illustrate this. Railroading was one of the most dangerous employments in the nation. In the switching service, for example, 1 in 7 employees over a ten-year period on the Illinois Central suffered a disabling injury, and 1 in 90 died; on train service the rates were, respectively, 1 in 20 and 1 in 120.[52] As Charles Russell observed at the turn of the century, "'The truth is that railroad employment in the United States is more perilous than the average soldier's life in war time . . . Of every ten trainmen at work today one will be killed or maimed within one year."[53] The companies had no formal compensation program for injuries and deaths and, indeed, were often indifferent to safety and fought employee claims for compensation with attorneys and court action. A reason workers joined trade unions, therefore, was because they offered mutual insurance for injury and death to members. Further, the unions pressured the companies to improve safety conditions and begin compensation programs.

The unions also negotiated for seniority systems. They were motivated to do so for several reasons. One was that the companies had a deliberate policy of weeding out employees once they passed their physical prime. Another was that promotion and layoff were done almost entirely at management's discretion and employees often perceived large elements of favoritism and capriciousness entering into this equation. Yet another was that the railroads increasingly converted to a piece-rate pay system in the mechanical shops and older employees were put at a significant disadvantage.

Compensation rules were also a prime subject of negotiation. The companies, for example, unilaterally changed the pay system for train drivers and conductors from a daily basis to a trip (mileage) basis.[54] Some drivers and conductors on short and/or fast routes were able to complete a trip in less than a day, thus realizing higher effective earnings; many others could not complete the trip in a day, however, and were penalized. Also a source of irritation and grievance was the fact that passenger train drivers and conductors were advantaged in this scheme over those on freight trains, as were drivers and conductors in rural areas versus urban areas. Particularly galling to all groups of train drivers and conductors was when equipment failures, bad weather, or other uncontrollable events caused trip cancellations or long delays, resulting in employees losing pay through no fault of their own.

Finally, the unions also sought to impose limits on apprenticeship programs. The companies deliberately sought to maintain an excess supply of labor in order to keep wages down; toward this end they would advertise for far more workers than they needed and would use apprenticeship programs and other more informal training methods to continually augment the supply of qualified workers. Said one union representative regarding the company's training program, " 'We feel that the system dictates a policy that ruins our future prospects,' " adding, " 'We feel the capitalists are doing this in order to flood the market with labor.' "[55] The unions, therefore, bargained to restrict the people admitted into the apprenticeship programs.

3

Contrasting HRM Strategies

Pullman and Baldwin

The case study of the Chicago, Burlington, and Quincy Railroad in chapter 2 indicates that as early as the 1880s railroad executives were debating different strategic approaches to labor management. Since labor was the largest component of total railroad cost, the truly surprising thing would be if these executives had *not* given at least some strategic consideration to alternative modes of labor management. The strategic dimension of late-nineteenth-century labor management is further highlighted in the case studies presented in this chapter. Examined are the labor policies and practices of, respectively, the Pullman Palace Car Company and the Baldwin Locomotive Works. The Pullman Company was the nation's largest manufacturer of railroad sleeping cars, and the Baldwin Works was the nation's largest manufacturer of railroad steam locomotives.

These two companies represent two quite distinct approaches to labor management and employee relations. The first approach, practiced by Pullman and most other employers of that period, was the *autocratic zero-sum* model, which led to one of the most tumultuous and destructive labor strikes in American history. The second approach, used by Baldwin and a modest number of other companies, was the *cooperative positive-sum* model. Many observers at the turn of the century thought Baldwin (a nonunion company) had one of the most perfected and harmonious employee relations systems of any large manufacturing firm in the country.[1] The large difference in the two companies' approach to labor management is particularly interesting and revealing since both companies were in the same broad industry (railway equipment manufacture), thus to some degree holding constant other perturbing influences such as differences in production technology and economic environment.

The Pullman Palace Car Company

The Pullman Palace Car Company was founded in 1867 by George Pullman. Pullman's business career was a real-life version of a Horatio Alger novel;[2] born into a poor family, Pullman started work at age fourteen as a store clerk, learned the craft of cabinetmaking, earned a sizable income elevating large buildings above the flood plain in Chicago, and then quit to prospect for gold in Colorado. Returning to Chicago during the Civil War, Pullman reflected on his nights spent in cramped and dirty railroad sleeping cars and decided to build a superior model. His new sleeping car was a tremendous success, embodying many new innovations (e.g., hinged upper berths that could be swung up during the day) and a level of craftsmanship and luxury heretofore unknown. By the early 1890s the Pullman Company had captured three-quarters of the sleeping car business and earned very handsome profits (dividend payments net of retained earnings to the 4,200 stockholders in 1893 equaled more than one-third the company's wage bill paid to its 14,500 employees).

In 1880 Pullman initiated an industrial experiment that would make him both famous and infamous. He purchased forty thousand acres of sparsely settled farm land twelve miles south of the Chicago business district and built on it a completely new set of manufacturing and repair shops. More newsworthy, however, was that he also built around the shops a completely new town, called Pullman.[3] The town, relatively isolated from other communities, was heralded as a marvel of the age and attracted national and international attention. A newspaper columnist said of Pullman, "'It is famous already as one of the wonders of the west,'" and thousands of workers traveled to Pullman to get jobs.[4] While many firms of that era built and maintained company housing for employees, no other company in the United States designed a town from top to bottom with as much meticulous planning, upscale design, and huge capital investment. It was akin to a nineteenth-century industrial version of Disney World. Out of the cornfields arose a model community with spacious paved streets; comfortable two-story brick homes; sewer, water, and gas service; municipal buildings and schools; parks and playgrounds; an ornate expansive building called the Arcade that centralized under one roof many of the town's retail stores (a forerunner of the modern-day mall); and a green stone church said to be the most beautiful structure in the community. Since the town was built almost exclusively to promote securing and maintaining the company's labor input, one can say that the Pullman Company made a major strategic investment in its people.

In the summer of 1893 the nation was hit by a financial panic. Orders for new sleeping cars quickly dwindled, and over a six-week period no new contracts were obtained. To bring in business, Pullman cut prices in order to meet competition. To maintain profit margins, Pullman also immediately acted to reduce labor cost. Many hundreds of employees were immediately laid off, wages were cut approximately 25 percent, and many workers were put on part-time schedules. At the same time, the company maintained the level of housing rents (judged to be perhaps 25 percent above rental rates for similar housing in Chicago) and utility prices, and did not cut either dividend payments to stockholders or salaries to executives. Many of the workers, after rents and utilities were deducted from their checks, had weekly earnings of $10 or less, substantially below what was at that time considered a family living wage. A number of the employees found themselves in growing debt to the company.[5]

In May 1894, a committee of forty workers met with George Pullman and petitioned for a restoration of the wage scale to the 1893 level and an end to various shop grievances. Among the major grievances were abusive foremen, the refusal of the company to reduce rents along with wages, the periodic reduction in piece rates (keeping daily earnings roughly constant even as workers' output doubled and tripled), and the policy of no pay for fixing defective work even when the defect was the fault of management or a supplier. Pullman said a wage restoration was impossible if the company was to capture new business, and he refused the demand. He promised that no member of the committee would suffer retribution and that the grievances would be looked into. Shortly thereafter, however, three members of the committee were discharged, greatly infuriating the workers.[6] Going against the advice of a representative of the newly formed American Railway Union (ARU), led by Eugene V. Debs, the workers went out on strike.[7] Several weeks later, to aid the Pullman workers the American Railway Union ordered its members to boycott all Pullman sleepers, effectively sidelining them from passenger trains. The boycott spread the strike across twenty-seven states, seriously disrupted the nation's rail traffic, and led to mob violence in places. The railway companies, eager to break the union, fired strikers, got court injunctions ordering the union to cease and desist, and convinced the federal government to send in federal troops. Ultimately the strike was defeated, the union was crushed, Debs was sent to jail, and the Pullman workers gained nothing.

These events, and the testimony of Pullman and other executives to a government commission appointed to investigate the strike, reveal several important facets of management philosophy and practice. One such facet was to look at labor as no different then any other commodity input. Pullman told the congressional committee, for example, " 'The wage question is settled by the law of supply and demand,' " a sentiment echoed by Thomas Wickes, the manager in charge of operations at the Pullman facility, who stated, " 'We go into the market for men just as we go into the market for anything else.' "[8] Pullman explicitly denied that there should be any connection between company profits and workers' wages (an ability-to-pay argument), noting, " 'I could see no reason why because the Pullman company happened to be prosperous, as you say, that it should pay higher rate of wages than other establishments in the same business'" (554). Wickes also denied that higher wages would pay back the company in the form of higher worker productivity (an efficiency wage argument), stating, "'I hardly think that that principle would be a good one'" (610).[9] Wickes went on to say that if a worker did not like the wages or working conditions, "'it is a man's privilege to go to work somewhere else'" (622), and if workers or their families suffered from hunger or lack of medical care this was "'unfortunate'" but not something that companies could remedy since they were operating as a business and not a charity.

Pullman and his subordinate executives also staked out an uncompromising position on the rights of management and their fiduciary obligation to maximize shareholder returns regardless of human consequences or sentiments. Pullman, for example, argued that the rights of property gave him sole authority to manage the business as he saw fit. He thus said it was "'impossible'" for him to consult with third parties (e.g., union representatives) or agree to arbitration since doing so would contravene "'the principle that a man should have the right to manage his own property'" (556). Further, Pullman claimed that all of his actions were mandated by his fiduciary responsibility to maximize shareholder returns. He told the investigating committee, for example, he could not pay higher wages because "'[the company] would not have a right to take the profits belonging to the people who own that property'" (554), a statement he reiterated, saying, "'I would have no right to take the stockholder's money to give one set of mechanics a higher rate than the market price'" (565). When pressed as to why he did not similarly reduce the salaries of his executives, he argued that this, too, was consistent with shareholder interests since the executives' skills and experience were too valuable to risk losing.

A third feature of Pullman's management approach was a marked tendency toward domination and control of employees, combined with a substantial degree of insensitivity toward concerns of fairness and justice.[10] On one hand, George Pullman claimed that he always sought justice for employees, and that employees "'are the most important element which enters into the successful operation of any manufacturing enterprise'" (529). Yet, on the other hand, he structured the workplace and managed the employees in such a way that he not only lost their confidence and loyalty but precipitated a bitter and lengthy strike.

To begin with, the employees of the Pullman Company felt that the company ran every aspect of their lives, including the churches they were allowed to attend, the books stocked in the library, the political candidates they could vote for, and who was allowed to come into and out of the town.[11] Political and social debate was tightly circumscribed, and people felt afraid to criticize the company lest their remarks be reported by company spies and informants. Commented one Chicago newspaper before the strike, "'None of the "superior," or "scientific" advantages of the model city will compensate for the restrictions on the freedom of the workmen, the denial of opportunities of ownership, the heedless and vexatious parade of authority, and the sense of injustice arising from the well founded belief that the charges of the company for rent, heat, gas, water, etc. are excessive—if not extortionate.' "[12] Reinforcing the perception that the company town was intended as an instrument of control and exploitation was Pullman's refusal to sell any of the town's property or homes to workers.

These negative feelings were then much inflamed by the perception that the company unfairly imposed most of the sacrifices entailed by the economic depression of 1893 on labor, and largely exempted capital. The company, for example, had $25 million in reserves while most working families had little or no savings, yet it was wages that were cut while dividends were maintained. Further, it seemed to employees to be patently unfair that the company cut wages but maintained housing rents and utility charges. They argued that if supply and demand were forcing down wages then shouldn't supply and demand also force down rents and utility prices—as well as executive salaries? The fact that rents and utility prices did not fall again pointed to the monopolistic control exercised by the company. The idea that the company was a coldhearted and selfish monopolist was then solidified when it refused to compromise on any of the strike demands and fired three of the strike committee representatives.

George Pullman advanced a variety of rationales in defense of the company: employees were free to live outside Pullman (a true statement, but one that neglected the time and cost of commuting, particularly in the 1890s, when available transportation was primitive), the housing was not earning a competitive rate of return on capital (the housing yielded a 3 percent return, not the 6 percent Pullman set as a target), and the worker representatives were fired without his knowledge. Thomas Wickes argued that giving workers special treatment would "'have a tendency to make men less independent'" and that it never occurred to him that the Pullman workers "'would want to be put on an exceptionally favorable basis. They would want to get there themselves, by their own efforts'" (611). Even if all of Pullman's claims were meritorious and Wickes's claims can be dismissed as rhetoric, Pullman and his executives nonetheless failed to strategically appreciate the corrosive and ultimately highly destructive effect that excessive company control and perceived unjust treatment had on employee attitudes. This conclusion was the one reached by the strike commission, noting that some accommodation by the company would have "shown good faith, would have relieved the harshness of situation, and would have evinced genuine sympathy with labor in these disasters of the times" (xxxiv), and in so doing might well have prevented the walkout that ended up costing Pullman shareholders a great deal of money.

A final feature of management's human resource strategy and practice at Pullman was refusal to deal with labor unions and a tendency to see labor unrest and strikes as the product of outside agitators. Pullman, like many employers of his era, claimed that the company made no discrimination against workers based on union membership. He told the investigating commission, for example, "'We have never discriminated against any labor union whatever'" and "'We have never made any question whatever on [a person's membership in a labor organization] in the hiring of the men'" (563). He noted, however, one exception, stating that "'the policy is that it [the company] will retain no one that belongs to the American Railway Union'" (564). That this exception was actually the rule was revealed under further questioning when Pullman admitted that to the best of his knowledge the only union ever active in his company was the ARU. Likewise, an employee contravened Pullman's testimony concerning nondiscrimination against union members, stating "'If a man belongs to a union, if the company knew it, he was discharged'" (417). In his testimony, Thomas Wickes justified not dealing with unions because it was a fundamental principle that the company "'have control of its own business'" and it would not allow its employees "'to dictate upon what terms it should do its business'" (604). This "dictation" theme was also cited by Pullman, who claimed that the ARU's goal was "'creation and duration of a dictatorship which could make all industries of the United States and the daily comfort of the millions dependent upon them, hostages for the granting of any fantastic whim of such a dictator.'"[13] Regarding the cause of strikes, Wickes told the commission, "'I think if our men had been left free of outside influences there would have been no trouble'" and "'the best of our men don't give us any trouble with unions or anything else. It is only the inferior men—that is, the least competent, that give us trouble as a general thing'" (622).

The Baldwin Locomotive Works

The Baldwin Locomotive Works was at the turn of the twentieth century not only the largest producer of steam locomotives in the United States but also the largest capital goods manufacturer. Employee numbers at Baldwin grew rapidly over the last two decades of the nineteenth century, going from around 3,000 in 1880 to over 8,000 in 1900.[14] Baldwin reached a peak in size and production in 1906 when it produced 2,666 engines—more than 8 locomotives each working day—using 17,000 employees working two shifts around the clock.[15] Most of these workers were concentrated in the huge Broad Street complex of erecting and finishing shops in Philadelphia. The Baldwin shops were considered by many to represent a modern marvel for their size, technological sophistication, and volume of production, and the company attracted visitors from across the country and world.

Baldwin faced many of the competitive problems that Pullman faced, but on a larger scale. Demand for locomotives, like sleeping cars, was highly unstable. During years of recession and depression sales plunged, while in boom years railroads rushed to place orders and clamored for quick delivery. The volatile nature of demand posed a huge challenge in staying solvent and managing the workforce. In the former case, the company's huge capital base saddled it with extremely high fixed costs, and when sales declined profit margins quickly disappeared and red ink gushed. Baldwin, like Pullman, responded by slashing prices in order to attract new sales and cover fixed charges, even if it meant working at a loss. Baldwin also sought to soften the impact of sales declines by colluding with other producers to maintain prices and allocate sales. In 1901, ten of its smaller competitors acted to further stabilize prices by merging into the American Locomotive Company (ALCO), allowing Baldwin and ALCO to collectively control 85 percent of the market.

The boom and bust in locomotive orders was hard not only on profits but on the workforce. With the onset of the Panic of 1893, Baldwin was forced within six months to cut the payroll from 5,052 men to 2,364, cut wages 10 percent, and put the remaining workers on part-time schedules.[16] The combination of the wage cut and reduced hours brought the weekly wages of workers down nearly by half, from $13.06 to $7.12. The company also suffered major costs when it had to resort to draconian layoffs since two-thirds of its workforce were skilled workers who were difficult to replace, expensive to train, and a valuable repository of nonreplaceable firm-specific training.

Despite the similarities of the business and macroeconomic environment, the labor relations climate at Baldwin was in many respects the opposite of that at Pullman. Baldwin was widely regarded as one of the most progressive employers in America and won plaudits for its employee relations. In 1902 the National Civic Federation sponsored an industrial conference to examine the causes and solutions to the Labor Problem. According to a participant by the name of E. Bingham, Baldwin was held up as a model of harmonious employee relations and labor representatives had to ruefully admit that unions could make no headway in organizing the workers. After visiting the Baldwin works, Bingham wrote up his conclusions in a magazine article and posed the question, "By what singular good fortune, or by what surpassing subtlety and skill, has the Baldwin Locomotive works been able, in the seventy-two years of its operation, utterly to avoid strikes and all labor troubles, and, with more than 13,000 men on its pay rolls now, to have proved invulnerable to proselytizing labor unions?"[17]

Based on this article and other historical sources, the answer appears to contain several parts.[18] One *not* present was any type of formalized personnel system or welfare program. Salaried management at Baldwin in both the line and staff divisions was kept to a bare minimum. An employment office was not created until the peak employment year of 1906, and the Baldwin executives were firmly against all forms of paternalism in the form of libraries, company magazines, and other accoutrements of the industrial betterment movement.[19] In its main outline, Baldwin used much the same top-down decentralized form of labor management that Pullman did. Hiring, training, rates of pay, and discipline and discharge were administered by twenty shop foreman and supervisors and subject to general policy guidelines and over-view by top company executives. The only "personnel staff" employed by the company were timekeepers and payroll clerks.[20] When possible, employees were paid piece rates, and discipline was strict and workers were fined for tardiness and spoiled work.

What *did* seem to account for the positive employee relations was a concerted effort by management to treat employees as partners in the enterprise, albeit distinctly junior partners. The partnership idea began at the top. From its founding in 1831 to the first decade of the 1900s, Baldwin was owned and operated as a tightly held joint partnership among a small number of long-time employees turned executives. At the turn of the century, six partners controlled the company and all had worked their way through the ranks, often starting as teenagers. From the founding of the company, new partners were carefully selected on the basis of dedication and skill toward making the company the premier manufacturer of steam locomotives.

This orientation toward company and product created a distinct management philosophy at Baldwin that fundamentally shaped employment strategy and tactics. John Brown calls the Baldwin management philosophy a "producer ethos."[21] Pullman, by way of contrast, had a "profit ethos" and, guided by this philosophy, managed the company to maximize shareholder returns. Toward this end, Pullman took a "market" (supply and demand) perspective toward labor where workers were not junior partners but "hired hands" and thus a short-run expense to be minimized. When curtailment and sacrifice were called for, Pullman sought to shift as much of the burden as possible to labor. At Baldwin, the emphasis was first and foremost on developing and building the strongest possible product line of locomotives, with the belief that profits would then follow. The emphasis was on the physical act of wealth creation through production and not the financial act of wealth creation for shareholders.

Brown observes that "the producer ethos became a tenet of management practice at Baldwin and the foundation of the company culture."[22] With regard to labor, the producer ethos caused the Baldwin owners to view employees—particularly the two-thirds of the workforce comprised of skilled workers—as indispensable junior partners whose knowledge, skills, and loyalty were the company's chief assets and source of competitive advantage. This partnership orientation was immediately noticed by Bingham when he toured the Baldwin shops, for he wrote,

> The Baldwin Company is not an incorporated company. There is no Baldwin stock. The concern is an old-fashioned partnership and from the front office to the ash heaps [where locomotive cinder boxes were emptied] the old idea of partnership and reward and promotion is realized in a fashion that makes the works unique among all the industrial enterprises of the country.[23]

This sense of partnership created what Bingham called the "Baldwin Spirit," which he described as a "feeling of self-respect, tempered with rare loyalty and enthusiasm." As John Converse, another news reporter, noted,

> A pleasing and noteworthy feature of the attitude of the men is the *esprit de corps* which prevails. They realize their employers are doing their best for them and only ask in return the best of the work of each man. Every man is proud of the establishment he works for, the oldest of its kind in the United States, and every man is proud to be known as a Baldwin man.[24]

How did Baldwin foster the partnership spirit? Converse captured the main points:

> The policy of the firm is to make the interest of the men identical with its own. Hard work is required, but high wages are paid, ingenuity is encouraged, and intelligent and faithful work is liberally rewarded. Piece rates are seldom cut, and then only on account of the introduction of a time-saving tool, in which case the workmen shares in the gain accruing. If one man shows especially marked ability, he may be shifted to another job, usually being made a contractor or sub-foreman. The policy of the establishment is to make promotions from within; foremen, bosses or superintendents are not imported. There are no hereditary rights to important positions.[25]

As indicated here, Baldwin viewed its workforce as a source of competitive advantage, much as depicted in the modern resource-based theory of the firm, and to protect and develop this investment adopted an HRM strategy that emphasized individual respect, a measure of self-control at work, a partnership corporate culture, and a mutual-gain compensation/employment policy. The company paid the highest wages in the country for the type of work done.[26] Further, it implemented wage cuts only as a last resort and only infrequently cut piece rates. When wage reductions were ordered, executives also cut their salaries, while parts of the savings from piece-rate reductions were shared with workers. Also of great importance, the company had a strong promote-from-within policy and gave first preference in hiring to Baldwin workers who had been previously laid off and had a good service record. Baldwin was such a desirable place to work that the company never advertised for labor and consistently had a supply of it at the shop gates where hiring was done (by individual foremen). Another by-product, already noted, was that the workers rebuffed the overtures of the trade unions—a remarkable feat since the core of trade union strength in that era was skilled craft workers. Notably, just as the workers rebuffed trade unions, Baldwin managers also rebuffed efforts to introduce the new practices of scientific management into the shops,[27] viewing it as incompatible with the producer ethos since it tended to substitute mechanical rules and formal processes for individual initiative and responsibility, antagonized employees with fears of regimentation and speed-ups, and added to the ranks of "unproductive" management staff and overhead cost.

Despite the much-touted advantages of working at Baldwin, life in the shops was not heaven on earth. In return for high wages and job security, the company had to earn back its investment through higher productivity. Part of this productivity advantage came from a grueling work pace. The company used piece-rate compensation wherever possible to elicit maximum work effort. During cyclical downturns, it also used the opportunity of layoffs to weed out the slowest performers (and those deemed troublemakers). Notably, Baldwin implemented piecework not only on an individual basis but also on a modified group basis in the form of inside contracting. The inside contractor system, widely used in the late nineteenth century as another device to decentralize labor management, contracted the manufacture of components of the final product to a skilled worker or foreman.[28] This person, acting as a quasi-entrepreneur and employer, used the firm's equipment but hired, organized, paid, and supervised a team of workers and produced the component, keeping the difference between the contracted price and the costs of production as a form of profit. Baldwin allowed workers and inside contractors to keep part of the higher compensation, rather than quickly cut the piece rate to bring earnings back to a market rate, as did many other companies, causing Horace Arnold (a noted writer on engineering subjects) to observe that "the Baldwin workmen do drive themselves, or allow themselves to be driven . . . precisely as the tools are driven to the limit of their powers."[29] By not cutting piece rates, Baldwin paid higher wages than did its competitors but avoided the problem of worker "soldiering"— the deliberate withholding of work effort as a counterresponse to the firm's exploitation of labor through piece-rate cuts and speeding-up—that so angered and frustrated Frederick Taylor. Apparently the bargain worked, for Arnold concluded, "Notwithstanding this high wage, the work is done very cheaply indeed, and in many cases at incredibly low prices."[30] Part of this low price and high output entailed another cost to employees, however, in the form of workplace accidents and fatalities. Over a ten-year period (1903–13) seventy-four men were killed in the Baldwin shops, and in one year 12 percent of the workforce was injured.[31]

It is instructive to note that Baldwin's exemplary employee relations climate started to deteriorate after 1906, the peak year of business. The most obvious and threatening sign was a strike by half of the company's workers in 1911, caused by their anger over a wage cut and the discharge of hundreds of union activists. How could the harmonious relations so quickly spiral downward?[32] One reason was that the producer ethos that had so long guided the company was gradually lost. To raise capital, the company incorporated in 1909, forcing it to pay greater attention to short-run profit and loss and the demands of shareholders. A second was that the company had grown so large that maintaining esprit de corps and monitoring the actions of supervisors and foremen had become increasingly difficult. A third was that the spread of piecework and pressure to increase productivity had led to an ever finer specialization and division of labor, causing a steady decline in the corps of skilled craft workers who had once formed the loyal backbone of the company. Complementary to this was a marked increase in foreign-born workers, reflecting the huge wave of European immigrants that were coming to the United States before World War I, and these workers were less acculturated to the individualistic work ethic at Baldwin and more willing to engage in collective action and trade union activity. Finally, dominating all of these things was a decline in the company's product market position and profitability. It had greatly expanded production capacity at a new site outside Philadelphia, only to find that sales languished for the next decade as railroad regulation by the Interstate Commerce Commission starved the rail companies of the cash needed to buy locomotives. Faced with the huge costs of expansion and stagnant sales, Baldwin had no choice but to tighten up on labor, albeit at the long-run cost of a slow erosion of the "Baldwin Spirit" of partnership. Unionization did not come to Baldwin, however, until the 1930s.

4

HRM and Alternative Systems
of Workforce Governance

Another dimension along which employment systems vary is mode of workforce governance. Governance includes how the rules of the workplace are formulated and implemented, provisions for due process in the administration of discipline and discharge, and the degree of influence and voice employees are given. In this chapter I will provide four short case studies that reflect four alternative regimes of workforce governance. These may be called the *autocratic*, *paternalistic*, *participative*, and *collective bargaining* models.

The Autocratic Model: The Fulton
Bag and Cotton Mills

The Fulton Bag and Cotton Mills company (FBCM) was incorporated in Atlanta, Georgia, in 1889 by Jacob Elsas.[1] Elsas had come to America as a penniless Jewish immigrant in the early 1860s and through dint of hard work and successful entrepreneurship gradually amassed enough capital to branch out into the manufacture of cotton towels, sheeting, bags, and other kindred textile products. He built a mill complex several miles from downtown Atlanta (visible from where I sit writing this, now turned into lofts and apartments) that was one of the largest and most technologically advanced manufactories in the area. In 1900, employee numbers topped 1,000, doubled again by World War I. Elsas built other mills around the country, and before he died he had turned FBCM into a Fortune 500 company.

Adjacent to the mill, Elsas bought land and constructed several dozen small houses (with "privies" in the back yard) for married employees; for unmarried workers he built a boarding hotel. Often two families occupied a three-room unit. Soon the area resembled a typical southern mill village, albeit less isolated. Employee relations were relatively tranquil while Jacob Elsas was involved in day-to-day management of the mill, but turned sour and contentious when his eldest son Oscar took over the reins after 1900.

Work hours in the mill were sixty-six per week in 1905. Workers normally rose around 4:30 or 5:00 a.m. to eat breakfast and walk to their work stations before the bell rang at 6:00. The quitting bell rang at 6:00 p.m. The employees got Sunday off, and only worked a half day on Saturday, starting in 1912. The labor force was largely drawn from poor whites, often illiterate or barely schooled, who had left the poverty of sharecropping and backwoods life in the Appalachian Mountains to seek a better life in the new mills and factories that were springing up in the South. While accustomed to hard work, they had never been "bossed" or put on a fixed work schedule, and most lived without electricity, indoor plumbing, or even running water. Often entire families worked in the mill, including children. Few African Americans, on the other hand, were employed in the mill, and then only in the lowest jobs. An attempt by Elsas to introduce black women into the folding department immediately led to a walkout and mob violence by the white employees. Most employees earned between $7 and $10 per week.

The life of the Elsas family provided quite a contrast. They lived in one of the most exclusive neighborhoods of Atlanta; their place of worship was a synagogue, not one of the Protestant churches attended by most of the employees. Son Oscar had attended the Massachusetts Institute of Technology, sent his children to Ivy League schools, and arrived at the mill each day in a luxury automobile driven by a black chauffeur. Oscar also had an "attitude." In the words of historian Gary Fink, "Oscar Elsas, who sometimes confused ignorance with stupidity, considered his employees shiftless and irresponsible and possessed of a strong inclination toward dishonesty and immorality. Such workers, he believed, needed discipline and close supervision."[2] Many years later, Douglas McGregor labeled Oscar Elsas's controlling and punitive style the "theory X" approach to employee management.[3] Elsas the son was also a strong believer in the sanctity of private property rights and the employer's right to govern, remarking, "'This is my business and I have the right to run it in my own way.'"[4] Fink observes, "Seldom was the social and economic gulf separating workers and employers—capitalists and workers—any deeper than it was at Fulton Bag and Cotton Mills."[5]

The type of labor management model used at FBCM was in broad outline quite similar to that at the Pullman Palace Car Company (see chapter 3) and many other companies of that era. Jacob and Oscar Elsas set the labor policy and acted as the final court of appeal in disputes, but delegated day-to-day labor management to supervisors and foremen. The paymaster often screened the job applicants who applied at the mill gates. FBCM also made an investment in various betterment and welfare activities. The company, for example, employed a full-time physician, ran a day-care facility for the children of mothers working in the mill, and financed a settlement house where educational and recreational programs were provided. What set FBCM apart was the particularly oppressive and autocratic manner in which Oscar Elsas implemented this model.

The turnover rate at FBCM was astronomical. In 1911 the number of employees was 1,200, but over 10,000 people had worked at the mill at some point that year, yielding a turnover rate of over 800 percent. By 1913 the turnover rate declined to "only" 368 percent. Surprisingly, however, half the mill's employees had worked there for five years or more. This pattern points to a distinctly two-tiered workforce composed of a group of long-tenured employees and another group of very-short-term and transient workers.[6] The latter group was known at the time as "floaters" and "seven-day men," the latter term derived from the practice of working at one employer only long enough to get a week's pay. The high turnover rate vexed Oscar Elsas, particularly since it greatly exceeded that reported by other mill owners in Georgia. One conclusion open to him would have been that the labor policies and practices at the mill were the source of the turnover and reform of these would reduce the problem. He concluded, however, that fellow mill owners were lying to make themselves look better and that the high turnover came instead from "peculiar" conditions affecting FBCM (e.g., the more competitive nature of the Atlanta labor market) and the undisciplined and lazy behavior of the workers. Thus, he sought to solve the turnover problem by tightening controls and increasing punishments. In hindsight, one can conclude that Elsas only compounded the source of his difficulties.

It was common in that era to have new hires sign a written employment contract (with an X for those who could not read and write). These contracts put into legal language the employment-at-will doctrine (i.e., that the employer is free to discharge the worker at any time for any reason); stated the rate, method, and timing of pay; stipulated terms and conditions governing company housing; often had language that absolved the employer of all legal responsibility in case of accident or death on the job; and, in a number of cases, committed the employee to refrain from joining a union (the "yellow dog" contract).

Elsas added additional clauses to the FBCM employment contract that were found at no other mill in Georgia. The most hated and controversial clause mandated that employees give the company one week's advance notice of their intention to quit. To enforce this rule, the company held back one week's pay and the employees forfeited it if they failed to give proper notice. This rule meant that employees worked the first week without immediate pay, which was a considerable hardship. Further, for whatever reason many employees quit without the requisite one-week notice and lost their pay—estimated to total over $2,500 per year (at a weekly wage of

$10, this implies 250+ workers worked one week "for free"). Finally, workers resented being "bound to the mill" by this punitive device. Despite much public criticism and employee discontent, Elsas declared, "'I have made up my mind on the subject, and I will not change the contract system until Hell freezes over.'"[7]

The employment contract also imposed a variety of other fines and punishments on employees that were either used not at all or much more sparingly at other mills. Management assessed fines for any work deemed defective or for even the most petty infraction of the rules. As one worker reported, "'The rules became so numerous that it was almost impossible to work under them. If you were so much as five minutes late, they would dock you thirty minutes. . . . The women don't like to be fined for going in the dressing room 5 minutes before closing time—they were docked 25 cents for this. They were even fined 25 cents for carrying water to one another at the machines.'"[8] Over a fifteen-month period the fines and deductions amounted to $1,500. Also hated was the company's policy of giving employees cash rewards if they "ratted" on other workers' defective work or infraction of the rules.

Numerous other sources of dissatisfaction festered among the workers. The piece-rate system of pay, for example, led to charges of "speed-up" as the base rates were cut so that workers had to work faster to make the same earnings. Also, the company housing was allowed to deteriorate until the city of Atlanta condemned the mill village as a health hazard. Yet Elsas again rejected blame, saying, "'[W]e are doing everything possible'" and the fault lay with the employees since they were "'seemingly not interested in their own welfare.'"[9] Other welfare activities also caused discontent. When an employee did not show up in the morning for work, for example, the family could expect a visit from the company doctor who was ostensibly checking on the person's health but was covertly searching for shirkers and malingerers.

Faced with these conditions workers could either use "voice" or "exit" to seek improvements. Voice was actively discouraged, however, and was indeed a sure way to get fired. Elsas maintained a paid network of informants who kept management fully apprised of the activities of the employees and the names and identities of troublemakers and union sympathizers. The company had no compunction about firing these people, per the statement of the paymaster and assistant superintendent that company policy dictated that "they get rid of people who were unsatisfactory on any grounds."[10] In one year, over five hundred workers were fired at FBCM. Finally, grievances and discontent came to a head and the workers spontaneously walked out in May 1914, precipitating a long, ugly, and ultimately unsuccessful strike and union organizing drive. True to form, Elsas expressed no doubts about the correctness of his position and instead lay the blame on outside union agitators. Regarding the strikers he said, "'In an acute situation where I had only men to deal with I'd just as soon get guns and mow 'em down as not.'"[11]

The Paternalistic Model: The Endicott-Johnson Company

A far different approach to labor management and workforce governance was taken by the Endicott-Johnson Company (EJC). The company—eventually one of the country's largest manufacturers of shoes—became nationally famous as a leading practitioner of industrial paternalism.[12]

The EJC was the successor firm to the Lester-Shire Boot and Shoe Company, started in 1888 and located a few miles outside Binghamton, New York. The labor management system of the Lester-Shire company was undistinguishable from most other companies of that era. Individual foremen did the hiring and firing according to their individual preferences. Although the number of employees in the 1890s was already over two thousand, no payroll office or written labor policies existed. The pace of work was highly seasonal, with brisk hiring and fifteen- to eighteen-hour days in the busy season (spring and early summer) and layoffs and short work weeks in slack seasons. The company also built extensive housing around the factory, but the combination of management and worker apathy let conditions quickly deteriorate. As a reporter from the *New York Herald* commented, "[H]ere conditions are also bad. The long, low tenements are crowded with persons who never knew what it was like to live in clean quarters" (18). This reference to never knowing what it was like to live in clear quarters reflected the origin of most of the workers; in the early 1890s most migrated to the factory from the surrounding countryside while after the mid-1890s a growing share were newly arrived immigrants from southern and eastern Europe. Part and parcel of the cramped and dirty living arrangements were other ills of urban life, including a burgeoning number of saloons and brothels.

In the 1890s the nation was awakening to the fact it had a major labor problem. The railroad strikes of 1877, the Haymarket Riot of 1886, the Homestead Strike of 1892, and the Pullman Strike of 1894 were only the most visible markers of what appeared to be growing class polarization and antagonism between capital and labor. A Binghamton newspaper noted this phenomenon, commenting,

> It is manifest that relations between labor and capital are seriously strained. Even when these relations are not marked by an occasional outbreak, there is still a sort of passive antagonism between the employer and the employee; the force that reacts upon them is a mutually repellant one, and this is due in great measure to the fact that conditions have conspired to array their respective sympathies in opposite sides. (1)

The newspaper was motivated to comment on the "labor question" in part because it had now reared its ugly head in Binghamton: in 1890, one-fourth of the town's entire workforce, most unaffiliated with a union, went out on a four-month strike in support of local cigar workers. Shortly thereafter union organizing started at the Lester-Shire shoe factory, and a union local was formed there in 1893. Discharges started immediately, and it appeared that a strike was on the horizon.

Into this volatile situation stepped George F. Johnson, who had gone to work at age thirteen as a shoemaker and gradually worked his way up to a position as foreman. The president of Lester-Shire hired Johnson to be assistant superintendent when the factory opened and, when labor troubles were threatening to erupt in 1894, replaced the general manager with Johnson. Soon thereafter Henry Endicott, the largest shareholder, bought out the president's equity interest and asked Johnson to join him as a junior partner. The company was renamed the Endicott-Johnson Company and under Johnson's three decades–long leadership became not only extremely successful but nationally famous for its harmonious employee relations.

After 1900, EJC became a leading practitioner of corporate paternalism. The word *paternalism* implies a family led by a benevolent father figure who is the acknowledged boss but uses his power and authority to promote the general interest of the family, protecting it from harm and promoting its prosperity and well-being. This was exactly the model practiced by Johnson at EJC.

Speaking of his early years as a foreman and assistant superintendent, Johnson commented,

> "I had at that time no particularly definite ideas upon the subject of man management. I had been brought up in the old, hard school in which the worker was considered somebody that the employer had to have just as he had to have leather. I imagined the best way to get work of men was to keep them going as hard as they would go and especially to see piece rates were low enough to force a man to do a good day's work in order to gain a living." (16)

As Johnson grew older, however, he concluded that this approach was neither the most profitable nor consistent with his social and ethical principles. Thus, he remarked,

> "I began to wonder if it would not be better to give more attention to the human side—that workers had hearts as well as hands and that a leader of industry shouldered certain responsibilities beyond pocketing the profits. Out of that thought grew our present plan of organization." (16)

The system of labor management used by Johnson was in certain respects highly similar to the traditional model first practiced at Lester-Shire. Labor management remained highly decentralized and informal. Foremen continued to hire and fire, and no written rules were developed, nor was there a centralized employment office. If employees had complaints or grievances they took them up with the foreman and then proceeded to Johnson's office if still dissatisfied. On some occasions, feeling they had not gotten redress, workers in a particular department would stage a short strike—a practice common among nonunion workers of this era as they sought to publicize their dispute and exert pressure on management. Even the welfare and betterment activities in the plants were for many years on a very modest and informal scale. Yet, compared to other firms, the employment model at EJC was not only quite distinctive but also quite successful at solving the labor question. As a Binghamton newspaper reported in 1900,

> The company pays larger proportionate wages than any other manufacturing concern in this region, while privileges and kindnesses are freely extended to the employees by the superintendent and his assistant that generally are unheard of in large establishments. Indeed, this company never allows any of its faithful employees to suffer through want or distress, neither does it allow the property of any of its men to be sold under process of law. Between employer and employees there exists a bond of warm friendship, and the interests of master and servant are identical. Herein lies the success which has rewarded the efforts of the managing officers. (21)

This passage captures the essence of corporate paternalism—through voluntarily bestowed generosity the company secured labor peace, a dedicated and loyal workforce, and freedom from unions or government. Key to this outcome was forging an identity of interest between company and employees so that all shared a common purpose and had an incentive to work hard for the company's success. Toward this end, Johnson and EJC consciously and relentlessly created a corporate culture that cast the company and its employees as "one big happy family" with Johnson as the father. This father image was woven throughout the company's communication's with the employees. Johnson often wrote letters to employees that began "To Members of the Happy Family," and the company marching band would play a song that carried the line "George F.'s the daddy of the family" (44). Later, when EJC started a company magazine, it often featured Johnson on the front cover benevolently talking with an employee at his work post or helping a wife or child. Johnson once commented, in a private letter, "'As I go among my foreign neighbors [immigrant workers and families], I am their 'Father'—even some of the older men and women, older than myself. They look to me for everything they lack, or think they need, to make life happy'" (44). The company's workers and their families were not only the recipients of corporate paternalism but EJC sought to bring into the "happy family" the entire community. The company built parks, paid for half the cost of a new fire department, sponsored a wide range of athletic and recreation programs, and the executives headed up numerous civic and philanthropic organizations, all in an effort to create a tight bond of solidarity between capital and labor.

All of this largesse, from the above-market wages to the employment security to the many favors and kindnesses, was partly done out of the philosophical conviction that management had "'an obligation for the wellbeing of its employees.'"[13] In the main, however, corporate paternalism was the instrument of hardheaded business objectives. Illustrative is the fact that the company referred to welfare expenditures as "efficiency expenses."

Corporate paternalism was expensive, but it yielded many benefits. The company was relatively free of labor troubles, and unions could not gain a foothold, even during the height of the union organizing fervor of the mid- to late 1930s. Also, EJC was viewed as a "plum" employer and thus was able to recruit and keep a higher quality of worker. Turnover was relatively low for that era, and many workers remained at EJC their entire lives (an early example of "lifetime employment"). The company also expected in return for its generosity hard work, loyalty, and responsible behavior, as well as a free hand to introduce new production techniques and capital equipment. These expectations were not left implicit but instead were made the corner-stone of what EJC called the "Square Deal."

The Square Deal became the company motto and mantra; it was embla-zoned on the company magazine, on all the factory bulletin boards, and even over the main entrance gate to the factory. The idea behind the square deal was quid pro quo—what the company gave it expected back in equal proportion. One benefit, as just described, was low turnover and loyalty. Thus, Johnson told fellow executives, "'If you can stabilize the workers, so they stick, and become regular and skillful, and through acquaintance with the policies of the Company, loyal, you have established, I think, one of the biggest assets in Industry, and one hard to estimate as to its value to the Company'" (42).

Another part of this quid pro quo was hard and conscientious work, framed as a "fair day's work for a fair day's pay." A company pamphlet dis-tributed to the employees made this part of the bargain explicit, stating,

> "This company and its Directing Heads, know their business. . . . Their busi-ness is to see that you give them a 'Square Deal'; which means fair return for what you receive—an honest effort to do the work well, and a fair and suffi-cient amount of it." (40)

Johnson spelled out this idea in another communication to employees, noting,

> "Your own selfish interest, now, demands that you protect this business. You would not stand by and see a burglar break into a house, or a pickpocket in a crowd get in his work. Certainly not. Then don't let anyone beat this 'old busi-ness of ours.' . . . I want to see the day when you will all be self-appointed, sworn in, 'special policemen,' to stop 'time killing,' and 'dead Beats,' and the 'leeches' which gather around every industry." (41)

Evident in these quotations are the reciprocal covenants and obligations that formed the essence of the bargain between employer and employees in corporate paternalism—the company promises to take care of the employees, but the employees must reciprocate by working hard and making the company successful. Seen in this light, paternalism was a strategic approach that sought to solve the problem of worker soldiering but without all the adversarialism and "push back" engendered by the autocratic and exploitative methods used by traditionalists such as the Fulton Bag and Cotton Mills.

The Square Deal also had its downsides, however. Over time employees developed a feeling of entitlement and their gratitude gradually shifted to expectation. Buying gratitude and loyalty thus had an ever-increasing price. Employees also became adept at extracting "more" from the company by holding up the Square Deal and arguing that a management "no" would violate the mutual understanding. The philosophy of the Square Deal, with its promise that employees would be taken care, also made it more difficult for the company to retrench in times of financial stringency. And, finally, the Square Deal required huge amounts of executive time and attention to employees. George Pullman could spend most of his time in Chicago and New York, but George Johnson had to be continually in the factories and have his office door open.

For many years EJC sought to avoid bureaucratizing employer-employee relations and, indeed, the "personal touch" was a cornerstone of paternalism. For this reason, for quite some time EJC avoided setting up an accident insurance program for its employees, preferring instead to have Johnson and other company officials personally visit injured employees and write checks to the families for their lost wages. As the company grew, however, this personal touch became increasingly difficult and burdensome. The company's hand was finally forced on this matter by the economic boom and unsettled conditions sparked by World War I.

The war started in Europe in 1914. The American economy, after an initial dip due to uncertainty and interrupted trade, started on a five-year boom. At EJC, employee numbers doubled from 6,500 to over 13,000 between 1914 and 1920. Accompanying the employment boom was a wartime inflation marked by a doubling of prices and a mushroom growth in union organizing and strikes. Toward the end of the war, fears of revolutionary Bolshevism also percolated through American society. These unparalleled social and labor-market conditions posed a major challenge to EJC's harmonious family employment system. Johnson's son George W. wrote a fellow executive about this period, noting,

> "You will recall at the beginning of the European War business became brisk and we soon ran into the most unusual times, (so far as Labor was concerned) that we had ever experienced. Wages doubled and trebled and many concerns offered all sorts of inducements, in addition to wage increases, that would tend to keep workers happy and contented. We were among those who did all that we could for our workers." (39)

To cope with the strains of the war, EJC inaugurated a number of new employment programs and activities. A centralized employment office was created to administer human resource flows into and out of the company (now expanded to include nearly two dozen separate manufacturing facilities in the local area). A Medical and Relief Department was also established; besides providing health care to all employees and their families, it administered workmen's compensation, old age and widow's pensions, sickness benefits, and food and fuel to needy families. The company's housing program was also greatly expanded and houses were sold to employees.

The year 1919 saw the greatest innovations. A company magazine, the *E.-J. Workers' Review*, was started in order to promote improved communication between management and workers. Company employment policies were also written up and distributed in a booklet called *An E-J Worker's Introduction to the Square Deal*. Promotion from within, previously a well-understood but implicit policy, now became a commitment in writing. Also started was a profit-sharing plan. All profits after the payment of dividends on common and preferred stock were divided between workers and shareholders on a fifty-fifty basis. Another new program was a stock purchase plan. Within a year, 17 percent of the employees owned shares in the company. Corporate paternalism thus became more formalized and systematized at EJC during and after World War I, but as a basic human resource management strategy it continued intact for several more decades.

The Participative Model: William Filene and Sons

The third case study of this section features a participative form of workforce governance. The example is William Filene and Sons, a department store company headquartered in Boston. Material for this case study comes from a book commissioned by the Russell Sage Foundation and published in 1930, written by Mary La Dame after a nine month on-site investigation.[14]

Filene's was founded in 1881 by William Filene, an immigrant to the United States. In 1901 he retired and turned management of the store over to his two sons, Edward A. and A. Lincoln. They shared executive control of the company through the 1920s and became very well-known and respected spokesmen for progressive causes both inside and outside the business world.

Filene's started out as a small-sized apparel store specializing in retail merchandising of women and men's wear, later growing into a more general department store. It became famous for its "Basement" section, which featured quality name brands sold at discount prices. By 1900 the flagship store in Boston had over 500 employees, and by the end of World War I that number had surpassed 2,000. The firm today has stores in many areas of the United States.

In the first paragraph of the book's introduction, La Dame outlines the close connection that existed between business strategy, organizational structure, and employee relations at Filene's. She writes,

Relations with employees, particularly the establishment of just conditions of work, records indicate, have ever been a subject of consideration by the owners of the store. These assumed proportions of significance at the very beginning of its history. For such relations, it was recognized, were inextricably tied up with the objectives of the business. Success, as the Filenes have always conceived it, largely depended on their workers. Accordingly, the very structure of the corporation and the organization of the store were determined with the relationship between employer and employee in mind. (45)

In particular, Edward and Lincoln Filene articulated a business strategy that involved three central goals: *permanence, profits,* and *service.* These goals were seen as working together synergistically—service (i.e., providing customers low-priced and high-quality merchandize in a pleasant shopping environment) ensured profits, and profits ensured the long-run growth and success of the company.

This business strategy, in turn, drove their industrial relations strategy. Thus, La Dame writes, "With their goal as to their customers defined, what, in the minds of the Filenes, was its relation to their present and future employees?" (70). She then provides a fourfold answer. First, permanence of the company was served by having permanence of employees, leading the Filenes to conclude, according to La Dame, that "[c]ertainly the first specification was. . . . security of employment." Second, maximum profit required creating an identity of interest between the company and its employees so that the employees were motivated to provide their full effort toward the company's success. For this reason, the Filenes also concluded that "profit was to be distributed among their employees partly, perhaps, as a matter of social justice, but more as a stimulus to and a reward for productive effort." Third, quality customer service was promoted by having "skilled and courteous assistance, particularly from salespeople,. . . . [with] a sound attitude toward their work and a correct demeanor." This goal, in turn, was served by careful employee selection, investment in training, and attractive rewards for good service. Fourth, and finally, a way had to be found to make sure that all of these industrial relations goals were effectively coordinated and accomplished, and aligned with the business strategy. According to La Dame, toward this end the Filenes were led to the most important component of their industrial relations strategy—*employee participation.* Thus, she writes, "More, however, than a statement of the identity of interest between employer and employee, as expressed by the aims of the business, would be necessary to get employees to put forth their best efforts to attain those aims. . . . To this challenge the Filenes very gradually responded with a threefold principle of procedures. In the phraseology of today, this was employee participation in management, in profits and, possibly, in ownership." La Dame goes on to add, "That the system of thought envisaged in employee participation in management, profits and ownership deserves to be designated as a philosophy [or *strategy*] of industrial relations, few if any will deny" (72).

The structure and implementation of the industrial relations program at Filene's in the late 1800s and early 1900s involved two central parts of the organization. The first was the personnel division. On the operation of this division La Dame writes, "Few companies have given as much emphasis and attention to the functions pertaining to personnel as has Filene's" (353–54). She continues, "From the very foundation of the Filene store, the problem of personnel has been one treated as permeating management. In almost all occupations represented in the organization, the human being is the important unit of production.... Personnel administration at Filene's has not been tacked on as a frill to management.... Furthermore, it was not stimulated by philanthropic feelings or sociological considerations. Rooted in a philosophy of cooperation, it has grown up as an organic part of management, cutting across its entire content...." (429).

For the first twenty years of operation William Filene and his sons personally performed most of the personnel functions. They interviewed job candidates, made hiring and firing decisions, conducted training, and heard employee complaints. As the store grew to more than five hundred people, however, this personal and largely informal approach to personnel management no longer worked. Hence, the Filenes started to establish a formal personnel function in the store.

An employment department—one of the first in the nation—was established about 1903. Early on, the employment manager was made a member of the store's board of trade (management committee). The employment department was responsible for employee recruitment and hiring, salary classification and job standards, transfer and promotion, and record keeping.

Several years earlier the store had also started various types of welfare work and appointed a welfare director to oversee them. In an early example of employee participation, in 1898 the company formed a joint worker-management insurance committee to develop and oversee an accident and health insurance program for employees. A savings program was also started that later evolved into the Filene's Credit Union. Other welfare activities included rest rooms and employee eating facilities, recreation programs, a library, a company newspaper and, at a later date, pensions.

A formal training program, directed by the welfare director, was begun in 1902. In 1906 the training function was separated from the welfare program and made into a separate personnel division. Training involved five activities: classes, conferences, efficiency bulletins, "blunder slips," and efficiency records.

Also starting in 1903 was the beginning of a profit-sharing plan. Profit sharing took the form of annual bonuses, the size of which depended on that year's profits. For the first ten years the bonuses were given only to executives and specialists (e.g., buyers), but in 1913 they were extended to all employees.

Another personnel policy adopted by Filene's was promotion from within. This policy was a long-standing practice that only later became codified.

Turnover and job tenure data are unavailable for years prior to World War I, but in the early 1920s over two-thirds of the employees (70 percent female) had been with the store more than two years, and 40 percent of them more than five years.

Another innovation, and one of the first examples of its kind in the nation, was Filene's in-house arbitration board, created in 1901. The mission of the board was to serve as the final court of appeal for all disputes between company and employees. In 1913 it heard seventy cases. In a significant act of faith on the part of management, the board was entirely composed of employees, and no management personnel were allowed to serve on it. On rare occasion, top management objected to a board decision and asked for a reconsideration. Evidence indicates, however, that the board operated with considerable autonomy and management forbearance. La Dame was able to locate summaries of 308 arbitration cases and found that 55 percent were in favor of the employee, 42 percent were in favor of management, and 3 percent were a compromise. In dismissal cases, management prevailed 54 percent of the time (272–74).

The second fundamental organizational structure at Filene's related to labor management, and the one that attracted the most national attention, was the Filene's Co-operative Association (FCA). As La Dame observes, "The Filene Co-operative Association, if not the original plan of employee participation in management set up in the United States, was among the earliest of such plans." She states that the beginnings of the FCA can be traced to two sources: "The first was the recognition by the Filenes of the value of the informal meetings with their employees inaugurated by their father. In these meetings workers found opportunity and were encouraged to express their ideas on all aspects of the work of the store. A spirit of intelligent and critical study of its routine was thus fostered." La Dame adds, "The second source. . . . was the realization by the owners of the store of the ineffectiveness of welfare work superimposed by them upon their workers." She then quotes Edward Filene: "'We had to acknowledge that our [welfare] work had been a failure. . . . We had tried to do the work for our people under well-meant but still despotically benevolent principles. But grown wiser and more democratic by our failures, we agreed. . . . to help them with all our minds and strength to do everything for themselves'" (119–20).

The FCA began to operate around 1898 and was formally established in 1903. It had a president, vice president, and treasurer, all of whom were elected annually by the membership. Most often the officers were managers or specialists. In the early years all important matters were voted on by the entire membership in a mass meeting. In 1905 this system was replaced by an FCA council composed of the three officers and nineteen employee representatives chosen by the employees in the nineteen divisions of the company. The council generally met once a month. The company paid all the expenses of the FCA, although it made proposals at several points that employees bear part of the cost through monthly dues. The FCA was also allowed to elect four representatives to sit on the company's board of directors.

The FCA's written charter stated the purpose of the organization to be the following: (1) "To give its members a voice in their government"; (2) "to increase their efficiency"; (3) "to add to their social opportunities"; and (4) "to sustain a just and equitable relation between employer and employee." Regarding these objectives, La Dame notes, "The second, to increase the efficiency of its members, was unquestionably the basic object for which the Association was established" (121). But there was also a broader purpose behind the FCA: to create a form of industrial democracy in the company. As is evident in the statement of the first objective, the Filenes looked at their company as a form of "government," albeit one located in the industrial realm. Just as political government has an executive, legislative, and judicial function, so does an industrial government. In most nonunion firms, all three functions are concentrated in the hands of the employer, making the company a form of industrial autocracy (or "monarchy"). Sometimes this autocracy is benevolent, such as at Endicott-Johnson, and other times is it is oppressive, such as at Fulton Bag and Cotton Mills, but in all cases the employer is the undisputed "ruler." The Filenes sought to democratize their company by creating the FCA and investing it with a significant measure of legislative and judicial power.

Regarding the legislative (rule-making) function, the constitution of the FCA stated that it may

> initiate new store rules or modifications or cancellations of existing store rules concerning store discipline, working conditions or relations, or any other matters, except policies of the business, either by a two-thirds vote of its entire membership or by a five-sixths vote of the File Co-operative Association Council. Such a vote shall have full effect unless vetoed by the president of the company. . . . [But] any measure may be passed over this veto by ballot vote of not less than two-thirds of the entire membership of the Filene Co-operative Association. (122)

The FCA exercised this legislative function primarily in several areas. One such area was in hours of work and vacation time. An early action of the FCA, for example, was to vote in 1902 that the store would close on Monday, July 5, giving the employees a three-day holiday. Later that year the employees voted against keeping the store open in the evenings before Christmas. The Filenes did not veto either measure, despite the fact that few if any other stores in Boston followed these practices. Over the years the FCA voted for additional holiday time off, shorter store hours, and winter vacations (in addition to the summer vacations the Filenes independently provided). A second area was in work rules and discipline. The FCA, for example, reviewed and approved the rule book distributed to all employees. It worked to get rid of time clocks and substitute an alternative "less mechanistic" system for keeping track of attendance and tardiness, and also successfully opposed a requirement that all employees at the time of hire pass a physical examination. A third area the FCA was active in was the company's welfare program. The association was represented on the insurance committee that helped design and administer the employee accident and illness benefits program. After losing money for a number of years on the employee cafeteria, the company also turned food services over to the FCA, which pushed it into the black.

One area in which the FCA had very little involvement or influence was wages. La Dame found almost no evidence that wages were a topic of discussion at FCA meetings. She concludes that the reasons were partly that the company did not encourage discussion on this topic and partly that the pay scale at Filene's was superior to that of competitors, and employees were thus relatively satisfied. The FCA, on the other hand, did take an active role in shaping the profit-sharing (bonus) plan.

The judicial (rule interpretation and enforcement) function of the FCA was lodged in the arbitration board. As noted earlier, the arbitration board was comprised of seven employees, all of whom were selected by the FCA. The FCA constitution gave the board a mandate of authority: "'On the application of any. . . . member it [the board] shall hear, determine and have final jurisdiction over grievances or disputes, including such questions as wages, discharges and working conditions'" (123). The operation and record of the board has already been discussed, but it is worthwhile to reiterate that it appears to have significantly circumscribed—and in some cases reversed—management decisions in discipline and discharge. Notably, one topic that almost never came before the board was antiunion discrimination by the company. Filene's not only did not discriminate against union members but voluntarily paid union wages and benefits to the workers in its employ (primarily building engineers and other skilled craftspeople) who did hold union cards—even though there was no union contract mandating that they do so. Eventually the nonunion workers filed a complaint with the arbitration board challenging the fairness of this arrangement!

Summarizing her study, La Dame concludes, "Judged by the criteria of profit, service to customers and provision for perpetuating the business, the policy of the Filene store in relation to employees seems to have been a success" (448). She also concludes, however, that the experiment in participative management was a mixed one, with positive and negative marks. On the positive side, the FCA and the arbitration board had given the employees a voice and influence in company policy far beyond that found at nearly any other nonunion company. On the negative side, while the employees expressed appreciation and satisfaction with the FCA and the company they also demonstrated little or no interest in the ongoing activities of the FCA and expressed little desire to become more involved in management. The general manager of Filene's was thus led to ruefully conclude, "'The truth has been brought home to us that the day of full self-rule in industry, as it is understood in government, is still far distant'" (333).

The Collective Bargaining Model: Coal Mining

The last type of industrial governance examined is collective bargaining between the employer and employees represented by one or more independent trade unions. At the turn of the century, the largest and most important locus of collective bargaining was the coal industry. This industry also best illustrates the impact of unionism on labor management practices in this early period, per the observation in the *Final Report* of the U.S. Industrial Commission that "[t]he influence of organization is nowhere more strongly exhibited than in the case of bituminous coal workers."[15] Unfortunately, no case study of labor management practices at an individual coal company exists for this era. As an alternative, I synthesize evidence for this industry from a number of sources, but with particular reliance on the report prepared by the presidential commission appointed to investigate the anthracite coal strike of 1902.[16]

The coal industry of the late nineteenth century was highly fractionated.[17] The industry was divided into two major coal product groups: anthracite coal and bituminous coal. Anthracite coal was located in a compact area of eastern Pennsylvania and was used mainly for home heating; bituminous coal was mined in twenty-six states and was used for a wide variety of commercial and industrial purposes. The bituminous segment, in turn, was divided into different but partially overlapping geographical markets, distinguished by product quality (e.g., purity, carbon content) and transportation cost. Anthracite production after 1900 was concentrated among a relatively small number of companies controlled by railroads and eastern financial interests and partook the character of a monopolistic cartel. The bituminous part of the industry, on the other hand, was comprised of more than a thousand companies and was highly competitive. Some producers were "mom and pop" operators with a few employees selling coal out of a pit or short shaft in a hillside; others were locally owned and operated companies producing out of one or several significant-sized mines with 100–300 employees, and yet others were large corporations headquartered in New York City or Philadelphia that owned many mining properties and employed thousands of workers.

Prior to unionization, labor management practices in both segments of the coal industry in the late nineteenth century were largely similar. In some respects they also mirrored practices at the mills and factories of that era, such as Pullman Palace Car Company and Fulton Bag and Cotton Mills, but in other respects they were considerably different. These differences turned on factors such as the geographical isolation of many coal mines, the technology and labor process used to produce coal, and the presence in most years of substantial overcapacity.

The HRM model used by coal companies was a classic example of late-nineteenth-century labor management: decentralized, externalized, and informal.[18]

Small- and medium-size mines were often owner operated, while larger mines were part of the holdings of a large corporation. In the latter case, the top executive in charge of the mine was usually the general superintendent, appointed by corporate headquarters and paid on a combination of salary, bonus, and stock. Here, too, was a major fault line in the industry, for owner-operators often had started out as miners and had some appreciation for the worker's point of view while corporate-appointed superintendents were often engineers who came to their posts with considerable technical expertise but little experience with human relations or appreciation of a miner's life.

Whatever the case, the superintendent or owner would have a small group of salaried managers, assistants, and clerks in the mine office to handle sales, accounting, purchasing, and other such matters. The owner or superintendent set general labor policy, but then delegated nearly all aspects of labor management to the mine foreman or "pit boss," who, sometimes with the help of subforemen, did the hiring and firing, set the pay rates, handled grievances, and so on. Neither the general labor policy nor individual HRM practices were formalized or put down on paper, and the pit boss had a free hand to practice labor management as he saw fit. This situation was similar to factories, except that most mines had only one mine foreman responsible for all underground operations, while large factories often had a dozen or more coequal foremen responsible for individual operating departments.[19] Also different was that large factories started to set up separate employment departments in the 1910s and full-fledged personnel or industrial relations (PIR) departments during or shortly after World War I, while PIR departments in the coal industry before 1920 were practically unknown and only a few large mines had so much as an office room for employment/hiring.

These differences between factories and mines reflected differences in the technology of the production and labor process. Factory production was under one roof, workers were closely bunched together and easily observable, and many tasks could be performed by unskilled or semiskilled workers. Coal production was considerably different; a coal mine often extended far underground, branched into different hallways three and four feet tall, and contained a number of separate rooms where coal was excavated. Miners often worked in small teams of two and three, with several helpers. For these reasons, supervision was difficult and expensive. Likewise, before mechanization came in a big way, coal mining was a skilled and physically demanding occupation. The miner had to be an expert at timbering, using explosives, undercutting the coal face, and sensing danger. These skills were another factor giving the miner freedom from the bossing and driving found in a factory. Thus, miners determined their own work schedules, including the days they worked, when they reported for work, and when they went home. In fact, the coal miner played the role of a lesser boss because he generally hired and supervised several assistants who did the manual work of loading the coal into cars and fetching supplies.[20]

The coal miner, therefore, worked as part of a small semiautonomous team and in certain respects was akin to an inside contractor. The major HRM device employers used to align the incentives of the miner and the company was a piece-rate system of compensation. In most nonunion mines, miners were paid per car of coal they brought to the mine surface each day. Other aspects of HRM were rudimentary or nonexistent. Training, for example, came on the job, often by father teaching son, while grievances were handled face-to-face between miner and pit boss. Partial exceptions concerned mine safety, company stores, and company housing. In the late 1800s a number of states passed mine safety laws and, although often weak and poorly policed, they forced coal companies to pay some attention to this area; often this entailed no more than a daily walk-around by the pit boss, but in some cases it involved hiring a safety engineer. Likewise, many mines were in remote and often mountainous areas of the Appalachians and companies had to set up from scratch an entire town—including a school, jail, store, and several dozen houses.

Among industry work groups in the nineteenth century, coal miners were among the most active and ardent in their pursuit of trade unionism and collective bargaining. Organizing started in the 1840s, and intensified after the Civil War. Similarly, among employer groups, few were as stalwart and uncompromising as the mine operators in their resistance to unionism. The inevitable result was a long history of animosity and conflict culminating in long and often violent strikes. These strikes sometimes paralyzed the industry for months, resulted in widespread property destruction and numerous deaths, and were ended only with the intervention of federal and state troops.[21] A classic example was the anthracite strike of 1902 that shut down coal production for five months, led to numerous acts of mayhem and murder, and was only resolved when President Theodore Roosevelt coerced the employers into accepting arbitration of the dispute.[22]

Consideration of the employees' and employers' position toward collective bargaining illustrates certain challenges and shortcomings of labor management in the late nineteenth and early twentieth centuries. This case also illustrates the two-sided nature of trade unionism and collective bargaining—on one side they are a potent source of conflict and adversarial employer-employee relations; on the other they have the potential to stabilize and harmonize the employment relationship.

From the employee's point of view, a coal miner's experience was one of constant insecurity, frequent periods of destitution, subjection to numerous petty tyrannies and injustices, and domination and control of all aspects of life by the employer.[23] Insecurity accompanied the miner everyday he went to work, for coal mining was one of the most dangerous occupations in the nation and each year hundreds of miners were killed and thousands seriously injured. The coal industry was also notoriously overdeveloped and seasonal, so coal miners often had three to six months of the year with no work or only part-time work. A full-time factory employee, for example, worked around 270–290 days a year, but the average coal miner worked only 180–200 days. When they worked, skilled miners' earnings compared well to those of other jobs, but the frequent slow periods caused annual earnings to often bump against or fall below the bare minimum for a family. This minimum family income level was called a "living wage" and became a major union demand. Further, during the long depression of the 1890s, coal wages fell 17 percent.[24] Some miners and their families left coal mining when things got particularly hard, but their spaces were quickly filled through the constant inflow of new immigrants from eastern and southern Europe, as well as through a smaller number of African Americans and Mexicans. Autobiographies of miners' lives reveal a continuing cycle of work and decent earnings for a few months or perhaps a year or two, layoffs or part-time employment, periods of scraping by on a thin meal a day and going into debt at the company store, and packing the family and few belongings on a mule-drawn wagon to find work at another mine over the mountain or down in the valley.[25] Also revealed is the pressure on poverty-stricken parents to send their children to full-time work in the mines as early as the age of ten.

Miners also had a number of other burdens and grievances.[26] Pit bosses, for example, maintained discipline and loyalty through rewards and punishments that could be arbitrary and unjust. For example, the foreman could assign a miner to the largest or cleanest part of the coal face where he could easily produce five or six cars a day, or to a thin or dirty part of the face requiring much more physical work and yielding only two or three cars of coal. Miners also often felt cheated because their rate of pay was based on a car of coal, but some pit bosses demanded that the car be heaped with coal rather than just filled level to the top (the difference between a "short" ton of 2,000 pounds and a "long" ton of 2,400 pounds). Mechanization of the mines was another source of grievance, for while machinery reduced some of the physical hardship of mine labor it also turned the miner from a skilled craftsman with considerable control over work speed into a semiskilled machine operator tethered to the speed of the machine.

The company store and housing were also perennial sources of complaint. Although the factual evidence is mixed, miners often complained that the prices at the company store were inflated or they were coerced to buy from the store lest they be fired or discriminated against.[27] Likewise, company housing was frequently not much more than a series of shacks, and the miners and their families knew they had to avoid trouble or face eviction. Coal companies hired their own police and security guards, and they patrolled the housing camps with armed weapons, arrested suspicious people, and denied entrance to undesirables. Critics of the companies compared the running of the coal camps to ancient feudalism. Completing the sense of domination and control was the widespread perception that the companies had bribed or pressured the local courts, politicians, and sheriffs to serve their interests.

   Given these conditions it is easy to appreciate why coal miners frequently
wanted representation and collective bargaining. Unionization of the industry would raise wages, making possible a decent standard of living. Higher
wages, of course, would raise costs for companies, but if all mines were organized then these costs could mostly be passed on to consumers in the
form of higher prices. Also beneficial was the fact that higher costs would
close down the marginal producers and help reduce the overcapacity problem and downward pressure on prices and wages. Stabilization of the anthracite industry was largely achieved by the early 1900s, when most of the
mines had been bought out by a handful of railroad companies, thus ending
the cutthroat competition that plagued both producers and workers.[28] Since
the bituminous part of the industry was too expansive for monopoly on the
producer side, stability could be accomplished by monopoly on the labor
side. A union also promised numerous other benefits. A union, for example,
could enforce stricter safety conditions and would lobby state legislatures
for stronger safety laws and enforcement. Again, as long as the higher safety
standards were uniform across firms, none would be at a competitive disadvantage.[29] Through collective bargaining, workers could also get another
prized demand—payment by the ton, documented by a neutral checkweighman. Also provided would be other benefits, such as a formal grievance
system, protection from arbitrary or unjust dismissal and punishment, regulation of training and apprenticeship, protection against speed-ups, and
death and accident payments. A union would, finally, offset employer
domination and give workers a voice at the workplace and political system. Although all of these gains benefited workers, the trade unionists and
their social reform allies claimed that the industry and society would also
benefit by greater production stability, the end of ruinous cutthroat competition, a more skilled and productive workforce, replacement of labor
wars with negotiated compromise, and greater democracy in the workplace
and polity.[30]
   Employers had a significantly different view of unions and collective bargaining. Most coal operators had a deep dislike for trade unions. Said one
coal miner, "'the company hated the union like God hates sin.'"[31] Part of
this dislike on the part of employers arose from unique American cultural
attitudes that made individualism, liberty, and the sanctity of property
rights core values.[32] The average employer believed that the business was
his property and no one had the right to tell him how to run it, including all
aspects of managing the labor. Freedom of contract was thus a deeply held
principle, and both unions and government regulation infringed upon it.
Employers, therefore, were deeply resentful when a union, viewed as an
outside third party with no investment stake in the business and often run
by radical and opportunistic leaders, forced companies to pay equal wages
to miners despite differences in their productivity, to hire only union members, and prove to a union officer that someone deserved to be fired. The
coal operators also had a deep belief in the efficacy of free markets and

unrestricted competition (at least for labor). They may not have read Adam Smith, but most accepted the principle that the labor market adequately protected the workers' interest and promoted the social welfare. If workers did not like being paid in company scrip rather than cash wages, the safety conditions at a particular mine, or the prices at the company store, they could readily quit and find a job elsewhere. This labor mobility from inferior to superior employers created wage differentials that compensated workers at the inferior employers for the less desirable conditions. It was these principles in mind that George Baer, a railroad executive, maintained in the 1902 anthracite strike that "'[t]he rights and interests of the laboring man will be protected and cared for, not by the labor agitators, but by the Christian men to whom God in His infinite wisdom has given the control of the property interests of the country.' "[33]

On purely pragmatic profit and loss grounds, most coal mine operators also felt they had good reason to resist unions. Coal mining was a highly competitive industry before 1900 and margins of profit were small and sometimes zero on a capital investment often of many millions of dollars. Anything that increased costs or reduced flexibility was not only a threat to profit but to survival itself. Two key issues that precipitated the 1902 anthracite strike, for example, were the union's demand for a 20 percent wage increase and a reduction in work hours from nine to eight per day. The companies asserted they had no choice but to take the strike, since this near 40 percent increase in labor cost would have either bankrupted many of them or forced them to drastically reduce output and employment and raise prices to consumers.[34] They also contended that there was no factual basis for the union's argument that wages or conditions were unduly low, since the companies were able to obtain all the labor they wanted. Stated one employer, "'The satisfactory character of the conditions prevailing has been conclusively shown by the fact that, without any effort on the part of this respondent, for many years those seeking employment have thronged the region.' "[35] The companies also leveled a number of other economic indictments against the union. According to one employer, for example, the union "'opposes the introduction of labor saving machinery; seeks to limit the supply of labor, and reduce all to the standard of the least efficient, and to systematically raise the cost of production. It sets up extravagant demands. . . . and enforces it orders and directions [by]. . . . sympathetic strikes, boycotts, picketing and the like.' "[36] Another said that since it began dealing with the union two years earlier, "'A depreciation in the quantity and deterioration in the quality of work followed, amounting to about 12 percent of the average output per man per day. During the past two years the members of the association [United Mine Workers union] brought about more strikes and interruptions of work than had occurred during the previous twenty-five years.' "[37] Related to the last quotation, employers often complained that the union did not honor its contracts and, in particular, either encouraged or refused to stop workers who walked out during a contract as part of a sympathy strike or opportunistic pressure tactic to extract yet additional gains.

One can sense from this brief overview that both the employers' and workers' positions had ethical legitimacy and a sound grounding in fact. This situation no doubt explains the conflicted state of public opinion on the general subject of unions in the late nineteenth century and more particularly the 1902 coal strike, as well as the "split the difference" set of recommendations proposed by the presidential commission.[38]

For the purposes of understanding the early history of HRM, three other more general lessons emerge. The first is that a strategy of positive HRM practices and mutual gain employer-employee relations is to a significant degree conditional on a stable and relatively full employment economic environment. It is not coincidental that the drive for unionization in the late nineteenth century was most persistent and intense in highly competitive industries such as mining, printing, and building construction. Employers had little control over production and prices, typically earned small profits, and were continually facing the threat of new entrants. Combined with large swings in the business cycle and long periods of recession and depression, these conditions led to great instability in production and employment, hypervigilance to keep down cost, frequent wage cuts, and emergence of a short-run commodity outlook on labor.[39] Such an environment made it difficult for employers to justify expenditure on positive HRM practices and, indeed, forced them in a "dog eat dog" world to control and exploit labor wherever and however possible. Thus, without absolving coal operators of moral responsibility, one can nonetheless appreciate that intense competition in a market situation of excess production capacity and abundant labor made it very difficult for the individual coal company to resist the "low road" (but economically "best practice") strategy of child labor, excessive prices at the company store, and cheating miners on their coal tonnage. Significantly, these problems abated in the anthracite portion of the industry after it was effectively cartelized after 1900 (at the expense of higher prices and declining demand and employment), while they remained severe in the competitive bituminous sector.

. This lesson from the coal industry sheds considerable light on a second insight, which is the importance for successful collective bargaining of taking labor cost out of competition.[40] An important reason individual coal companies so stoutly resisted unionization was that they feared some competitors would remain nonunion, have a cost advantage, and gradually take over the industry. This factor was particularly relevant in the bituminous sector, given the huge number of competing firms. Between 1898 and 1904 the United Mine Workers (UMW) union was able to organize most employers in what was called the "central competitive field," encompassing states stretching from Illinois to Pennsylvania, as well as in a number of western and border states. Once organized, many of these coal companies grudgingly accepted the union because they recognized that monopoly on the labor side could help stabilize the industry and benefit both capital and labor. The problem was that in the next few years the union failed to organize much of West Virginia and several southern states. As the UMW raised wages and labor costs in the central competitive field, these employers came under growing competitive threat from the nonunion sector and finally had to either mount another "labor war" to break the UMW's hold or watch themselves slide toward bankruptcy. Both happened in the decade and a half leading up to World War I, followed by another industrywide strike in the prosperous year of 1919 as the union once again tried to resuscitate collective bargaining by organizing the entire market.[41]

A final lesson from the coal industry is the large social and private costs that often accompanied the struggle over collective bargaining. In several industries in the late nineteenth and early twentieth centuries, a union was able to organize the entire product market, and for a decade or more collective bargaining proceeded relatively peacefully with few strikes. Two examples are the stove industry and the printing industry.[42] In most industries of this era, however, unions were able to organize only a portion of employers, such as in the bituminous coal-mining industry. The result was that unionization threatened to raise the individual firm's labor cost and make it noncompetitive, and this prospect—abetted by ideological opposition to unions—elevated union avoidance as one of employers' highest strategic goals. The combination of intense opposition to collective bargaining and frequent resort to hardball union suppression techniques, when combined with labor conditions such as the drive system and hire-and-fire HRM that often drove workers to want the protection of a union, inevitably created deeply conflictual and strike-prone employer-employee relations.[43] For this and other reasons, the United States witnessed a growing number of bitter, destructive strikes between 1900 and 1920. The costs were quite large, not only in economic terms but in terms of satisfying work relations and human life. The economic costs are suggested by the anthracite strike of 1902. A presidential commission estimated this one strike cost coal operators and railroads $46 million and $19 million in lost revenue, respectively, while workers lost about $25 million in wages.[44] Given that the average miner earned $600–$800 a year, this was a huge loss due to inability to structure the employment relationship in a more positive and mutual-gain manner.

5

HRM in the Industrial Heartland I

The United States Steel Corporation

Part 1 of this volume closes with two case studies of early labor management practices in the industrial heartland of the American economy: the steel and auto industries. These industries exemplify the transformation of America from a nineteenth-century agricultural- and natural resource–based economy to a modern, technologically advanced twentieth-century industrial economy. By the end of World War I, steel was the core of the manufacturing sector and the automobile industry was at the leading edge. The case studies focus on two particular firms in steel and autos, the United States Steel Corporation and the Ford Motor Company. A good argument can be made that these firms were the two most important and influential in the entire nation in terms of their labor management practices.

The United States Steel Corporation and the Steel Industry

The United States Steel Corporation (USSC) was formed in 1901 from a merger of eight independent companies.[1] It controlled two-thirds of steel industry output and employed over 160,000 people. For the next thirty years the "Steel Corporation," as it was commonly known, not only dominated the country's largest and most important industry but was also widely regarded as the single most influential employer in terms of setting basic labor policy.

The story of labor practices in the steel industry, and how they changed with the formation of the USSC, must begin twenty years earlier. It also has to include the remarkable person Andrew Carnegie.

The story starts with a crucial difference: iron versus steel. Production of iron originally dominated the industry and was only surpassed by steel in the early 1890s. The advantage of steel was a much higher tensile strength, making it far stronger and more durable in applications such as rails, structural beams, and machine tools. But steel was also more complicated to produce because it required higher heat and a more sophisticated technology. Only with the invention of the Bessemer converter in 1856 did steelmaking become practical, and even then it took another thirty years for the technology to develop and diffuse. Until then, iron production was king.

The key feature about iron production was that it could not be fully mechanized and, for this reason, operated at a relatively modest scale. A typical iron rail mill, for example, had an annual output of 12,000 tons, while a steel rail mill produced nearly ten times as much.[2] The major constraint in iron production was that every batch of molten iron from the blast furnace had to be stirred by hand in another furnace to bring impurities to the top where they could be skimmed off as slag. This process was done by skilled workers known as "puddlers." The craft of puddling required considerable experience and expert judgment, thus making puddlers relatively scarce and expensive to train.[3] This also gave puddlers strategic control of the pace of the work, which they used to regulate the daily and weekly "stint" (the number and size of iron batches from the furnace).[4]

Having a strategic position in the labor market, the puddlers sought to leverage it through collective action and to do so they formed the Amalgamated Association of Iron and Steel Workers. The Amalgamated grew to be one of the largest and most powerful unions of the 1870s and '80s and successfully organized many of the iron producers. The largest of these iron producers was the Carnegie Company, owned by Andrew Carnegie. Carnegie was for an initial period friendly to the Amalgamated and signed collective bargaining contracts with it. The reason, however, had mostly to do with shrewd business acumen and provides an early illustration of how human resource strategy can align with and promote business strategy.[5] Carnegie's business strategy was to build the largest and most modern mills, "run them full" to gain lowest unit cost through economies of scale, and use his superior cost position to underprice rivals and gain market share and further scale economies. He used the Amalgamated to advance this strategy since the union's high wage rates and work restrictions (detailed in fifty-eight pages of "footnotes" to the contract) raised unit costs proportionately more at his smaller scale rivals and thus gave him a further pricing advantage. (The bulk of unskilled workers were not represented by the Amalgamated, but to maintain worker solidarity during strikes it also demanded higher wages for them.)

Two things happened, however, to turn Carnegie toward an antagonistic position.[6] The first was that the Amalgamated's coverage of the industry and thus its ability to take labor cost out of competition was slipping, thus turning unionization of Carnegie's mills from a competitive advantage to a competitive disadvantage. The second factor, largely responsible for the first, was that steel was rapidly displacing iron, and steelmaking could be entirely mechanized because it did not require puddlers. These events led to the famous strike at Carnegie's Homestead, Pennsylvania, mill and the ousting of the Amalgamated.[7]

The deunionization of the iron and steel industry, coupled with the depression of 1893–96 and Carnegie's policy of gaining market share through aggressive pricing, led to intense price competition among the companies and numerous bankruptcies and mergers. Greater competition in product markets inevitably rippled into labor markets, leading to wage cuts, longer hours, and intensification of work efforts. In particular, Carnegie and a number of rivals had shifted their mills to three eight-hour shifts in the 1880s, but in the 1890s went back to a schedule of two twelve-hour shifts operating seven days a week. Also more evident was work intensification. The deskilling of labor arising from rapid mechanization, coupled with the influx of immigrants, led to expansion of the drive system.[8] Greater speed of work was also induced through wider application of piece-rate pay systems, accompanied by periodic cuts in the piece rates. As an English industrialist remarked in 1897 after visiting American mills, "'The "bosses" drive the men to an extent that the employers would never dream of attempting in this country.' "[9]

All of these factors set the stage for the formation of the United States Steel Corporation in 1901 and the emergence of a new labor regime. From 1898 to 1902 the nation was swept by an unprecedented wave of horizontal and vertical mergers, aimed in part at greater integration along the supply chain and attendant economies in production and also toward higher and more stable prices through the elimination of competition in product markets. Thus was born a number of huge trusts, formal pooling arrangements, and monopolies. The largest and most spectacular of these was the USSC. Financier J. P. Morgan and lawyer turned corporate executive Elbert Gary bought out Carnegie, combined Carnegie's empire with seven other companies in the world's first billion-dollar merger deal, and installed Gary as the new head.

Labor policy at USSC, and across the steel industry, evolved into an interesting two-part pattern perhaps best characterized as the "iron fist in the velvet glove." Writing in the 1930s, for example, Carroll Daugherty, Melvin de Chazeau, and Samuel Stratton observed,

> Labor management and control in the iron and steel industry has in fact had these two aspects. The list of things that has been done 'for' labor [i.e., the program that was developed in order to secure the cooperation and loyalty of the workers]. . . . was impressive and seldom equaled elsewhere in American industry. At the same time, it must be said, the industry had attained an equally impressive and eminent position in the use of harsh and repressive measures against those who appeared as obstacles to the realization of its labor objectives.[10]

The velvet glove comprised several steps, such as avoidance of wage cuts where possible, paying modestly above market wages (especially at the

USCC), selective improvement of safety and other working conditions, and extension of a variety of welfare benefits. The iron fist was composed of strict control of labor, unremitting hostility to trade unionism, and continued commitment to the twelve-hour day. Implementation of this labor policy proceeded, in turn, in a highly uneven pattern with only modest development of a formal labor management function. Before getting to this part of the story, however, some background is required.

Since steel is primarily a commodity business, cost of production is a key source of competitive advantage, as Carnegie realized and exploited so well. After the creation of the USSC and the consolidation of the industry, competition and pricing was "coordinated" in a "follow-the-leader" style with the USSC setting the standard, thus eliminating the worst tendencies toward cutthroat price reductions. Increased stability in pricing resulted, in turn, in increased stability in wage rates (more so among the major producers, less so among smaller firms and independent producers). Yet competition remained intense and the quest for profit drove the companies in an unceasing search for economies. As David Brody well describes, the steel companies sought to maintain and expand profits by working on two margins—raising labor productivity and holding down labor cost.[11]

The principle route taken to raise productivity was technological innovation and greater mechanization. The aim was to integrate and simplify production processes everywhere so that throughput was sped up and direct labor was eliminated. Converting to continuous furnaces in the finishing mills, for example, reduced labor requirements by two-thirds, while productivity in unloading iron ore boats increased fifteenfold when people with shovels were replaced by mechanical scoopers. Significantly, not only were per-unit labor requirements substantially reduced but the new technology and machinery greatly changed the type of jobs and average skill levels. In earlier days steelworkers were divided largely into two groups: a minority group of skilled workers who possessed knowledge and experience crucial to making the product and a majority group of unskilled workers organized in labor gangs who primarily contributed physical effort to haul, shovel, lift, and perform other weighty tasks. Between 1900 and 1920 the new technology and equipment greatly reduced the need for skilled workers and their ranks and power fell sharply, while mechanization also eliminated many of the lowest level unskilled jobs. The result was that skills and knowledge were transferred from labor to the capital equipment and the mass of steelworkers comprised semiskilled machine tenders and operatives and unskilled helpers and kindred employees, all of whom could learn their jobs in a matter of days or weeks. Remarked another English observer, " 'The various operations are so much simplified that an experienced man is not required. . . . The workmen in America do not act upon their own judgment, but carry out the instructions given to them.' "[12]

The steelmakers were also vigilant about holding down labor costs wherever possible. They did this through a variety of methods. On the shop floor, they used the drive system, which was widespread across industrial America before World War I, to extract maximum work out of their employees.[13] A mill superintendent gave this succinct description of the drive system: "'Catch 'em young; treat 'em rough; tell 'em nothing.'"[14] Sumner Slichter has described the drive system as "the policy of obtaining efficiency not by rewarding merit, not by seeking to interest men in their work, not by fostering their good will nor by seeking to obtain their *cooperation*, but by putting pressure upon them to turn out a large output. The dominating note of the 'drive' system is to inspire the workmen with awe and fear of the management." He goes on to observe, "The 'drive' policy by its very nature renders discord and ill-feeling inevitable. The management attempts to get as much out of the workmen as possible . . . , they retaliate for the speeding up by limiting output."[15]

A graphic description of the drive practice in operation in a steel mill is offered by Whiting Williams, a personnel director who took a year leave of absence and disguised himself as a manual laborer and worked in a variety of factories for a year.[16] His first job was at a 10,000-man steel mill. He relates, "the gang bosses, at least those of the labor gangs, seem to be the worst of the what-the-hell philosophy. . . . Our bosses can put into it [directing labor] an amount of heat and steam which makes it really terrifying to the tired worker. . . . After a long turn of work, I rested a moment. Their notice was the usual 'Hey, dere! What da hell! Do you t'ink dis sleeping place?'" Williams goes on to observe that "the men, of course, get to feeling that their work is never done. They have not the slightest interest in what it means or how it affects the operations of the mill . . . It is just a matter of doing as little work as the boss will allow."[17]

A complement of the drive system in the steel industry was the twelve-hour day and seven-day workweek. Probably no other aspect of USSC labor policy drew more attention and social critique than this.[18] Steelmaking is a continuous production process so a full complement of employees is required around the clock. The practical choice of alternatives open to the companies was two twelve-hour shifts or three eight-hour shifts. Until pressured to change by the administration of President Warren G. Harding in 1924, the major steel companies opted for not only the twelve-hour shift but also a seven-day workweek for the core of production workers.[19] Thus, blast furnace and open-hearth workers would do the day shift for two weeks from 6:00 a.m. to 6:00 p.m. and then would move to the twelve-hour night shift for two weeks, working a full twenty-four-hour day (the "long turn") each fourteenth day. Not only were the resulting work hours extremely long but the nature of steel work in many parts of the mills was very arduous, unpleasant, and dangerous.[20] The steel companies, led by the USSC, claimed that the twelve-hour/seven-day week was not only a cost-saving necessity but also one desired by the majority of the workers who wanted to make as much money as possible. The cost-saving aspect came from the fact that converting to an eight-hour shift would require hiring a third crew of workers, while the existing workers would demand a raise in wages to offset their reduced hours. Abandoning the seven-day week was also resisted because of the extra men, and extra scheduling complexity, that such a move would entail. Critics and reformers, including some steel executives, claimed that the "twelve/seven" work schedule was not only inhumane but also cost-raising, since workers were far too tired and dispirited to produce at their maximum.[21] In effect, said the critics, the steel bosses did not know their own self-interest. These arguments were stoutly resisted, however, until threatened government intervention forced a change.

In addition to long hours and driving gang bosses, the steel companies held down labor costs by holding the line on wages. Their ability to do so before World War I was greatly aided by the combination of skill-saving technological change and the flood of immigration. At the USSC, in 1902 the number of employees was 168,000, and by 1913 that had grown to 230,000, yet the average real wage (in 1914 dollars) had only slightly increased from .235 to .266 cents.[22] The combination of rapid productivity growth and relatively flat wage rates allowed the steel companies to capture most of the gains in the form of higher profits. While steel industry wage rates were modestly above the all-industry average in the United States, the marked irregularity of employment in the steel industry often reduced weekly and annual earnings to a level that left the majority of steelworkers and their families close to or below what experts at the time considered a minimum family wage.[23]

The role of immigration in holding down wages has been mentioned, but immigration had a far more pervasive influence in other ways. It influenced every aspect of human resource management strategy and work life in steel mills of this period. The period from 1900 to World War I brought the peak in European immigration to the United States. In this short time span over twelve million people arrived on American shores—an amount equivalent to the entire population of the Scandinavian countries, adding in some years 1 percent or more to labor force growth. This wave of immigration provided the steel companies with a seemingly inexhaustible labor supply for their low-skilled and semiskilled jobs, evident in the throngs of foreign-speaking men that congregated outside the mill gates seeking jobs at the shift turns. As a result, by 1911 nearly 60 percent of the steel industry's workforce was foreign born, and it would not be unusual to find workers of more than two dozen different nationalities—often able to speak only their native tongue and little or no English—in a single mill.[24] Further, after 1900 the bulk of new immigrants came from southern and eastern European countries and had poverty-stricken, preindustrial peasant backgrounds. Most had never worked in a factory, many were illiterate and could only speak a few words of broken English, and many had what seemed like crude manners and primitive customs. To native-born Americans the new immigrants, often derogatorily called "dagos," "wops," and "hunkies," were a lower order of humanity. Because of their poverty and ignorance (and the plans of many to return to their home countries after saving a decent-sized nest egg in America), these new immigrants were more amenable—or less resistant—to long hours, harsh conditions, and authoritarian management methods, while many of their American employers argued that such policies were necessary to keep order and induce the men to work.[25] These immigrants also provided a bulwark against unionization since ethnic divisions and language differences impeded collective action.

Another source of immigration, albeit internal to the United States, came from the millions of African American workers who moved from the South to the North in search of better economic opportunities and more political freedom. The hiring practices of steel companies, and indeed nearly all employers of that period, were blatantly and openly discriminatory against the foreign-born, women, and African Americans. Foreign-born workers, particularly from eastern and southern Europe, were hired only into lower-grade jobs and were generally passed over for promotion, while women were hired only for a narrow range of clerical jobs.[26] But no group faced more severe and uncompromising discrimination than African American workers.[27] Until World War I most steel companies had only a handful of such workers and then only in the most menial or unattractive jobs. During World War I, however, the severe labor shortage created by war production and the military draft partially broke down the barriers of discrimination and steel companies began to actively recruit and hire African Americans, albeit still into the lower-paying and less desirable jobs.

Given this background, we can proceed to labor management practices in the early days at the USSC and other steel companies. In 1900 the labor management practices of steel companies were not in any significant way different from those at the Pullman Palace Car Company (see chapter 3) or most other large manufacturing enterprises of that day.[28] Supervisors and foremen in steel mills had significant autonomy to run the production process as they saw fit, subject to meeting the oft-stringent time deadlines and cost constraints imposed on them by their superiors (and which they missed at risk of losing their own jobs). The companies claimed the workers had a readily available "open door" to higher officials if they had a complaint, but often they were intimidated from using it.[29] As in other industries, the individual foremen and gang bosses handled hiring and firing and set pay rates. The decentralized process of wage setting led to a pay structure that was, according to contemporary observers, "extraordinarily complex and varied."[30] Training was also highly informal. In some cases the foreman or supervisor would take a few minutes to show the new worker how to operate a machine or perform a task, while in other cases workmates demonstrated how to do the job or the person simply learned through trial and error. To get jobs, workers would frequently exaggerate their experience or skills and then try to hide their inexperience and mistakes from the foreman. If discovered and the mistakes were significant, the foreman had an incentive to fire the worker so that his "hiring mistake" was quickly disposed of and out of the sight of his superiors.

The steel companies had set up the situation to make great profits, but they needed to maintain internal control of labor and keep out external threats in the form of unions and government regulation. Toward this end, under the leadership of Gary and the USSC, they crafted the "velvet glove and iron fist" HRM strategy.[31]

The first part of this HRM strategy was to secure workers' acceptance and loyalty through a carefully measured and circumscribed set of positive inducements, as well as to promote a "good trust" image for the corporation in order to win public approval and forestall government antitrust action. This was the velvet glove.

One element of the velvet glove was development of a promote-from-within policy. A concomitant of promotion from within was a measure of job security for workers who were loyal and hardworking and creation of a nascent form of internal labor market.[32] Charles Hook, vice president of the American Rolling Mills Company (a USSC subsidiary), expressed the company's position on this matter when he declared, "'One of the most important of these [hiring policies] is the policy of promotion within the organization. This is done wherever possible and has several advantages; the most important of which is that stimulating effect upon the ambitions of workers throughout the organization.'"[33] Others noted that the effect of promotion from within was to tie the worker more closely to the company, fragment working-class solidarity, and create a stronger unity of interest between workers and the company. In his 1908 field study investigation of labor practices at steel mills in the Pittsburgh area, John Fitch found widespread evidence of the promote-from-within policy in operation, noting, for example, that "[a] new man is put to work in the cinder pit; from here he is promoted to be second helper and then first helper." Fitch also notes, however, that promotion remained circumscribed to the extent that members of particular ethnic groups (e.g., Slavs) were seldom raised above a certain job level, such as to foreman or supervisor.[34]

A second element of the velvet glove was an expansive and highly publicized industrial welfare program.[35] The general aim was enunciated by USSC president Gary in these instructions to subordinate executives:

"Above everything else, as we have been talking this morning, satisfy your men if you can that your treatment is fair and reasonable and generous. Make the Steel Corporation a good place for them to work and live. Don't let the families go hungry or cold; give them playgrounds and parks and schools and churches, pure water to drink, and recreation, treating the whole thing as a business proposition, drawing the line so that you are just and generous and yet at the same time keeping your position and permitting others to keep theirs, retaining the control and management of your affairs, keeping the whole thing in your own hands."[36]

The program began in 1903 with what the company described as a "profit-sharing" plan but was in reality an employee stock subscription plan. The plan involved the sale of USSC stock to employees at reduced rates, paid for by monthly deductions. In addition to regular dividend payments, the plan also promised a five-dollar bonus for each of the first five years the employee remained with the company and retained the stock, and another five dollars at the end of the fifth year, provided he showed "a proper interest in its welfare and progress."[37] George Perkins, the USSC executive primarily responsible for the plan, called it "'Socialism of the highest, best and most ideal sort, a Socialism that makes real partners of the employer and the employee.'"[38] Besides promoting partnership between capital and labor, the plan ostensibly channeled part of the large profits made possible by monopoly pricing, stable labor costs, and rapid productivity growth back to employees. Also, the bonus feature of the plan provided an incentive to stay with the company while the "proper interest" clause was an oblique warning not to become involved with labor unions and other radical causes. Although the stock subscription plan was much touted by the company and favorably reviewed in the press, the reality was that never did more than one-fourth of the employees participate, and often those that did owned only one or several shares.[39]

The next major welfare initiative was in 1906 when the USSC inaugurated an accident prevention and workplace safety program.[40] It was supplemented in 1910 by a voluntary accident relief fund that made cash payments to injured and killed employees and their families. The safety and accident program was in terms of scope and activities groundbreaking and is widely regarded as having inaugurated the industrial safety movement in American industry. Steel mills were extremely dangerous places to work, and the fatality rate among steelworkers was over twice that of laborers in general.[41] As Gary instructed subordinates, "'Nothing which will add to the protection of the workmen should be neglected. The safety and welfare of the workers are of the greatest concern.'"[42] Toward this end, the company created a cascading series of committees charged with investigating accidents and improving safety. At the top level was a permanent committee on safety comprising the director of the corporation and the president of five subsidiary companies. The committee appointed inspectors who visited all corporation facilities and made recommendations on actions needed to improve safety and working conditions. Each USSC mill, in turn, formed its own plant safety committee consisting of the plant superintendent and other executives and front-line managers who met weekly to discuss accidents and safety work. At the shop floor level, workmen's safety committees were created, composed of several rank-and-file workers who made periodic inspections of the plant and investigated accidents and safety violations. Workers who came up with new safety measures received cash rewards.[43] From its inception to the end of World War I the "Safety First" program, as it became widely known, succeeded in reducing by one-third to one-half the injury and fatality rates in the USSC mills.[44] Although these gains were laudable, critics pointed out that they were less a product of corporate social responsibility or enlightened employee practices and more a result of the USSC's desire to minimize the growing costs of lawsuits from injured employees and families of killed workers as well as employee claims under newly enacted state workmen's compensation statutes.[45]

The next major welfare initiative was in 1911 when the USSC created a companywide employee pension program.[46] At the time of his retirement in 1901, Andrew Carnegie gave a gift of $4 million to create a pension fund for his employees. In 1911, the USSC added $8 million to the fund and extended pension eligibility to all corporation employees. The USSC pension program was not the first in the nation, but it was by far the largest at the time. Critics again found shortcomings, however.[47] The original Carnegie plan provided pensions after age sixty with fifteen years of service; to limit costs the USSC gradually tightened eligibility rules. In 1915, for example, pension eligibility was changed to sixty-five years of age and twenty-five years of service. Further, it was charged that companies such as the USSC often found a pretext to layoff workers who got close to their pension date. As a result, in 1919 the USCC had only 2,940 pensioners, or only 1 percent of the total employed ranks, and a number of these were from the managerial sector.[48] Furthermore, the company tied pension benefits to previous earnings, yielding a decent monthly benefit for managers and executives but only $200–$300 a year for production workers.

During World War I, USSC and other steel companies established a wide array of other welfare programs. A major investment was made in company housing, including the building from the ground up the town of Gary, Indiana (the site of a new steel mill). Other examples include schools, playgrounds, recreational facilities, plant doctors and medical facilities, libraries and reading rooms, and locker and shower rooms.[49]

The velvet glove sought to win the cooperation and loyalty—or at least acquiescence—of the steelworker rank and file through positive inducements. These were complemented by a number of more punitive sanctions and coercive tactics that collectively represented the iron fist, which was directed toward both the individual worker and any collective action on the part of workers that threatened the company's control. The locus of the iron fist's power was the worker's fear of losing the job.[50] Steel jobs, while they might involve very long hours and arduous conditions, were nonetheless coveted because they paid above-average earnings and promised some room for advancement. In most years, the number of job seekers considerably exceeded the number of jobs, as was clearly evident to steelworkers every morning and evening when they passed into and out of the mill gates and saw the throng of applicants eager for work. Having little savings and often a family to support, most workers saw the job as not only their principal asset but also the only thing separating them from homelessness and hunger.

The steel companies used the workers' fear and vulnerability to cow them into compliance and docility.[51] The USSC and the other companies, for example, employed undercover spies and agents to circulate through the mills and mill towns and report to managers anyone who said unfavorable things about the company or advocated trade unionism or radical politics. Many of the mills were also in company towns or in communities where steel employment provided the bulk of jobs. In these communities the steel companies exercised a pervasive control.[52] City officials were either employees of the companies or handpicked by them. The companies also had large private police forces that, along with the town's often-compliant judges and municipal police, were ready to use force and intimidation against those deemed troublemakers. Union organizers had difficulty finding any place willing to let them hold a meeting and could expect within a few days to be roughed up and run out of town, while company agents recorded the names of workers attending union meetings and they were immediately fired or warned to cease and desist. Also providing a potent source of leverage for the companies was their control of much of the steel communities' stock of housing and the knowledge of workers that if they lost their jobs they also lost the roofs over their heads.

For these reasons the atmosphere in steel communities was repressive and charged with fear. One contemporary observer mockingly called the mill towns "our benevolent feudalism."[53] John Fitch, in his yearlong field study of the steelworkers, reported,

> I doubt whether you could find a more suspicious body of men than the employees of the United States Steel Corporation. They are suspicious of one another, of their neighbors, and of their friends. . . . The fact is, the steel workers do not dare openly express their convictions. They do no dare assemble and talk over affairs pertaining to their welfare as mill men. They feel they are living always in the presence of a hostile critic.[54]

Fitch goes on to relate that individual workers would only talk about their jobs and mill conditions if no one else was present and with a promise of anonymity, quoting one worker who commented,

> "We cannot tell about these things ourselves; we cannot write for the papers about our long hours and the unjust restrictions; but we want the public to know and we are glad to tell you—but never mention our names. We must not lose our jobs, for that is all we have."[55]

The steel companies exercised control through other means as well.[56] One tactic was to promote an excess supply of labor in the mill towns by widely advertising job openings or overstating the number of positions available. A second was an open policy of disinvesting in and closing unionized mills. A third was to infiltrate local union lodges with company agents (and in some cases the lodge presidents or officers were secretly on the company payroll). A fourth was to exploit ethnic rivalries and divisions to forestall worker solidarity or undercut a union drive. Examples of this divide-and-conquer strategy were the policy of segregating departments or job groups by nationality and bringing in trainloads of African American workers from the South to break strikes.

Having outlined the basic contours of the labor policy and practices of the USSC and other major steel companies, the final topic to consider is the evolution of organization and administration of the labor management function. On this topic very little has heretofore been written.

First, it should be evident that the USSC practiced an early version of strategic HRM, for the corporation's labor policy was carefully considered and crafted by top corporate executives. The profit sharing, safety, accident insurance, and union avoidance programs originated at the executive level, were adopted to promote and align with long-run business goals, and were structured as a synergistic package with the purpose of mutually achieving cooperation and control. Critics might argue that the steel executives adopted the *wrong* strategy, but few would argue that they *lacked* a strategy.[57]

Having a labor strategy did not mean, however, that the steel companies required a formal labor management function to administer it. The USSC and most other steel companies were, in fact, laggards in the movement during 1900–1920 to create personnel and industrial relations departments. Indeed, even though in the World War I years employment grew to over 230,000 at the USSC, the company never created a corporatewide labor management department. Most other steel companies followed the USSC in this regard, the major exception being Bethlehem Steel—for interesting reasons that will be discussed shortly.

As described in chapter 4 of *Managing the Human Factor*, most of the personnel and industrial relations departments created in this period were formed to provide centralized oversight and administration of three separate but related labor management functions: employment, "service" (welfare/benefit activities), and joint relations. Only the service (welfare) function was extensively developed at the USSC and most of the other steel companies before 1920, while the employment and joint relations functions remained informal and decentralized or nonexistent. It is reflective of this state of affairs when Daugherty, De Chazeau, and Stratton remark that "'personnel management,' as that term is commonly used, was very unevenly developed in the [steel] industry." They go on to add, "Employment, training, and promotion techniques were rather simple in the industry [while] . . . welfare programs were extensive."[58] They could have added that joint relations were also generally simple and undeveloped.

Starting in the first decade of the 1900s, the larger steel companies appointed people to serve as welfare directors and safety directors. The safety director was typically a safety engineer or a medical doctor. At some point many companies combined the two functions into one. The USSC, for example, formed a bureau of safety, sanitation, and welfare, while the High

Beam Steel Company (discussed in chapter 13) created the position of director of safety and labor. This person reported, in turn, to the company's general manager.[59]

The employment function, oriented around hiring, firing, training, and record keeping, remained relatively underdeveloped at steel companies through World War I. An "employment management" movement began in the United States in the early 1900s and achieved widespread publicity. Many hundreds of companies created an employment management department and appointed a middle-level management person to serve as director. This movement largely bypassed the steel industry. The authoritative source for developments in the steel industry in this period is the monthly journal *Iron Age*. While dozens of articles were devoted to safety and welfare programs in steel firms between 1910 and 1918, none were devoted to the employment management function or gave a case study example of an actual employment department in a steel company.[60]

Below the surface, however, a very modest movement was made in this direction. It occurred at two levels. The first was among small specialty steel producers, foundries, and fabricators. These firms typically belonged to an industry association, such as the National Metal Trades Association (NMTA). In about 1905 the NMTA formed a central labor bureau to assist its eight hundred member companies in recruiting skilled workers.[61] Gradually each of the NMTA's fifteen local branches established its own labor bureau to help member firms in its locality. The labor bureaus served as a "hiring hall" for workers. Member firms sent the labor bureaus requests for workers of certain qualifications, and the bureaus would direct available workers with these qualifications to the companies. Each firm recorded on individual index cards the name, address, job, work record, and date of hire and termination of its employees and sent updated cards to the labor bureau. The bureau kept a complete file of these cards and used them to fill requests for new hires submitted by the companies. The labor bureau also used this system to police a "no pirating" agreement in which member firms agreed not to hire away an employee or apprentice of another member firm without its consent. The labor bureau also served as a recruitment center for companies wanting to find workers to use as strikebreakers.

The second development in the employment areas was among the large steel companies. Without much public notice, they gradually set up centralized hiring or employment offices in the individual mills. These offices attracted little comment because they were usually staffed by low-level employment clerks who took "job orders" from foremen, did a perfunctory interview of candidates, and sent likely prospects to the nurse or physician for a physical examination.[62] A picturesque description of this process at an unidentified steel mill is provided by Whiting Williams:

> After lying awake most of the night in a dirty, top-story, stale-smelling, enormously noisy three-dollars-a-week room, I went over to that same plant gate

again at six-forty-five, and after an endless hour tried to wig-wag the labor gang-boss and later the works superintendent. "Nothin' doing to-day," was the answer. "Try again at six this evening." The same thing at another big mill a few doors down. By luck a [street] car came by just then, labeled for a famous steel town; so I jumped on and shortly found myself in an employment office filled to the ceiling with a coughing, swearing, smoking, ill-smelling gang of fifty representatives of all the known races, including Mexicans, negroes, Indians, and Turks. Up at the window finally I was taken on as "labor."

The boy was slow enough in asking all manner of questions—talking through two misplaced holes in plate-glass certainly makes a bad go for any real exchange of facts or ideas. The young clerks supposed to do the hiring gave most of their time to tickling the backs of the necks or the much-exposed chests of the young stenographers, while my newly hired or unhired associates looked on and let out grunts of impatience and disapproval in as many tongues as Babel ever knew. Finally a policeman came in and very roughly ordered "Everybody out—clean outa here, you!—Unless you got a ticket—or are a-waitin' to see the doctor." Nobody could tell if it was because they had hired enough for that day or what.[63]

The third leg of the new personnel and industrial relations departments of that period was joint relations. The traditional form of joint relations was collective bargaining, but as already indicated, the USSC and other major steel companies practically eliminated trade unionism from the mills. An entirely new form of joint relations, however, had just sprung up in the World War I decade and it was management of this activity that most often formed the third leg of the PIR triad. This new type of joint relations was variously known as a works council, shop committee, employee representation plan, or industrial democracy plan. The most famous and influential of the early representation plans was at the Colorado Fuel and Iron Company (CF&I), started in 1915 by corporate owner John D. Rockefeller Jr. in order to foster cooperation and rapprochement in employee relations after a disastrously destructive strike (the "Ludlow Massacre"). While the organizational details differ, the common denominator among these employee representation bodies is that they are some type of labor-management committee created by employers as an alternative form of nonunion voice and representation for purposes of fostering greater bilateral understanding, communication, efficiency, morale, and dispute resolution.[64]

Gary at the USSC and executives at most other steel companies did not follow Rockefeller at CF&I and opt for employee representation, partly because of the prevailing ethos of managerial authoritarianism and partly because of fears that employee representation would quickly evolve into full-fledged collective bargaining. After America entered World War I in 1917, strikes and union organizing broke out at a number of steel mills, threatening to paralyze urgently needed war production. To restore labor peace, the National War Labor Board, created by President Woodrow Wilson, ordered several of the steel companies most impacted by strikes to establish shop committees. The most important of these was Bethlehem Steel, but this also included smaller companies such as Lackawanna Steel and Midvale Steel.[65] After initial resistance and stonewalling, Bethlehem put in employee representation plans broadly based on the CF&I model. After the war ended, most companies quickly disbanded the shop committees but Bethlehem (and CF&I) kept them, albeit in a weakened form in the case of Bethlehem.

Bethlehem Steel, thus alone among the major integrated steel producers, had at least two of the three legs of the PIR triad. Not surprisingly, Bethlehem also went the furthest in establishing a centralized corporate industrial relations function. In about 1920 the company, following the model pioneered at Standard Oil of New Jersey, created a new top-level executive position, assistant to the president, and appointed Joseph Larkin to it. Larkin's sole duty was to coordinate and administer the corporation's industrial relations program.[66] He acquired his experience in employment work at Bethlehem's Fore River Shipbuilding division, where under direction of the Emergency Fleet Corporation set up by the Wilson administration during World War I an employment services department had been set up to promote greater efficiency in labor utilization and resolve disputes before they led to strikes. The labor department started at Fore River then moved "upstream" to the parent corporation.

Bethlehem was also the only steel company to join the Special Conference Committee, an association of ten leading corporate practitioners of Welfare Capitalism formed in 1919, and Larkin was the only steel executive to take a leadership position in the newly formed Industrial Relations Association of America—a practitioner association dedicated to advancing the practice of personnel and industrial relations in industry, and served as its president in 1920–21.[67] Most other steel companies, on the other hand, chose to stay with traditional labor practices put in place before the war. One of these was the twenty-four hours per day/seven days per week work schedule, which was a major cause of a several month industrywide strike in 1919.[68] Led by the USCC, the companies defeated the strike, repulsed unionization for another seventeen years, and kept the "24/7" work schedule until 1924.[69]

6

HRM in the Industrial Heartland II

The Ford Motor Company

If the steel industry symbolized the industrial core of the early-twentieth-century American economy, automobiles symbolized its future and leading edge. The automobile was an invention of the mid-1890s and a decade later was still a high-priced luxury item beyond the means of all but the affluent. The cheapest models started around $800, and the most popular were over $2,000. The entire output of the auto industry in 1904 amounted to 22,800 cars, produced by 12,000 workers.[1] Over the next fifteen years the industry was transformed by a cascading series of new innovations in every aspect of the business, including product design, factory layout, technology, machinery, and management. By 1919, total auto production fell just shy of the two million mark and the industry employed 340,000 wage earners. Before the great inflation of World War I arrived, entry-level cars were selling at the cut-rate price of less than $400.[2]

Leading this revolution was one person and one company—Henry Ford, and the Ford Motor Company. Arguably Henry Ford joins Frederick Taylor as the two people who had the deepest and most profound impact on business and industry in the twentieth century. Of the two, Ford achieved more widespread fame and public hero worship, becoming in his day an iconic figure known and lauded across the world.[3] The product that made Ford famous and rich was the Model T. But to produce the Model T at the rate of 1,100 per day at the price of $350 required genius and a complete transformation in automobile manufacturing.

Ford's most famous contribution toward this end was perfecting the assembly line and the art of mass production.[4] But theese innovations also required a markedly different employment system, and here, too, Ford made pioneering contributions. As Allan Nevins notes in his authoritative account of the early years of the company, "Thus the Ford Motor Company, which in 1911 had no labor policy at all," possessed three years later the most advanced labor policy in the world."[5] This labor policy combined in one integrated program four components not heretofore found elsewhere in any major company: principles of scientific management, an advanced program of industrial welfare, a centralized employment function and use of formal personnel management techniques, and a formal mechanism for employee voice and dispute resolution.

As indicated by Nevins, before 1913 the labor policy at Ford was quite traditional and in this respect mirrored that at most other manufacturing firms. The reason, in turn, is that the production system at Ford was also in most respects traditional for the late nineteenth and early twentieth centuries.[6] In its early years, auto manufacturing relied on the craft system of production widely used by other manufacturers, such as Baldwin Locomotive Works (see chapter 3). Three-fourths of the Ford workforce before the introduction of the assembly line were considered skilled workers, and the workforce was centered on its skilled craftsmen. These craftsmen, working individually or in teams along with helpers and assistants, were in charge of assembling the product from start to end. Thus, the Ford engine assembly room was organized into row upon row of assembly benches where a skilled worker put together individual motors one part at a time, with helpers bringing in engine blocks, taking away finished product and running back and forth to fetch components. The normal production rate was one engine per day. The job of the engine assembler required considerable skill and judgment, partly because there were many complex steps in making an entire engine and partly because he had to use a variety of metalworking tools to get all the parts to fit together smoothly.

The craft system of production was inherently subject to high cost and low productivity and volume. It also limited management control. Because the skilled craftsman was an indispensable part of production, he gained autonomy and power and thus commanded a high wage, effectively set the pace of work, and had a vested interest in protecting his "secrets of the trade." It was not unusual for skilled craftsmen from this era to work with an apron over a white shirt and tie.

The traditional craft system of production encountered a brilliant and determined opponent in an industrial engineer named Frederick W. Taylor. Taylor worked for the Midvale Steel Company in the 1880s and later for Bethlehem Steel, where he developed his principles of scientific management. Taylor's ideas had relatively little impact there, but in the early 1900s and onward they were to have a profound effect on American industry and the practice of management. As highlighted in a case study in *Managing the Human Factor* (161–63), the Joseph and Feiss Company, a manufacturer of men's suits, received national attention shortly before World War I as a leading example of scientific management in action. However, the Ford Motor Company went even further and in the public's eyes most completely exemplified the broad principles and practices of scientific management applied to modern manufacturing, although by most accounts Henry Ford had only passing knowledge of Taylor's ideas and more or less independently worked his way to the same conclusions.[7] For this reason the terms *Taylorism* and *Fordism* have become indissolubly linked.

Taylor and scientific management are examined in more detail in *Managing the Human Factor*. In broad outline, however, Taylor sought to dramatically reorganize management and production, with his theories ostensibly based on objective scientific principles. One of these principles was to increase efficiency through the specialization and division of labor; a second was to use engineering principles to determine the most efficient way to perform a task; and a third was to gain greater work effort and cooperation from employees by incentive pay schemes that better linked reward to productivity. In his own way, Henry Ford implemented each of these and not only in the production system of his company but also in the employment system.

Henry Ford revolutionized the process of automobile manufacturing and ushered in the era of mass production. Ford, like the owners of Baldwin Locomotive, was motivated by a "producer's ethos." Further, he had a deep dislike for "mere moneymakers."[8] His goal was not to maximize profit, although he became one of the wealthiest men in America, but to perfect the manufacturing process in order to turn out the highest volume of low-cost but quality-built cars possible. Ford framed his end goal as a "motor car for the multitude."[9] His first step toward this end was relentless standardization and simplification. Only one basic version of the Model T was ever produced—exemplified in Ford's famous remark that customers could have any color they wanted as long as it was black, and its parts and construction were engineered to be as simple as possible. Model T's could thus be produced via a "cookie-cutter" approach. Next, in 1913 Ford introduced the moving assembly line. Instead of having an engine or car body assembled on a stationary bench, Ford stationed workers along a moving line and had each one perform one task repeatedly as the engines or car bodies passed in front of them.

In this one innovation, Ford accomplished what Taylor had long sought—to transfer the knowledge and skill of production from the worker to the expert and the machine, to dramatically increase productivity, to save labor cost by replacing skilled workers with unskilled or semiskilled machine operators and assemblers, and to prevent workers from soldiering. Illustratively, the time required to assembly a chassis fell from 12½ hours to 1½ hours. The deskilled nature of the work process is indicated by the observation of John Fitch that "Fifteen thousand men work in gangs on the track system. Each gang, and each man on the gang has just one small thing to do—and to do over and over again," while a member of a group from Yale University who toured the Ford plant commented, "Division of labor has been carried on to such a point that an overwhelming majority of jobs consist of a very few simple operations. In most cases a complete mastery of the movements does not take more than from five to ten minutes." Regarding the pace of work, another person in the Yale group observed, "From the time you become a number in the morning until the bell rings for quitting time you have to keep at it. You can't let up."[10]

The shift to a new production system also necessitated a shift to a new employment system. Consistent with the practice of most other employers of that period, Ford and his managers at first gave primary attention in their quest for greater efficiency to the mechanical elements of production, such as factory layout, new machinery, and redesign of the production process. Once this new system was in place, however, they discovered that its efficiency was still seriously constrained by something to that point largely neglected—the human element. In this regard, one of Ford's managers noted that "'we began to realize something of the relative value of men, mechanism and material, so to speak, and we confess that up to this time we believed that mechanism and material were of larger importance and that somehow or other the human element or our men were taken care of automatically and needed little or no consideration.'"[11] But Ford managers soon discovered the human element needed just as much attention as the mechanical element. In other words, Ford discovered it had a "labor problem."

The mass of jobs at Ford had become highly routinized, monotonous, and fast-paced. Ford also drew roughly three-fourths of its workforce from the immigrant population. Additionally, the labor market in Detroit in most years was quite strong due to the industrial boom, allowing a person "to quit his job in the morning and find employment in another factory at noon."[12] Through 1913 Ford paid production workers wages that were roughly comparable with those of other auto companies. Ford also used fairly traditional labor management methods. Foremen continued to have authority to hire, fire, and establish pay rates, although as at steel companies hiring was funneled through an employment office.

One result of this system was a complex wage structure with over sixty different rates of pay in the plant. On this system, a Ford manager commented, "'We, like other employers, had gone on for years, hiring men at the back door for as little as we could get them, putting them into the shop and making them work at the same job for as long as they would stick, and not giving them an advance until we had to.'"[13] Another was a haphazard assignment of workers to jobs, and a penchant on the part of foremen to promote their pets and fire others who for some reason incurred their disfavor. Said a visitor to the Ford plant, "'Some men advanced rapidly because of their efficiency; others, because they knew how to handle their foreman and were self-assertive in their demands. Other men of a retiring nature in the same department hesitated to ask for higher pay and went on working at a lower rate when they really merited more.'"[14]

Of far greater concern and cost, however, was a sky-high rate of employee turnover. In 1913 the turnover rate at Ford reached a staggering 370 percent—almost twice the level at some other auto companies. This meant that Ford had to hire more than 52,000 workers to maintain a workforce of about 13,600 employees.[15] Some days the employment department had to process and assign jobs to over 500 people. One person estimated the cost of turnover at $35 per person, implying that turnover cost Ford over $1.8 million per year.[16]

Further complicating the life of Ford managers was an extremely high rate of absenteeism. In 1913 the daily absentee rate was 10 percent, meaning that in a typical day managers had to scramble to fill 1,300–1,400 positions.[17] This level of turnover and absenteeism was costly in any kind of production system, but for an integrated assembly line operation like Ford's it was hugely expensive since a slowdown or interruption at any one point quickly ripples through the entire operation.

Yet another problem, discovered to the consternation of Ford managers, was that even with the new assembly line technology and the deskilling and individualizing of jobs, workers were still able to successfully restrict output and soldier on the job. Labor economist John Commons noted that workers such as Ford's were holding back to protest their dissatisfaction with conditions, in effect "conducting a continuous, unorganized strike."[18] The workers developed group norms of what constituted a fair day's work and used social ostracism and physical violence to enforce them. Talking about workers who exceeded the work norms, a Ford manager noted that "'no one would talk to them. Every time one of them went for a drink of water or to the washroom, the belts on his machine were cut, the grinding wheel smashed, his personal tools damaged, the word 'RAT' was chalked on his machine in block letters. They were treated in the way union building craftsmen treat a scab on the job.'"[19]

In 1913 Ford put John R. Lee in charge of reforming the company's employment program.[20] Lee became the company's first employment manager and one of the nation's pioneers in this new management profession. The company sent Lee on a nationwide tour of other manufacturing plants to benchmark what other companies were doing in the employment area. The *Detroit Tribune* reported that "it was found that conditions were generally the same all over the country. After Mr. Lee's return an entirely original system had to be worked out."[21] This new system combined important parts of scientific management and welfare work and added to them a revolutionary new form of wage payment and a formal channel for employee voice. The first phase of the new program was announced in October 1913.

One of Taylor's principles of scientific management was dividing tasks into functional specialties, thus exploiting gains from specialization, and assigning each specialty area to a "first class man," thus reaping the gains from comparative advantage. Toward this end, Taylor proposed in his 1903 treatise *Shop Management* that firms create a "planning department" where experts work out the "one best way" to organize and execute production. Taylor further suggested that within the planning department should be an "employment bureau" in charge of a "competent man" who should "inquire into the experience and especial fitness and the character of applicants and keep constantly revised lists of men suitable for the various positions in the shop."[22] Taylor also advocated replacing rules of thumb and informal and arbitrary decision making with scientifically determined standards that were uniformly applied and administered by competently trained experts.

Whether Lee was familiar with Taylor's writings is uncertain, but he implemented the idea of functionalized employment management at Ford.

The original employment office was upgraded to an employment department. Where the employment office served as little more than a clearinghouse for labor, the new employment department was given control of hiring and put in charge of an elaborate (for that time) record-keeping system.[23] The new department was in charge of one head, who had one assistant, one interpreter, one record keeper, and one typist.[24] The entire process of hiring, performance management, transfer/promotion, and termination was formalized and systematized through the use of eleven written employment forms. For example, foremen who needed labor sent a written requisition to the employment department stating the number of people needed and their type of job and skills. The department was responsible for screening and selecting candidates, conducting physical examinations, and escorting successful candidates to the appropriate foremen. For each new hire the department completed a written employment record form, a medical record form, and a time clock form, and gave the new employee a metal badge with an employee number. [A medical department was established a year or so before the employment department, most likely in response to Michigan's enactment of a new workman's compensation statute.] Workers clocked in and out each day and the time clock forms were used by the payroll department to issue checks once every two weeks. Once on the job, the employment department periodically checked the person's pay and advancement record and if lack of satisfactory progress was found then contacted the foreman for an explanation. Additional written forms were filled out for recommendations for transfer, promotion, or discharge. Within six months of implementation the employment department had written records on 108,000 employees.[25]

Lee also replaced rules of thumb and informal procedures with formal and expertly designed personnel practices. The centerpiece of the first phase of labor reforms at Ford in late 1913 was a new "skills-wage classification system."[26] The first objective of this skills-wage system was to rationalize the company's wage structure and base it on objective criteria; a second objective was to provide an incentive for workers to stay with the company and upgrade their skills. Critics charge there was a third—to fragment worker solidarity and quell mounting discontent with the regimented work process.[27] Lee stated that the purpose of the system was "'to grade the men in our employ according to their efficiency and to see that every man gets a square deal and receives the wage he is entitled to as soon as he reaches our different standards of proficiency progressively arranged.' "[28] The system, using an embryonic form of job evaluation based on job tasks and skills, established six ranked groups or grades of workers (e.g., skilled operatives, operatives, helpers, etc.), and within each group workers were further ranked into three skill levels (first class, average, beginner). Uniform pay rates were attached to each grade/skill position and the pay rates rose with movements up the grade-skill hierarchy. The employment department monitored each worker's progress and, in cases where progress to a higher grade was absent or unduly slow, required that the foreman provide an explanation and remedial plan of action. Laggards, rather then being fired, were investigated and where possible the problem was corrected through counseling, training, or transfer to a different job. When a worker still failed to progress then he or she was discharged for failure to meet the minimum level of efficiency.

Another new labor management practice added in 1916 was a company-financed training program. Called the Ford Trade School, it enrolled dozens of young people and trained them to be skilled machinists and mechanics. Students rotated between one week of classroom instruction and two weeks of practice on the shop floor.[29]

The company also started new welfare programs.[30] Henry Ford had always stressed clean and safe working conditions, but the new employment reforms expanded and strengthened the company's safety program and made it a leader in the industry.[31] At about this time the company also started an employee magazine called the *Ford Times*. Another new initiative was an employees' savings and loan association. The business objectives were to reduce turnover and absenteeism and build a greater steadiness of character in the workers. These goals were to be accomplished by giving workers in need of emergency cash a place within the company to secure a quick and low-cost loan and to encourage thriftiness and long-term employment by giving them a place to save and earn a reliable return. The company paid the costs of the savings and loan association and distributed part of the interest paid on loans back to depositors as an extra dividend for saving. Another noteworthy welfare measure that Henry Ford took a personal interest in was hiring crippled and disabled workers. The employment department was directed to examine the work requirements of all jobs in the plant—7,288 in all—and to determine which ones could accommodate disabled workers. In 1917 the company provided gainful employment for 1,700 disabled workers and between 4,000 and 5,000 workers partially disabled by disease.[32] Ford was also considerably more liberal in hiring and promoting African American workers than other auto employers.[33] Started in 1917 was a legal aid department with four attorneys. In one month it provided advice to over 2,000 Ford employees.[34]

A final innovation was to take the authority for hiring and firing away from the foremen and give the workers some greater opportunity for voice and due process in the resolution of disputes. Lee headed a new committee that investigated each foreman's recommendation for the discharge or major discipline of a worker. According to an outside observer, "'Now if a man fails to get along with his foreman he comes before the court, is carefully questioned, plainly talked to if at fault, and sent back to work in another department. Often it is a case of a 'square peg in a round hole,' and the man is shifted around until the work that he can do best is found.'"[35] Lee observed of this policy that "'it is a great deal cheaper for us to take him from one department to another than to discharge him,'" while John Commons enthusiastically concluded, "The Ford scheme of industrial government has nothing of unionism, or shop committees, or collective bargaining, or 'industrial democracy.' It is just old-fashioned autocracy. . . . [But] why should there be any industrial democracy or workmen's grievance committee, or labor organization, when nobody can be fired anyhow, and when this advisory committee of thirty is always on the job investigating trouble long before it ripens, and when the management always has a line on foremen who have too much trouble?"[36] In a remarkable turnabout, in one month in 1913 the company discharged 1,276 workers, while three years later only seven workers were discharged in six months![37]

The reforms of October 1913 went part way in solving Ford's labor problem. In January 1914 the company announced a second phase of labor reform that was so unprecedented and daring that it quickly made Henry Ford one of the most famous men in the world. That month the Ford Motor Company announced that it would share profits with workers and establish a minimum wage of five dollars per day. The new pay system quickly became known as the "five-dollar day."

Reasons for adoption of the five-dollar day are tangled and subject to some controversy.[38] One motive was apparently altruism and public relations. The company's profits had exploded since 1910 and Henry Ford felt pressure to distribute some of the surplus to employees. His initial estimate was that the five-dollar day would cost the company $10 million, compared to corporate net income in 1913 of $27 million and dividend payments of $5 million. A number of other more economic/business motives also appear to have played a role. Although diverse, they all tie into the fact that the company was the first to install a mass production system and was thus the first to also fully perceive the necessity for uninterrupted production.[39] Along this line, one business motive of the five-dollar day was to further reduce turnover and absenteeism or, as one person put it at the time, "'to put an end to floating.'"[40] In this aspect the plan was greatly successful, for turnover declined to a miniscule 16 percent by 1916, while thousands of job seekers lined the street outside the employment department. Ford also expected an increase in efficiency and hard work from his employees, stating, "We expect to get better work and more efficient work as a result."[41] A year later Ford told the Industrial Relations Commission that efficiency had indeed increased, on the order of 15–20 percent, while the company in internal documents concluded that once productivity improvements were factored in the actual cost of the program in the first year was not $10 million but only $5.8 million.[42] And, finally, the company also sought to use the profit-sharing plan to remold the attitudes, habits, home life, and social behavior of its employees—particularly the immigrants and unskilled workers—on the belief that making its employees better people and citizens outside the factory would also make them more efficient and reliable workers inside the factory. In this respect Ford embarked on a broad plan of not only efficiency engineering but social engineering. Fitch observed in this regard that "a man is entitled to his wages, if he is kept on the payroll," but that "he is entitled to profits only in the case of adhering very strictly to the rules laid down."[43]

The company was not shy about promoting the unprecedented nature of the plan. The initial public announcement stated, "The Ford Motor Company ... will on January 12, inaugurate the greatest revolution in the matter of rewards for its workers ever known to the industrial world."[44] In 1913 the average wage at Ford was $2.50, so the new program effectively doubled the rate of pay, particularly for workers in the lower pay grades. At the same time, Ford also announced a cut in work hours from nine to eight per day. Fellow industrialists reacted with disbelief and dismay, fearing that they, too, would come under pressure to raise wages and cut hours, and many forecast a bad end to what they regarded as Ford's folly. (So many job seekers flooded the Detroit labor market after Ford's announcement that the other auto producers actually benefited from a substantial increase in labor supply.) Public reaction was overwhelmingly favorable, and some of it bordered on the ecstatic. The *London Economist*, for example, declared the five-dollar day "'the most dramatic event in the history of wages'"; in a similar tone the *New York Herald* called it "'an epoch in the world's industrial history,'" while socialist and muckraker Upton Sinclair was moved to call Henry Ford "one of America's national heroes."[45] A worker interviewed outside the Ford plant observed that instead of building libraries for workers that few ever used, "'wouldn't it have been great if Andrew Carnegie had used his money that way?'"[46] For his part, Ford called the profit-sharing plan "not charity [but] efficiency engineering" and later stated the five-dollar day was "one of the finest cost-cutting moves we ever made."[47]

The five-dollar day plan maintained the company's existing wage scale but added a supplement to bring the worker's daily pay up to a minimum of five dollars. To qualify, however, workers had to meet certain objective and subjective criteria. Objective criteria included being a married man of any age or a single man over the age of twenty-two (or any age with dependents), being a resident of Michigan for at least six months, and employment at Ford for at least six months. Soon women were included in the plan (of the 16,000 workers at Ford's main factory in 1914, only 250 were women), as were Ford employees in other states. The subjective criteria were more complex and controversial. When the profit-sharing plan was announced, the company initially gave only general guidelines. Henry Ford stated, for example, that profit sharing was a monetary incentive for "proper living."[48] A somewhat expanded definition came from James Couzens, a Ford vice president and reputed cocreator of the five-dollar day idea, who stated, " 'Thrift and good service and sobriety will be encouraged and rewarded.' "[49]

Soon the company came face-to-face with the realization that it had to not only better define the subjective criteria it would use to award profit-sharing bonuses but also create some mechanism or agency for determining who did and did not meet both sets of criteria. In late 1914, therefore, Lee created the sociological department to administer the profit-sharing program.[50] The term *sociological* was used in industrial circles of that era as a general descriptor of programs and activities aimed at bettering the lives of workers. Ford may have borrowed the term from a similar department created at the Rockefeller-controlled Colorado Fuel and Iron Company—a company almost as famous at the time for a different kind of human resource management innovation (employee representation).[51]

The sociological department began with a staff of 30 that within a year expanded to over 150.[52] Its jurisdiction was every employee at Ford making less than $200 per month and its mandate was to determine whether each met the criteria for profit sharing and, if not, to suggest corrective action and monitor compliance. Each investigator, equipped with a car, driver, and interpreter, was assigned a district in Detroit—selected as much as possible to include a limited number of ethnic/language groups—and visited the homes of Ford employees. Besides determining a person's age, marital status, and other such characteristics, investigators were also instructed to check on factors such as "properly supporting wife and family," "home conditions good," "habits good," and "thrifty." Also looked for was evidence of specific vices, such as excessive drinking, gambling, and "immoral" behavior. To determine these matters, the investigators entered the living premises, interviewed family members and neighbors, and examined financial statements such as bank records and insurance policies.

After the first round of investigations was completed in April 1914, 10 percent of the employees did not meet the objective qualifications (job tenure, etc.) and 40 percent did not meet the subjective criteria.[53] This 40 percent were retained as employees, paid their straight wage, and given instructions on remedial actions expected of them. If these employees did not improve after six months, they were subject to discharge. The prospect of a five-dollar day apparently had great incentive effect, for two years after the program's start 90 percent of the workforce qualified for profit sharing.[54] As can be imagined, some employees and social critics found the Ford methods excessively intrusive and paternalistic and, most certainly, in some cases the investigators crossed the line or used heavy-handed tactics. Nonetheless, Nevins concludes, "The conditions imposed . . . appear reasonable; all could be met without more than temporary hardship; they were for the good of the workers in the long run, and the good of the Detroit area. . . .

The real question is whether it was better than a laissez-faire course. . . . To that question the answer is clear."[55] This statement might be discounted as the glossy assessment of a Ford company apologist, but even the famous progressive muckraker Ida Tarbell came away singing the praises of Henry Ford, saying, after a personal inspection, "'I don't care what you call it—philanthropy, paternalism, autocracy—the results which are being obtained are worth all you can set against them, and the errors in the plan will provoke their own remedies.'"[56]

The Ford labor reforms peaked in spirit and content shortly before U.S. entry into World War I. Then a hardening in philosophy set in, accompanied by a dismantling of the sociological department and a regression toward a more hard-line approach to labor discipline and control.[57]

The most notable new activity in the labor area taken on by Ford before the war was a mammoth educational program directed toward the "Americanization" of the foreign-born part of its workforce.[58] The Young Men's Christian Association (YMCA) was at this time very active in promoting industrial betterment activities and had an industrial service department with staff that worked with companies to start up and operate new welfare initiatives. In April 1914, Ford hired Peter Roberts, a young YMCA educator, to begin teaching English language classes to immigrant employees. The program was soon integrated into the work of the company's sociological department and enrollment and graduation from it became a key hurdle for foreign-born workers to overcome in order to qualify for profit sharing. Thousands of Ford employees were soon enrolled in what became officially labeled as the Ford English School. Classes were offered after work and were taught by supervisors and other men from the shop floor. Consistent with the aim of the sociological department to remold the attitudes and behavior of immigrant workers, the classes combined language training with lessons on personal and civic virtue. Thus, one lesson during the course was "Table Utensils," while another was "Going to the Bank." The Ford program was soon copied by numerous other companies and cities and an Americanization boomlet followed for the next decade.

The entry of the United States into World War I in April 1917 created economic and political conditions that greatly strained the labor reform program started in 1913. After the war, much of the program was scaled back or eliminated.

Part of the problem was that the costs of the labor reforms started to balloon and their effectiveness in dealing with new labor problems waned. The labor market in Detroit quickly tightened with the interruption of immigration, the military draft, and a surge in war orders and hiring to meet them. The number of employees at Ford, for example, mushroomed to 32,000 in 1917. To attract and hold employees, auto companies started raising wages. In 1917 Ford had to boost its basic labor rate to $3.44, and to $4.00 in 1918. This increase in basic wages, however, successively reduced the profit-sharing bonus received by workers and the attractiveness and incentive effect of the five-dollar day. The company at first tried to keep up with the labor market and adopted a six-dollar day. At the height of wartime inflation, however, it would have had to move to a ten-dollar day, and Ford was unwilling to do this.[59] Of course, turnover and absenteeism worsened (turnover moved up to 51 percent in 1918), but this was apparently considered less costly than a further boost in profit sharing. The postwar depression of 1920–21 forced Ford to close its factories for a month and take severe cost-cutting measures. One of the casualties was the profit-sharing program, which was phased out.[60]

The massive increase in employment also made the operation of the sociological department an increasingly burdensome and expensive proposition. At its peak the department had over 150 investigators. Cost-minded executives came to regard it as an excessively large and nonproductive overhead expense. Further, the war significantly reduced the inflow of new immigrants to America and by the war's end most of the Ford foreign-born workforce had passed through the Americanization classes and qualified for profit sharing. Ford executives were also increasingly sensitive to the charge of social critics and disgruntled workers that the investigations of the sociological department were overly intrusive and paternalistic. To blunt this charge, the department was renamed the educational department. Nonetheless, when the depression of 1920–21 arrived the department was also a victim of cost-cutting.

Also entering into the shift of labor policy at Ford that commenced with the war was a resurgence of trade union activity. Henry Ford had a deep antipathy for trade unions and was determined to keep them out of his shops. During the war, trade union activity in Detroit blossomed: forty thousand workers joined the Auto Workers' Union, and fifteen auto plants were hit by strikes. Workers felt aggrieved because their wages lagged behind inflation. The decline of the profit-sharing bonus also made Ford workers less willing to remain quiet and toe the company line. While pay and job security at Ford's were far above average, a visiting industrial engineer also noted that workers were expected to be "'absolutely docile'" and insubordination was "'absolutely intolerable.'"[61] Such tight control, and the feeling of repression and subordination that accompanied it, came into growing conflict with the government's drumbeat propaganda campaign justifying the war as necessary to "make the world safe for democracy" and the movement for industrial democracy that it spawned. In addition, a particular source of grievance among Ford workers was the grueling pace of work and the constant pressure for "speed-up." Said one observer of the Ford plant, "'You've got to work like hell in Ford's,'" while a ten-year veteran of the Ford plant remarked, "'Many healthy workers have gone to work for Ford and have come out human wrecks.'"[62]

Ford shifted from paternalism and generosity to hardball tactics. Industrial espionage had been used at Ford since 1906 and was reportedly continued even during the heyday of labor reform. When the trade union threat multiplied during World War I, so was the investment in espionage. At the height of the war Ford had over a hundred people working as undercover agents and informants in its Detroit plant. The sociological department co-ordinated the espionage network and seventeen operatives were stationed in the employment department.[63] The industrial spy campaign was partly justified on patriotic and national defense grounds as a means to ferret out German sympathizers and saboteurs among the immigrant portion of the workforce, but in practice any persons expressing dissatisfaction with the company or sympathy with unions were reported to company managers. Some were quickly fired.

A final factor that explains the rise and fall of labor reform at Ford is the shift that took place in managerial philosophy. As Henry Ford grew older and became fabulously famous and rich, he also became isolated from the shop floor and his employees, while the generous and humanitarian side of his personality gradually gave way to a more mean-spirited and prejudiced temperament.[64] Illustrative of this is that in the 1920s Henry Ford became an outspoken anti-Semite. Ford also replaced his early team of executives, many of whom had shared his earlier instinct for a humane and generous approach to labor, with a new team that emphasized cost control and the bottom line. It was not long before the most distinctive and famous parts of the labor reform program were eliminated and work at the FordMotor Company was not much different from work at any other Detroit auto plant.[65]

PHOTOGRAPHS

1. The Carnegie Steel mill complex.

2. Mill workers tapping an open hearth furnace.

 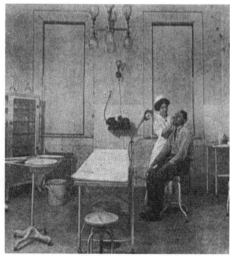

3 and 4. Newly installed safety guards on barbed wire machines; an operating room in a U.S. Steel emergency plant hospital.

5 and 6. Community bread line for unemployed steel workers and families in the 1908 depression; private lodging house room for immigrant mill workers on twelve-hour shift. Often workers on the next shift sleep in the same beds.

7. Henry and Edsel Ford with the new Model A.

8. Ford workers on the Model A assembly line.

9. Job seekers outside the Ford factory.

10. The Ford employment office.

11. The Square Deal Arch built by Endicott Johnson workers in appreciation for profit sharing.

12. Eviction of striking workers from company housing at Fulton Bag and Cotton Mills.

13. CF&I employee representatives with John D. Rockefeller Jr. (middle, front).

14. Federal troops guard the Arcade building at Pullman during the strike.

15. Interviewing job applicants in the employment office.

16. Scientific management in action: production monitoring board for employees.

17. A company-sponsored athletic program.

18. An English class for immigrant women employees.

19. A coal town: company store (foreground), company housing (middle), and mine (background).

20. Child labor was widespread. Here "breaker boys" remove slate waste from crushed coal heading to rail cars.

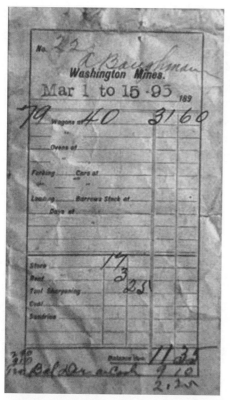

21. The miner's pay envelope, 1895. He worked two weeks (Sundays off), mined and loaded seventy-nine coal wagons (395 tons) for gross pay of $31.60. After deductions from the company store, for housing, for tool repair, and for the doctor, he received net pay of $2.25, or a wage of about one-half cent per ton.

22. The miner's check-in board. Each miner had a brass tag with an employee number and put it on the board before entering the mine and then removed it when leaving work. Idle mine days were also announced here.

Part II

THE PRACTICE OF HUMAN RESOURCE MANAGEMENT, 1920–1930

7

Industrial Relations Counselors, Inc.

P_{art} 2 of this book transitions to human resource management (HRM) programs and practices in the 1920s. Six case studies are presented. All come from consulting reports prepared by the staff of Industrial Relations Counselors, Inc. (IRC) and its predecessor organization, the industrial relations (IR) section of the law firm of Curtis, Fosdick, and Belknap. These reports provide what are certainly the most detailed and in-depth portraits in existence of how HRM was organized and practiced at American firms in the years before the Great Depression.

The full story of the birth, activities, and accomplishments of IRC is contained in the organization's seventy-fifth anniversary commemorative volume, *Industrial Relations to Human Resources and Beyond*. (Also worth consulting is the fiftieth anniversary volume, *People, Progress, and Employee Relations*).[1] Brief review, however, is called for, not only to situate the case studies but also to highlight the significant but greatly underrecognized contributions IRC has made to the development of modern human resource management.

As described in *Managing the Human Factor*, employers had used labor consultants for many years but largely in a negative capacity as strikebreakers, union busters, and in-house spies. Only with the birth of the employment management movement after 1910, and then the personnel management and industrial relations movements in the latter part of the decade, did labor consulting firms of the modern and more constructive variety emerge. One of the first was the firm of Tead, Valentine, and Gregg, established in 1915. Tead and Valentine in particular were early and well-known participants in the progressive/liberal wing of the scientific management movement and Taylor Society.[2]

Their firm pioneered the "labor audit," an HRM tool that became the template for the IRC consulting reports done in the 1920s. The labor audit was an "A-to-Z" overview and evaluation of the client company's labor management program, typically performed through extensive on-site investigation and personal interviews with managers and employees.[3] The audit describes the company's labor policy (philosophy and approach to labor and employee relations, roughly what is called HRM strategy today), the organization and staffing of the labor management function, and the operation and practices of each subfunction, such as staffing, compensation, benefits, safety, and employee relations. Also provided is a detailed diagnosis of what parts of the HRM program are functioning well and what parts are underperforming or causing problems and a detailed set of "action recommendations" for company management.

IRC owes its existence to John D. Rockefeller Jr. and, in particular, to Rockefeller's deep-felt commitment to promoting progressive labor management and employee representation in industry. Also important was that he was the son of the world's richest capitalist, John D. Rockefeller Sr., and he thus had the financial resources to underwrite IRC's establishment and consulting activities (performed on a nonprofit basis).

John D. Rockefeller Jr. had little interest in or knowledge of labor management until the calamitous strike at the Colorado Fuel and Iron Company (CF&I) in 1914.[4] CF&I was almost wholly owned by the Rockefellers, although they remained largely absentee owners and let company executives run nearly all aspects of the business. In 1913 the United Mine Workers union started an organizing campaign in the southern Colorado coalfields that quickly precipitated a massive strike at not only CF&I but numerous other companies. (CF&I had coal mines to supply fuel for its steel mill in Pueblo.) The strike was long and bitter and finally ended in a pitched battle when state militia, widely regarded as quasi-agents of the companies, stormed a miners' tent colony in Ludlow, Colorado, leading to the death of more than a dozen people, including a number of women and children. A shocked nation quickly dubbed the disaster the Ludlow Massacre and the Rockefellers were excoriated across the nation as bloodthirsty capitalist exploiters.

As a defensive measure, Rockefeller hired Canadian labor expert William Lyon Mackenzie King to counsel him on how to contain and repair the situation at CF&I. King was an experienced labor mediator and a progressive in labor management and employee relations. He soon realized that Rockefeller knew little about labor and that part of the reason for the strike was the company management's arbitrary and hardfisted approach to managing employees. So he undertook schooling Rockefeller in a more progressive approach to industrial relations and to convince him to fundamentally reorganize and reform labor management at CF&I. Rockefeller not only agreed to King's proposals but became a "born again" convert to the cause of a more humane and liberal approach to labor management.[5] The linchpin in the new Rockefeller/King program of industrial relations was *employee representation*—a nonunion system of joint governance and collective employee voice, similar to but broader than a works council or shop committee.

Rockefeller was soon enmeshed in another labor war when strikes broke out in 1915 and again a year later at the Bayonne, New Jersey, refinery operated by his flagship company, Standard Oil of New Jersey (SONJ). Both strikes led to great violence, property destruction, and radicalization of relations between management and men. Rockefeller had to face the reality that "business as usual" in labor management was a recipe for disaster for both public relations and the profit and loss statement, and with King's guidance Rockefeller also overhauled corporate management and the conduct of industrial relations at SONJ.

As part of this program, in 1918 Rockefeller brought in Clarence J. Hicks to become SONJ's new executive in charge of industrial relations. Hicks became involved in labor management in the late 1890s through welfare work with the Young Men's Christian Association's railroad division, then worked in the labor management function at International Harvester (the company was connected to the Rockefellers through marriage), and later was hired away by Rockefeller to manage the new employee representation plan at CF&I.[6]

At SONJ, Hicks created one of the most advanced industrial relations programs to be found in an American company. George Gibb and Evelyn Knowlton, in their history of SONJ, note, "The conclusion is scarcely debatable that in one mighty surge of effort the Jersey directors, prodded by Rockefeller, Jr., and led by Hicks, had pushed the company almost overnight to a position where it could be regarded not just as a good employer but as among the most progressive in the field of labor."[7] In a similar assessment, labor historian Irving Bernstein calls Hicks's PIR program at SONJ "the most ambitious and enduring monument of the welfare capitalism of the 1920s."[8] Hicks arguably became the nation's most influential HRM executive in the 1920s, marked for example by his chairmanship of the Special Conference Committee (SCC), an association of ten of the nation's largest welfare capitalist firms that was financed in part by Rockefeller.[9] The SCC later became the Cowdrick Group, named after Edward Cowdrick, its long-time secretary, and after Cowdrick's death in the early 1950s was run by IRC. When Hicks retired from SONJ in the early 1930s,[10] he became director of the board of IRC. Hicks also took a lead role in establishing the first autonomous IR centers in North American universities, including Princeton University (1922) and the Massachusetts Institute of Technology (1937) in the United States and Queen's University (1937) in Canada.[11]

Rockefeller sought to extend progressive labor management practices and employee representation to his family's other industrial concerns. At first he utilized King for this mission, but King was increasingly unavailable as he began consulting for other large corporations and also reentered Canadian politics. In 1919 King won a seat in the Canadian Parliament and was elected leader of the Liberal Party; in 1921 he became Canadian prime minister. At this point his work in industrial relations, particularly for the Rockefellers, effectively came to an end.

Rockefeller next turned to Raymond Fosdick to serve as his counselor and "eyes and ears" on labor matters at his companies. Fosdick was a young attorney whom Rockefeller had met before World War I when both served on a grand jury investigating the white slave trade. Impressed with Fosdick's abilities, Rockefeller employed him as a personal advisor and, in 1920, as his legal counsel. Rockefeller had Fosdick visit several of his companies and write up reports on labor conditions and employee relations.

As the volume of labor work increased, Fosdick could no longer handle it on an individual basis so he recommended to Rockefeller that a special industrial relations section be created in his law firm Curtis, Fosdick, and Belknap, located in New York City.[12] Such a section was established in 1922, with George Anderson (formerly managing director of the New York Employing Printers Association) hired to direct it, and by 1923 the section had a staff of ten people. The section undertook several in-depth industrial relations audits at various companies Rockefeller had financial interests in, and also started to do consulting and counseling work for other organizations. In 1924 Anderson resigned and was replaced by Arthur Young, formerly executive in charge of industrial relations at International Harvester. By 1925 the volume of industrial relations work had grown so large that the personnel of the IR section outnumbered the rest of the people in Fosdick's law firm.

Upon Fosdick's recommendation, Rockefeller approved taking the IR section out of the law firm and setting it up as an independent nonprofit corporation. Thus, on May 1, 1926, the consulting firm Industrial Relations Counselors, Inc. was established with its headquarters in New York City. Young remained director, and IRC staff soon totaled more than a dozen people, augmented by specialists hired on an as-needed basis for large-scale projects or special research reports. Some of these specialists, such as Henry Metcalf, Mary Gilson, Canby Balderston, and Sumner Slichter, were among the best-known practitioners and academic experts of that era on matters of personnel management and employer-employee relations.

Several points about IRC's creation deserve mention. First is its name. The term *counselors* was that era's term for consultants. The term *industrial relations* was used because in this period industrial relations conveyed a meaning that was both more strategic and broad-based than any other.[13] In the 1920s (and through the 1950s), industrial relations was defined to cover the entire employment relationship, including personnel management/HRM and labor relations (rather than just the latter, as is common today). Thus, IRC's twenty-fifth anniversary conference proceedings state, "In terms of content 'industrial relations' has come to include all contacts between labor and all grades of management, which are connected with or grow out of employment. Specifically, it covers items usually classified as personnel work, such as recruiting, hiring, placement, transfer, training, discipline, promotion, layoff, and termination of employees."[14] In this early period, therefore, industrial relations effectively subsumed personnel management and what is today called human resource management and imparted to both a broad-based, strategic perspective. IR was more broad-based because it explicitly included all areas of employment, including private and public, union and nonunion, and it was more strategic because it explicitly included the top executive function of creating and administering the firm's labor policy (i.e., a statement of labor philosophy and principles and how these supported and complemented the mission of the firm). The concept of labor policy has, since the early 1970s, evolved into the related concept of strategy and now forms the basis for the academic subfield Strategic Human Resource Management (SHRM). The strategic nature of industrial relations circa the 1920s is indicated in this statement by Cowdrick: "In many companies the duties of the labor manager had little visible connection with management in general. The personnel man was not expected to have much knowledge about—sometimes not even much sympathy with—the business affairs of the employer—The result [of the industrial relations movement] has been an enlarged conception of labor management as an essential part of general management, not to be separated from the other policies of the corporation."[15]

Second, the objective of IRC was to promote scientific progress and mutual gain outcomes in employment relationships. Its stated mission, for example, was to "advance the knowledge and practice of human relationships in industry, commerce, education, and government." Toward this end, IRC engaged in three principal activities—consulting, research, and training. More on each of these will be described shortly. Also part of IRC's mission was to remain scrupulously neutral in matters of unionism. From the very start IRC informed clients that it would not counsel or assist in antiunion activities, either directly or indirectly (e.g., such as through the establishment of an employee representation plan to serve as a union substitute), and my investigation of the company's internal memoranda and written reports reveal no exception to this policy.[16] IRC was thus a proponent of what at that time was called the model of "industrial liberalism," which is to say a "high road" and "high performance" model that sought to gain competitive advantage and profitability through superior employment practices and the creation of cooperation and unity of interest between employer and employees. Crucial to the model of industrial liberalism was some formal method for employee voice and participation, such as a plan of employee representation, thus turning workforce governance from "autocracy" to "liberalism." An effect of industrial liberalism was frequently to substantially reduce workers' desire for union representation, but this was regarded as a beneficial indirect outcome arising from constructively eliminating sources of employee dissatisfaction.

Third, while Rockefeller continued to financially support IRC for another decade (such support totaling approximately $1.5 million), the organization was intended to become financially self-supporting, albeit on a nonprofit basis. To accomplish this, IRC quickly began to recruit business from companies outside the group owned by or connected to Rockefeller. The result was that by the late 1930s IRC had consulting relationships with a wide cross-section of American companies, including many of the "blue ribbon" firms in corporate America. Based on the evidence, it is fair to say that while other labor/personnel consulting firms started before IRC, no other before World War II had IRC's reach and influence.

As mentioned earlier, IRC had three principal activity areas: consulting, research, and training. In the training area, IRC offered courses and classes in aspects of industrial relations management at a variety of sites across the nation. The capstone training class was an annual two-week "IRC Management Course in Industrial Relations" in Williamsburg, Virginia, for fifty to sixty top and middle managers in industrial relations.

IRC also carried out an extensive research program in industrial relations, and by the late 1930s was widely viewed as one of the leading labor/employment research organizations in the country.[17] IRC's research program was carried out both by in-house staff and academic people recruited to undertake specific studies. Among the latter were J. Douglas Brown (Princeton University), C. Canby Balderston (the Wharton School at the University of Pennsylvania), Sumner Slichter (Cornell University), Herman Feldman (Dartmouth College), and Richard Lester (Princeton University). Balderston, for example, authored reports on wage setting and profit-sharing, while Feldman and Lester wrote on the pros and cons of experience rating in unemployment insurance programs.

More significant, however, was the industrial relations research generated by IRC's in-house staff. This research grew out of the growth of IRC's consulting business, which quickly developed a major thrust in the area of benefits and pensions. During the 1920s a number of firms established accident, health, unemployment, and retirement insurance plans. Lacking internal expertise in these matters, they hired IRC to advise them on setting up the actuarial, financial, and administrative/organizational aspects. By the mid-1930s IRC had a team of experts in the benefits/insurance area that was recognized as the best in the nation.[18] Given IRC's mandate to promote science and research in industrial relations, the organization encouraged its staff to disseminate their knowledge of "best practice" through books and monographs. As a result, from 1930 to the 1940s IRC staff published eleven monographs in the two areas of unemployment insurance and pensions. When President Franklin Delano Roosevelt formed the Committee on Economic Security to draft what later became the Social Security Act (1935), IRC staff members Bryce Stewart and Murray Latimer were appointed to high-level positions.[19]

This brings us to the third IRC activity—and the one that bears most directly on this volume: industrial relations consulting.

From the very start, IRC undertook consulting projects on specific and relatively narrow and well-defined IR topics, such as wage evaluation plans and pensions. But for the first twenty years or so this was not IRC's central consulting activity nor what it marketed to clients as its forte. Rather, IRC specialized in full-scale "A-to-Z" labor audits, or what it called "industrial relations surveys." In these surveys, a team of IRC staff, often about three in number but sometimes as large as a half dozen or more, would spend several months on-site at a company. They would interview all ranks of management and employees about IR matters, examine internal company records, and go out in the field to see personnel and employee relations in practice. They would then return to IRC, write up a draft of their findings, observations, and recommendations, send it to the company for review and comment, and generate a final draft.

The end product was an industrial relations survey that to an academic person most closely resembles a PhD dissertation. Particularly for the first decade or so, these IR surveys were massive in-depth reports on all aspects of the company and its IR program with the end product encompassing 200–300 pages, always with numerous tables and charts and sometimes black-and-white photos, and then bound in reddish-brown leather. These early surveys were in part meant to educate and inform top corporate executives about labor conditions and practices in their companies, since many (like Rockefeller before them) had little knowledge of these matters due both to lack of information (personnel record keeping was generally primitive and fragmented) and the great distance that often separated the executive suites and the shop floor.

One must see the bound industrial relations surveys to appreciate their impressive size and depth of detail.[20] I still vividly recall the first time I visited IRC headquarters at Rockefeller Center in New York City and saw them. I was led into a large conference room and along an entire wall were the many hundreds of IRC consulting surveys and reports arrayed in chronological order, starting with the first report in 1923 done by the IR Section staff of Curtis, Fosdick, and Belknap. They were behind locked glass doors and, I was told, never made available to an outside person because of legal confidentiality requirements with the client companies. This was a truly awe-inspiring sight for any person with an appreciation of the drama and events of American labor history and, to me, was akin to opening the door of a newly discovered Pharaoh's tomb containing never-before-seen written records of ancient Egypt.

Through good fortune, I was invited to help IRC plan a commemorative seventy-fifth anniversary two-day conference at Princeton University in 2001. As fate would have it, the conference began on the morning of September 11, and was brought to an abrupt end about 9:30 that morning, for tragic reasons that need no recounting here. In the context of that relationship, I was given access to the consulting reports as an aid for preparing my conference presentation and subsequent chapters for the anniversary volume on the history of IRC.[21] Later, I was given permission to write up synopses of the contents of the early reports, which are presented as the case studies that follow in this volume. For reasons of legal confidentiality I cannot identify the names of the companies in these case studies so I have given each a pseudonym.

The early IR surveys were organized with a fairly standard format, although the location of individual chapters sometimes varied. A typical survey began with an extensive overview of the history of the company, its principal lines of business, and recent operating and financial results. Then the survey of the company's industrial relations programs and policies followed, organized into separate chapters. A typical volume had these chapters:

- Organization and administration of industrial relations (including policy)
- Employment, wages, and hours
- Training and education
- Medical and health services and insurance plans
- Housing, sanitation, and employee activities
- Other employee benefits, including savings and investment plans
- Accident and fire prevention
- Pensions
- Joint relations

Chapters in later surveys typically had three parts: good practice; present conditions; and conclusions and recommendations.

The IRC survey reports, to the best of my knowledge, give the most detailed and in-depth accounts available of IR/HRM practices at individual American companies in the years before World War II. They also provide valuable company-level data on certain employment outcomes, such as turnover rates, job tenure, and hiring costs, that are otherwise quite difficult to obtain. I believe, therefore, the case studies that follow significantly expand and elaborate our knowledge base regarding early American HRM programs and practices. Not knowing whether these IRC reports will ever be available to other researchers, I also decided to err on the side of inclusiveness and present a more detailed description of the specific HRM activities and programs in these companies than I other wise would. Readers uninterested in this level of administrative detail may pass it by.

The IRC reports also have their limitations and unique features that need to be briefly mentioned. For example, in the period up to the early New Deal (the ending point for this volume), there are not a large number of IR surveys to choose from, and a significant number come from two principal industries—oil and coal, or idiosyncratic industries (e.g., Hawaiian pineapple growers). Beginning in 1923, IRC did an average of about two large-scale IR surveys per year, which then largely ceased during the worst Depression years of 1931–1933 (when an IR survey became an unaffordable luxury, amid rampant wage cutting and layoffs).

Accordingly, I have selected six surveys that as much as possible provide interesting variation in HRM programs/policies in terms of industries covered, degree of HRM formalization, and "quality" of employer-employee relations. These case studies include an oil refining company, a large-size coal company, a medium-size specialty steel producer, a vertically integrated coal and steel company, an electricity generation and distribution company (a utility), and a company with a main line of business in consumer electrical equipment manufacture (e.g., radios and phonographs). Ideally, one would wish for IR surveys in several other industries, such as automobile manufacturing, industrial electrical equipment, and banking, but such is not available.

The reports also contain some unfortunate—but perhaps revealing—omissions. For example, the HRM system is explained and examined with very little attention to the parallel production system, such as the nature of the production technology, its impact on the job structure, and the job structure's psychological, social, and skill ramifications. In effect, the production system and job structure are treated as largely invisible "givens" and the IRC consultants then proceed to analyze HRM programs and practices largely without reference to these other parts. This omission helps explain why the HRM function often had (and may continue to have) difficulty establishing a strategic role in the company because the operations core of the business was typically developed and run by industrial engineers and production managers and the HRM function was brought in to handle lower-level administrative and programmatic aspects of personnel and employer-employee relations in an after-the-fact role.

Also missing from the reports are accounts of the day-to-day reality of work and work relations on the plant floor or observations and experiences as related by the employees. The preface and introduction to the reports state that the IRC consultants interviewed numerous employees, but very little of what they learned is conveyed in personal terms through quotations or examples. The consultants also undoubtedly witnessed firsthand what it was like to work in these plants, mills, and mines, the nature of the employer-employee interactions, and the problems that resulted, but only hints (either good or bad) make it into the reports.

The IRC reports also provide interesting evidence on the degree and extent to which PIR in this period was (or was not) practiced strategically. It is a mixed record.

A modern definition of strategic HRM is "the pattern of planned human resource management deployments and activities intended to enable an organization to achieve its goals."[22] Scholars then distinguish two dimensions of SHRM: *vertical alignment* (aligning the firm's HRM practices to maximally support attainment of its business goals) and *horizontal alignment* (arranging individual HRM practices into a coordinated and synergistic whole).

The evidence is clear in the case studies presented in the following chapters that IRC conducted the surveys from a strategic perspective, albeit couched in a somewhat different idiom than is commonly used today, and counseled the client companies to think about their PIR programs in a comprehensive and integrated manner. Further, the evidence reveals that at least some companies in the 1920s actively and consciously took a strategic approach to labor with attention to both vertical and horizontal fit. This is most obvious in the advanced welfare capitalism firms, where achieving cooperation and unity of interest with employees were explicit strategic goals, and toward this end were crafted integrated, synergistic packages of HRM practices, such as fair wages, job security, generous benefits, and a formal collective employee voice.[23]

The strategic perspective taken by IRC toward the practice of PIR is illustrated in this passage that (with some variation) opens the preface to several of the early reports:

> In all industrial organizations, the attainment of results is ultimately dependent upon human labor, in its many variations of skill and experience, from the common laborer to president. Because of this fact, it is desirable to provide administrative machinery which will make full use of all the possibilities inherent in the working forces. The accumulated experience, with methods of control and co-ordination of the labor force in an industry, is defined by the term labor administration. From a technical standpoint, labor administration has to do with the intricate and complex problem of obtaining the most effective use of the labor force, thus securing the maximum return from payroll expenditure. It ranks in importance, therefore, with finance, engineering, manufacturing, marketing and other major functions of management.
>
> There are, however, other compelling aspects in labor administration brought about because, more and more, public opinion is demanding that company officials also conduct their businesses in ways that are socially justifiable. As a result, labor administration takes on special significance expressed by the term "Industrial Relations," which is defined as the direction of co-ordination of human relationships in industry for maximum necessary production, with minimum friction and with proper regard for the genuine well-being of the workers."

The downside to the IRC reports—and, to some significant degree, to the industrial practice of that era—is that the strategy idea, though grasped, was for the most part weakly articulated and thinly implemented. Illustratively, the introductory chapter in the surveys provides an overview of the company's products, markets, operations, and financial performance, but exactly how these relate and influence the shape and practice of HRM is typically not well developed. The result, if one wants to be critical, is something of a functional "silo" perspective. Horizontal linkages across individual PIR practices fare somewhat better (e.g., the link between successful employee representation and job security), but again the elaboration of these linkages remains superficial.

Another part of the debate in modern SHRM concerns *universalistic* versus *contingency* theories of HRM and firm performance.[24] Some scholars argue that firms always attain higher performance (i.e., profits or return on capital) when they adopt HRM practices that create strong commitment, high involvement, and a highly skilled workforce. In effect, these companies get not only the workers' time and muscles each day but also their hearts and minds, giving them a big productivity edge. Frequently cited "high performance" HRM methods are employee involvement programs, job security, mutual gain pay systems, extensive training, and formal dispute resolution procedures. Other scholars argue, however, that the HRM practices that work well in one firm (e.g., Microsoft) may be a failure in another (e.g., McDonald's) because HRM has to be tailored to a variety of important contingent factors, such as the nature of the production technology, characteristics of the customers, required skills and knowledge of the workers, and the state of the economy. During an economic depression or in poultry processing plants, to cite two examples, firms may get higher profit not by using "high road" HRM practices such as employee involvement and extensive training but by using "low road" practices such as child labor and driving foremen.

The IRC reports render an interestingly mixed verdict on this debate. On one hand, the reports clearly state there is no "one best way" in HRM, and human resource programs have to be tailored to fit each company's situation. The key desiderata in designing an HRM program is that it has to pass the market test, meaning that it contributes to or at least does not subtract from profits and the survival and growth of the enterprise. With this consideration in mind, it makes no sense to recommend a full-fledged, advanced HRM program if it is economically infeasible. Thus, even though IRC was a strong supporter of employee representation, the consultants did not recommend it to some clients because the companies' economic situation or employee relations climate was not right. Also, IRC emphasized that a particular HRM outcome, such as reducing absenteeism or raising employee morale, can be accomplished using either formal or informal procedures— for example, a written handbook statement promising job security for good performance or an implicit but well understood psychological contract— and that in all matters the *spirit* in which HRM is conducted is more important than the specific nature of the procedures.

On the other hand, IRC also took a universalistic or "best practice" approach in certain areas. Every report, for example, counsels the employer that efficiency and profits are improved by creating a more rational, formalized, integrated, and professionally conducted HRM function and, further, that success in medium-to-large firms requires that the HRM function be the sole responsibility of a high-level executive. Another constant theme is that companies must recognize that their HRM policies have to not only pass the dollars and cents market test but also the social and moral legitimacy test as seen by their employees and the wider community.

Receiving most attention, however, was a third "best practice" idea. Every IRC report states as a fundamental principle that enterprise performance is always and everywhere enhanced by HRM methods that promote closer *cooperation* and greater *unity of interest* between employer and workers.[25] Indeed, the themes of cooperation and unity of interest, and the many benefits that flow from them—such as higher productivity, lower turnover, better citizenship behavior, and reduced conflict—run through IRC publications, reports, speeches, and articles by Rockefeller, Hicks, and Young like a mantra. IRC identified, in turn, four key ingredients for creating cooperation and unity of interest: a culture of *fair treatment*; bona fide opportunities for *employee voice and participation*; performance-related *mutual gain* practices in pay, benefits, and promotion; and a well-articulated and conscientiously practiced policy of *employment security*, conditional on good job performance and a minimum necessary level of profit. Not all firms could fully or perhaps even partially implement these four ingredients because of the contingencies noted earlier (e.g., nature of the industry, state of the economy), but IRC's strong conviction was that *every* company—no matter if a McDonald's or Microsoft or in an economic depression or economic boom—had room to make improvements in these four areas and *every* company and workforce will benefit by doing so in a carefully planned and consultative way.

I now proceed to the case studies. Readers should note that because the company names are confidential I am precluded from presenting other material about these companies and their HRM programs, such as from other scholarly works and the periodical literature, that would necessarily reveal their identities. I am also constrained by my material to outline each report in a relatively descriptive chapter-by-chapter manner. As much as possible, I let every report speak for itself and only occasionally interject commentary or observation. For ease of exposition, I also refer to surveys done by the staff of Curtis, Fosdick, and Belknap as IRC reports, although technically the two groups are separate. Finally, while I outline the HRM programs of all companies in these reports, only for one do I also describe the set of recommendations made by the IRC consultants. I do this because many of the major recommendations are fairly standard across reports and thus need be described only once.

8

The Human Resource Model in a Welfare Capitalism Firm

The Top-Grade Oil Company

Our first case study is of a large oil refining company headquartered in a major eastern city. This firm was an industrial relations pioneer, was widely recognized as having one of the most advanced and far-reaching human resource management (HRM) programs in the nation, and typifies the leading edge of labor management practices among firms in the welfare capitalism movement of the 1920s. Of the six IRC case studies, this one best represents the *human resource* model in operation.

In this case study and the ones that follow, I write the text in the present tense just as it is contained in the IRC report. This particular IR survey was done in 1923.

Background

The Top-Grade Oil Company (hereafter "the company") is composed of a parent organization and a number of subsidiaries in the United States and numerous foreign countries engaged in all branches of the petroleum industry. Total employment in 1923 is 68,000. The parent organization consists of refining, marketing, and marine divisions and is not engaged in the production of crude oil. It operates six refineries, employing 10,500 people.

The company experienced strikes in two years shortly before World War I at an East Coast refinery that resulted in considerable acts of violence, destruction of property, and the use of National Guard troops to restore order. In 1917, with encouragement of the principal shareholder, new and more forward-looking management was installed, including a new chairman of the board and president. One of the chairman's first acts was to create a new position of executive assistant to both the president and the chairman of the board in charge of all phases of industrial relations work. The position was filled by a man hired from outside the company who had considerable past experience in industrial welfare work, employment management, and employee representation. Under this person's guidance, the Top-Grade Oil Company put in place one of the most comprehensive and progressive industrial relations programs in the nation.

The IRC report provides a telling description of labor conditions and practices at the company prior to the new industrial relations program. I quote at length:

> Previous to 1918, the Top-Grade Oil Company had formulated no definite labor policy. The general attitude of the company had been distinctly conservative. During 1917 and 1918, with the accession of Mr. [X] as President, and later as Chairman of the Board of Directors, the labor policy of the company changed. The Company decided that it must be progressive in labor management as well as in financial development, and that it was good business as well as socially just, not only to give employees fair wages, hours, and working conditions, but also to insure a form of representative dealing with management.
>
> There had been no uniform labor policy, local management being left to conduct labor administration as it thought best. Conditions in some of the eastern refineries had been chaotic. In one large eastern refinery, labor graft had abounded, political privilege was prevalent, and serious labor disturbances had occurred. Gradually, however, there came a change in labor policy. The World War, in to which our country had entered at that time, surely had its effect, but the way alone could not bring about the tremendous changes which took place. Possibly the bad conditions existing in some of the eastern refineries were more vital factors. At any rate, there came a change in vision on the part of the leading officials of the company. There was a realization that if the company was to be thoroughly modern in its administration, it must be progressive in labor management as well as in financial management; that wage earners must have just and representative dealings with management; that wages must be fair and in accord with changing living costs; and that working conditions must be decent. However, the new policy was not adopted for mere sentimental reasons but because it was good business. The officials of the company realized that it was sound investment, not mere welfare, to spend considerable money in creating healthy and safe working conditions; in voluntarily paying benefits to sick, injured, and superannuated employees or their dependents; in adjusting wages in relation to the cost of living; and in striving for industrial justice.
>
> This change in the labor policy should be emphasized most clearly. If one talks with the old employees, he will realize what this change has meant in the attitude of employees toward the Company. Where formerly antagonisms and bitterness existed, today there is substantial loyalty. The effect does not end with employees, but permeates entire communities in their attitude toward the Company. Today officials agree that the present labor policy of the Company has not only paid for itself but has contributed greatly to the prosperity of the Company.

Another statement of the company's labor policy is provided in a booklet issued by the company outlining the industrial representation plan adopted in 1918. In it the industrial relations director states, "The labor policy of the Top-Grade Oil Company is based upon certain well established principles which have been developed on the fundamental proposition of a 'square deal' for all concerned: the employees, the management, the stockholders, and the public."

The New Labor Policy

The IRC report proceeds to outline the major principles and practices of the company's new labor policy, based on statements provided in various company documents and a written handbook distributed to all employees. The handbook begins with a message to employees from the company's president. Note the emphasis on cooperation, mutual gain, fair treatment, and a long-term employment relationship (and, immediately below in item 1, voice and participation). It reads in part,

> It is the policy of the Company that the interests of its employees shall be safeguarded in every reasonable way. The several plans described in this booklet for the protection of the employees' health, earnings, and personal rights are matters of direct interest to each employee. . . . In a company as large as this an employee often thinks he is a very small part of a large machine and that what he does will hardly be noticed. We want you to know, however, that each employee has an opportunity to become an important part of the Company; that your career with us is limited only by your ability; and that the Company offers you a chance for life service under favorable conditions. We hope it will be a pleasure, not a task, to give the best that is in you. We are counting on your cooperation in all matters that make possible the success of the individual employee and the prosperity of the Company.

The principles and practices of the new labor policy are then outlined. They are the following (condensed, but left in the language of the original as much as possible):

1. *Collective Bargaining through Industrial Representation. The Company accepts the principle of collective bargaining made effective through the Industrial Representation Plan. The Company believes in the establishment of contact between management and men through the opportunity of joint conferences between company and employee representatives.*
2. *Employment Policy*
   a. Non-discrimination: The Company makes no discrimination against any employee on account of membership in any organization or union.
   b. Age Limitations: Except with specific approval of the Board of Directors, the age limitation for applicants is 45 years for men and 35 years for women. The Company states that it has made this age limitation in order to effectively safeguard its annuity policy.

c. Physical Examination: All new employees are required to pass a physical examination by a Company doctor.

d. Recognition of Length of Service: The Company recognizes the length of service of employees of more than ten years' service by means of special service buttons.

e. Layoffs: The Company in laying off employees takes into consideration the following conditions: efficiency, length of service, citizenship, and number of dependents. Efficient employees receive an advance notice of one week and are, if possible, placed upon a temporary layoff list.

f. Ninety-day Inactive Period: Employees temporarily laid off, sick, or on leave of absences, are placed upon an inactive list for a period ranging up to ninety days. Efficient employees placed upon this list do not become permanently laid off until the end of the ninety-day period.

g. Casual Employees: In order to safeguard its Annuities and Benefits Plan, the Company is seriously considering the limitation of the status of regular employment to those employees who have worked at least twenty days in twelve consecutive months.

h. Discharges: All discharges conform to certain rules contained in the joint agreement of the Industrial Representation Plan.

3. *Wage Principles. The Company accepts two basic principles in regard to wages: first, that wage rates should be equal to or higher than the prevailing scale for similar work in any community; and second, that wages shall be dependent upon the rise and fall of the cost of living in any community, as indicated by the Bureau of Labor Statistics. The Company pays a basic rate of $.48 for common or unskilled labor, raising this rate to $.53 after three months' service and to $.57½ after one year's service. The Company did not reduce wage rates for common labor below this basic scale throughout the period of industrial depression. This farsighted policy has curtailed labor turnover and built up a strong and loyal common labor group. The payment of fair and just wage rates by the Company has been thoroughly satisfactory from a business, as well as a social point of view, and is one of the strongest factors in the success of the present labor policy.*

4. *Hours. In the refineries of the Company, there is a universal eight-hour day and forty-eight hour week. The Company changed from a two-shift to a three-shift basis in refineries in 1915.*

5. *One-Day's-Rest-in-Seven. The Company believes in one-day's-rest-in-seven, preferably Sunday, or the equivalent of such a period. Officials of the Company state that six-day labor is now universal in all refineries and marketing areas, of the parent company and in the producing fields.*

6. *Working Conditions. The Company strives for healthful and sanitary working conditions and, through a medical services and safety organization, is constantly safeguarding the health and lives of its employees.*

The Industrial Relations Program and Its Administration

The next section of the IRC report is devoted to a description of the administrative structure and component parts of the Company's industrial relations program. I provide here only a skeletal outline of the IR program since most components are described in more detail later in this chapter. They are (in the order listed in the report):

1. The Industrial Representation Program
2. Personnel and Training Department
3. Medical Services
4. Sickness
5. Safety
6. Accidents
7. Annuities and Benefits
8. Stock Acquisition Plan
9. Housing
10. Publications
11. Cafeterias
12. Bands
13. Recreational and Social Activities

The organizational structure and administration of the industrial relations program is depicted in a chart in the IRC report. At the corporate level, the industrial relations department is organized into six major subdivisions: Industrial Representation, Personnel and Training, Medical, Annuities and Benefits, Safety, and Service (administering items 8–13 in the list above). The corporate IR program is headed by the executive assistant to the president and board of directors. This executive position was unique at this time in American companies for its high level in the corporate hierarchy and direct access to the highest decision makers in the firm.

The organization of the IR function at the refinery level mirrors that at the corporate level. An assistant to the superintendent in charge of industrial relations reports to the plant superintendent, with a "dotted line" to the corporate-level executive assistant for industrial relations, and supervises the same six IR subdivisions.

The industrial relations function is seen as a staff function and, in the words of the IRC report, all IR staff are acting as "counselors and advisors" to the operating units of the company. There is thus a clear separation between staff and line and industrial relations belongs to the latter.

The implementation of the industrial relations program is not uniform or comprehensive across the company. The percentages of the company's personnel covered under the six parts of the program are as follows: industrial representation plan (30%), personnel and training (66%), medical services (66%), annuities and benefits (66%), safety (30%), and stock acquisition

(50%). A number of the subsidiaries not covered under various parts of the IR program are located in foreign countries, while the maritime division follows the personnel practices of other shipping companies.

The parent company does not attempt to dictate labor policy to subsidiaries. The report gives two reasons: "In the first place, unless executives are 'sold' on the labor policy, the application of the various features of the industrial relations program is impracticable. The hearty cooperation of local management is the essential and primary basis for successful local administration. Without the necessary esprit de corps, all plans fail. . . . In the second place, there is often resentment of any interference by the Company with the internal affairs of subsidiaries." The report goes on to observe, "In general, labor policy has been adopted in subsidiaries not because of mere financial control, but rather on account of alignment with the spirit and attitude of the parent Company. The future advancement of the industrial relations program will be proportionate to the acceptance of labor policy by the subsidiaries, and is limited by the attitude of subsidiary executives, as well as the sensitiveness of the subsidiary in accepting policies laid down by the parent Company."

Finally, the report notes, "It has been the purpose of the Top-Grade Oil Company to keep away from a formal type of industrial relations frequently found in large industrial corporations. . . . Fundamentally, therefore, the administration of the labor policy is informal: it depends for its success more upon the spirit than the letter."

The Industrial Representation Plan

The Top-Grade Oil Company considered its employee representation plan to be the foundation and linchpin of its industrial relations program. The plan was established in early 1918 when the new company president sent a letter to the employees of three eastern refineries inviting each employee to take part in the election of representatives. The first meeting of the representatives took place shortly thereafter and the Industrial Representation Plan was formally adopted. Over the next four years the plan was adopted in nine other facilities or divisions. As of 1922, the plan covered 20,300 employees.

A booklet outlining the purpose and provisions of the Plan is given to every employee. The purpose is stated in the first paragraph (1921 edition):

Justice is the underlying purpose of the Industrial Representation Plan of the Top-Grade Oil Company which has been in effect since April 1st, 1918. Its main object is to provide a point of contact between the management and each employee, and regular opportunities for collective action between representatives of the employees and of the management on all matters of mutual interest. It grew out of a belief, on the part of the Directors, that a system which would create an opportunity for the honest expression and fair consideration of the views of all, which would send men about their work with the consciousness that so long as the industry flourished their interests were safeguarded, must, in the long run, bring results in contentment, efficiency, cooperation, harmony, and mutual profit.

Structure and Operation

All employees in units where the plan is in effect, except salaried workers, are eligible to vote and to hold office. No restrictions regarding length of service, color, nationality, position, or membership in a religious or labor organization are made. In this regard, the IRC report notes that some representatives from skilled craft groups are known to be union members. The basis of election is one representative for every 150 employees, with at least two representatives in each division. The general basis of selection is an occupational group or department. As an example, in one refinery the thirty-seven representatives have been chosen from fourteen divisions, composed of groups such as boilermakers and blacksmiths (2); carpenters, painters, leadburners, and machinists (2); masons, pipefitters, tinsmiths, railroad, and hoisting engineers (3); common labor (3); still cleaners (2); barrel factory (3); cooperage department (3); paraffin process (3); and so on. The election of representatives is by secret ballot and is done annually. The report notes that in a southern refinery twelve white and four "colored" representatives served on the plan, while in another southern refinery the representatives included twenty-six white and thirteen "colored." At this time, most independent trade unions had a strict color bar that excluded black workers.

The meetings of the joint conferences are held at least once quarterly, sometimes monthly. All matters of mutual interest may be put on the table. Joint secretaries, one from management and the other from employees, take minutes. The minutes are reviewed by all representatives and then forwarded for inspection by the work's superintendent and the company president and board of directors. The meetings are chaired by a management representative. Once a year a companywide meeting is held with the management and employee representatives in attendance. A dinner is held in the evening with top company executives in attendance.

Topics

The report provides several tables that give a breakdown of topics discussed in council meetings. One such table shows the percentage distribution of topics discussed among fourteen areas for six time periods between adoption of the plan in the spring of 1918 and the spring of 1922. The report gives no further commentary on these tables or on the resolution of these discussions, so what we know are the summary figures in the table. Wages were the topic at meetings 30 percent of the time; also important were hours (10%), working conditions (10%), industrial representation plan (10%), and "general" (15%).

The report discusses two aspects of the wage question with respect to the representation plan. The first is with respect to wage reductions. It notes that the company granted two wage "bonuses" of 10 percent each during 1918 and 1919 to compensate for the rapid increase in the cost of living (pursuant to its new policy of adjusting wages with respect to price increases). However, staring in early 1920 the national economy went into a steep recession and prices dropped sharply. Thus, in early 1921, the company took back one of the 10 percent bonuses. Later in 1921 the company proposed removal of the second bonus, but the official cost of living had not declined by the full additional 10 percent. Appearing to being formally blocked from proceeding further, the company formed an ad hoc committee of employees and managers and surveyed wage rates at adjacent companies. It was found that company wage scales were 18 percent above prevailing local scales. According to the report, the company pointed out to the employees that it had good reason to propose a cut in the base wage rate to bring it into line with local rates. To avoid this possibility, employees consented to removal of the second 10 percent wage bonus.

The second wage-related topic discussed in the report with respect to the representative plan is the wage standardization program. According to the report, in early 1922 an employee representative stated that first-class painters in two of the eastern refineries were not receiving the same rate of wages. A committee was appointed to investigate the matter, and evidence was presented that not only painters received unequal wages but that this problem was a general one among all grades and classes of labor. Hence, at a plan meeting a resolution was adopted that stated (in part), "The wisdom and necessity of uniform job classifications for identical work at the company's refineries is apparent. . . . To eliminate unnecessary rates and to properly classify the remaining rates will undoubtedly involve, in individual cases, some rate reductions, as well as some increases, and the cooperation of employees' representatives will be invaluable."

Under the direction of the manager of personnel and training, a complete job analysis and wage study was done in each of the three refineries. Toward this end, a detailed two-page "job analysis" sheet was designed that measured a host of employee and job characteristics, such as education, physical attributes (weight, height, etc.), working conditions, skill requirements, supervision required, and responsibility. In the last week of 1922, the committee reported its investigation and recommendations before the joint conference of employee and management representatives. A total of 4,916 jobs were included in the wage studies. Of this total, wage rates were increased for 1,380 and decreased for 536. The wage decreases were held in abeyance, however. The wage rate for common labor after six months was established at $.53 and at $.575 for common labor after twelve months.

Summarizing the results of the wage standardization program, the report states, "*The main point is that about two hundred different wage rates have been discontinued and twenty wage rate levels have been instituted* [emphasis in the original]. This wage standardization plan is the most important step that the Company has undertaken in the field of industrial relations during the past year. It is an attempt to place wages and jobs in a fair and equitable relationship."

Summary

The report ends its discussion of the industrial representation plan with this short statement: "The Industrial Representation Plan, during the nearly five years of its establishment, has proven successful in bringing matters to the attention of local management for the settlement of grievances, and for the promotion of a closer spirit of cooperation between management and men. Through a period of unequaled fluctuations in wages, the Plan has made possible the adjustment of both wage increases and wage reductions with but one serious labor disturbance [an unsuccessful strike of boilermakers in a southern facility in 1920 over a demand for union recognition]."

Personnel and Training

In introducing the personnel and training function, the report states, "The institution of the various features of the progressive labor policy necessitated the creation of an efficient Personnel Department to handle employee records and to provide the means of personal contact with the individual employee. In addition, the Personnel Department . . . has complete oversight of the various educational features, including training courses and Americanization work." The manager of personnel and training is given control of hiring of all employees, including office help and salaried executives up to $7,000 per annum; is given authority over all personnel work in the refineries and marketing fields of the parent company; and acts in an advisory capacity to subsidiaries. Foremen, supervisors, and department heads often make recommendations for individual wage adjustments, but these require the approval of the Personnel Department before becoming effective.

Written Statements of Employment Policy and Practices

Most companies in this time period had no written statement of labor policy or terms and conditions of employment. Similarly, beyond a time/ attendance sheet and payroll record, few companies used written employment forms as part of their internal administration of labor. The Top-Grade Oil Company was a pioneer in both areas.

The company provides all employees with three booklets pertaining to employment and terms and conditions. The first is an employee handbook, the second outlines the industrial representation plan, and the third describes the annuities and benefits plan.

In internal labor management, the company developed what at that time was perhaps the most elaborate set of written employment forms/records in American industry. Fourteen separate forms were used: an application for future employment; an interview notification; an immediate employment form and index cards; employees' record cards; a references investigation; an instruction book; a requisition card; a list of persons employed; a list of persons transferred; a list of persons terminated; a list of permanent transfers; a list of temporary transfers; a termination slip; an application of change rate card; a temporary pass; a daily labor turnover card; a monthly labor turnover card; an absence report; an employee's rating report; an employee's pass; a notice of absence card; an advance notice of temporary layoff; and a visitor's pass.

Hiring Process

The first step in the hiring process is for a foreman or department head to submit a "requisition card" to the personnel department requesting an employee for a particular job. Applicants are reviewed by the employment manager and screened into "acceptable" and "unacceptable" categories. From the group of "acceptable" applicants, one is selected and sent to the company doctor for a physical exam. The report indicates this decision is made by the employment manager; whether the foreman/department head has any input in the matter is not indicated. If the applicant passes the physical exam, reference checks are made by the personnel department. Upon passing this step, the person is hired as an employee of the company, and the employee's record card is filled out, and the employee receives a copy of the employee handbook. A person from the personnel department then introduces the new employee to the foreman and the person is assigned to the job.

Turnover

The company had for several years calculated labor turnover figures, but the data were not comparable across subsidiaries due to differences in reporting forms and requirements. Beginning in mid-1921, however, employment records were standardized across the company and comparable turnover data was thus made possible. Turnover was calculated using both the average number of employees listed as active and inactive (on temporary layoff).

From mid-1921 to mid-1922 the annual labor turnover rate in the company and subsidiaries was 85 percent. If only active employees are used as the denominator, the ratio was 95 percent. Turnover experience varied greatly across divisions and subsidiaries, however. In the parent company, turnover was 36 percent, but it was 124 percent in the subsidiaries. The report provides only meager discussion of these disparate trends. Within the parent company, for example, two subsidiaries had turnover rates of 193 percent and 132 percent, respectively. These high turnover figures were said to stem from rapid local development projects (e.g., opening a new oil field) and subsequent layoffs when the work was completed. A reasonable conjecture, I think, is that the relatively low turnover figure for the parent part of the company vis-à-vis certain subsidiaries reflects in part the more far-reaching adoption and implementation of the new IR program in the former.

The general economy in 1921 was very depressed, which had a divergent impact on turnover. Given the scarcity of jobs, turnover from resignations was no doubt lower than usual while layoffs from lack of work were higher. Labor turnover from "discharges for cause" was the lowest of the major categories, averaging only 2.5 percent at the parent company. This figure also varied considerably across divisions and subsidiaries, with the report noting that it was higher in areas of the company experiencing rapid growth (given greater hiring of young and inexperienced workers) and where African Americans comprised a larger fraction of the workforce.

Although economic activity was generally depressed during this twelve-month period, the substantial turnover rate necessitated continual hiring of new workers. For the combined company and subsidiaries, average annual employment was 34,172, but over this twelve-month period 30,443 new employees were hired. The volume of new hiring was much larger in the subsidiaries.

As part of its new industrial relations program, the company established preferential recall rights for former employees. Employees on layoff went into a ninety-day "inactive employee" list and were considered first for recall. Recall was contingent, however, on satisfactory past service. In the parent company, 55 percent of new hires came from reemployment of former workers, a ratio that fell to 39 percent in the subsidiaries.

Wages

The average annual earnings per employee in 1922 for the entire company were estimated at $1,600. This figure does not include earnings of people classified as "casuals." Average earnings at the parent company were $1,690, and at the subsidiaries, $1,512. Annual average earnings per employee at the company in 1922 were 9.3 percent lower than in 1920, reflecting the two wage reductions in 1921.

Training

Managing and delivering training programs was another responsibility of the personnel and training department. The report states, "The Top-Grade Oil Company has been one of the pioneer industrial organizations to grasp the value of training employees for larger service in the various phases of its work throughout the world." From the inception of the various training courses in 1920 to January, 1923, employees receiving training numbered 4,711. The report lists the following courses with the number of people currently enrolled or graduated (in parentheses, both completed and currently enrolled): Foreign training course (142), foreman training (278), Americanization (254), refinery process course (375), apprenticeship (121), illustrated lecture course (700), "Top-Grade Oil" course (750), special gasoline meeting (503), general petroleum course (890), general accounting course (110), and standard products course (588).

The refinery process course was technical in nature and studied subjects such as pipeline mechanics, boilermaking, and shop mathematics. The general accounting course provided office employees training in office procedure, accounting, and stenography. Originally the foreign service course recruited men from outside the company, such as from colleges and technical schools, but this policy was reversed and all enrollees were current employees.

Another company training program was the one on "Americanization," whose classes were confined to the two largest refineries, since these plants had the largest foreign-born contingent. At the largest eastern refinery, among the approximately 4,000 employees were 610 noncitizens and 554 who were assessed as illiterate.

Medical Services

In 1917, before the advent of the new industrial relations policy, medical work was confined to taking care of accidents on a first-aid basis. In 1918, a medical director's position was created and, in the words of the report, this person now "directs a vast medical work in the properties of the parent Company." The report goes on to say about the medical service, "From being regarded as incidental, the work has grown to be a vital feature of the program of the company. This development has come because it is realized that every feature of medical work pays in dollars and cents, as well as in life and health."

The Medical Service program is directed from company headquarters. As of 1923, each refinery had one full-time doctor, one full-time nurse, and one full-timer first-aid person or clerk. Facilities included dental equipment, X-ray machines, and equipment for blood and urine analysis. For employees engaged in field operations, medical service is contracted for on a fee basis. Although as earlier noted, the parent company strove to give subsidiaries considerable autonomy in matters of industrial relations policy, in the matter of medical service "the power of the Medical Director in purely medical matters is unlimited" and "No feature of the industrial relations program of the Company appears to be more effective in binding the subsidiaries closer to the parent Company than the Medical Service."

The Medical Services department is responsible for the administration of physical examinations to all new employees. The staff also performs first-aid and, in case of serious injuries, surgery. Employees suffering from various kinds of sickness are also examined and then referred to outside doctors or hospitals. A company doctor or nurse makes home visitations each day.

During the first two and one-half years of operation of the Medical Service, the company and subsidiaries spent $745,000 on this activity, an amount that was equal to .45 percent of total payroll and $.63 per employee per month. The report notes that the benefit to employees of this expenditure is considerably greater than if the money had instead been distributed directly into their pay envelopes.

As noted in the next section, the company had earlier instituted a death benefit plan. Of 15,536 employees eligible to receive death benefits, in 1922 there were 99 claims, representing a death rate per 1,000 of 6.37. The number of cases of serious sickness (lasting more than eight days) among employees was 1.55 per 100 employees per month.

In 1920, the medical staff at the largest eastern refinery estimated that the cost of the medical service at the plant was $21,890 and that it resulted in reduced labor cost of $117,791. A subsidiary company estimated a return of 270 percent on every dollar spent on medical service.

Safety

Beginning in early 1921, the Top-Grade Oil Company created the position of chief safety inspector. Commenting on this development, the report says, "Up to this period there had been little appreciation on the part of the officials of the Company of the worth of organized safety work. Safety work had been confined merely to improvement of working conditions in compliance with state compensation laws and the rule of insurance companies." But with the advent of the company's new IR program, and particularly the benefit and annuity program and medical service program, the virtues of a formal safety program soon became apparent.

The chief safety inspector has direct supervision over all safety work in the company. But, in keeping with the spirit that industrial relations staff should be counselors and advisors, the inspector can conduct investigations and make recommendations but does not have executive authority to mandate action. Within individual refineries, safety work is the responsibility of local safety inspectors. The inspectors work with a joint safety committee, typically composed of managers and employees under the aegis of the industrial representation plan.

The refinery-level safety program focuses on the following four aspects of the problem:

Inspection. The refineries are divided into zones and two men from the safety committee are assigned as a team to inspect conditions in four zones one week and the other four zones the next week.

Accident investigation. A person from the safety committee attempts to reach the scene of each accident as soon as possible and ascertain its cause. A written report is prepared, including recommendations for preventing future such accidents.

Accident prevention. One or more members of the safety committee review with employees of the affected work zone the cause of the accident and steps to avoid a repetition. A written summary is also distributed to all foremen and subforemen, who discuss it with the employees under their charge.

Education. Safety awareness and education is carried on through meetings, lectures, plant papers, and statistical reports. Large bulletin boards are placed near the refinery entrances with charts showing accident frequency per month and across the various work zones.

In the parent company the accident rate per 100 employees per month in 1920 was .53 (approximately one accident among 100 employees every two months). After the start of the safety program, the accident rate dropped significantly—to .39 in 1922 (one-quarter decrease).

The report summarizes the benefits and costs of the safety program. In 1922 there were 374 fewer completed accident cases than in 1920. Since each completed case cost $103 in benefits and compensation in 1920, the total amount saved in this area was $38,522. Further, there was a reduction of 6,998 days lost on account of accidents, which was equivalent to the full year's time of 23.3 employees (evaluated at 300 annual workdays). Multiplying this figure times average annual earnings of $1,690 yields an additional saving of $39,377. In addition, there was a decrease of $5,112 in accident benefits paid in 1922 in contrast with 1920. Total savings, according to the report, was thus $83,011. The exact dollar cost of the safety program is said to be unknown, but "at most is a negligible sum in comparison with the saving effected through the reduction of accidents."

Annuities and Benefits

A major part of the company's new industrial relations program is in the area of employee benefits. The report states in this regard, "The Top-Grade Oil Company has one of the most complete plans in existence for the care of disabled and superannuated employees."

Annuities for Retirement

Annuities are granted to men over sixty-five (and women over fifty-five) who have had twenty or more years of service. Special retirements may be granted to men over fifty-five (and women over fifty) with thirty years' service; to men over sixty with twenty years' service; or to any employee of over ten years' service whose physical condition points to total permanent incapacity. The amount of payment is calculated as 2 percent times the years of service times the average annual pay during the five years preceding retirement. The minimum payment is $300 per year; the maximum is 75 percent of average annual pay.

Death Benefits from Sickness

The beneficiary of all employees of one or more years' service suffering death from sickness or off-duty accidental injury receives a death benefit. The minimum benefit is $500, the maximum is $2,000, with the amount depending on length of service.

Death Benefits from Workplace Injury

All employees regardless of length of service are covered by accidental death benefits. Where state workmen's compensation laws apply, the settlement is made under the terms of such laws; where such laws do not apply the benefits are made in accordance with the workmen's compensation law of a certain eastern state.

Accident Disability Benefits

All employees regardless of length of service are covered. The company covers the cost of all medical service and provides full pay for the first sixteen weeks and two-thirds pay for the next thirty-six weeks of temporary total disability. Payments may be withheld upon evidence of willful negligence by the employee.

Sickness Disability Benefits for Wage Earners

After seven consecutive days of sickness, wage earners of one or more years' service (with thirteen weeks of consecutive service prior to the disability) receive one-half wages, dating from the first day of sickness. The time limit on receipt of benefits is determined by length of service: persons with one to two years have a limit of six weeks of benefits; two to three years have eleven weeks, and so on, with person having over ten years of service eligible for a maximum of fifty-two weeks of benefits.

The total cost of the annuities and benefits program from January 1, 1920 to July 1, 1922 in the parent company and subsidiaries was $2,626,282, which translates into 1.59 percent of payroll and $26.78 per year for each employee ($.52 per week). The actual payments to employees totaled $2,365,137, or 1.44 percent of payroll and $.47 per hour (excluding the subsidiaries, the payment per employee in the parent company was $.57 per week). For the parent company, retirement annuities cost $466,812; death benefits costs $386,222; accidental benefits $230,648; and sickness benefits $331,200. As of the end of 1921, 207 workers were receiving retirement annuities (averaging $93 per month) and 90 death benefit claims had been paid over the previous twelve months (averaging $1,447). The sickness rate per 100 employees was 1.56 and the average days out from work per case was 26.1. The report concludes, "If the total cost of the Annuities and Benefits Plan had been turned back into the pay-roll and divided among the employees, it would have meant an increase of a little more than $.50 a week, which would have been of little benefit to the average employee, and less to the sick, disabled, and superannuated workers. The expenditure of the present sum for annuities and benefits, therefore, is of slight cost to management but considerable value to the men for relief and to the Company in upbuilding the morale of the employees."

A separate sickness and accident benefit program was initiated in 1920 for salaried workers. A salary worker disabled by sickness or accident with two years of service, for example, is eligible for four weeks of full salary and seven weeks of half salary.

Employee Service Features

Under employee service features are grouped seven activities: stock acquisition plan, housing, publications, cafeterias, company stores, bands, and recreational and social activities. Each is briefly described below.

The Stock Acquisition Plan

A stock acquisition plan was established upon employee request in December 1920. The reasons given are two: to provide a vehicle for employee savings, and as a way for employees to become partners in the company.

The employees participated by authorizing deduction from pay of up to a maximum of 20 percent to be invested in a fund composed entirely of company stock. The company then contributes in the employee's name an additional deposit equal to 50 percent of the original. The company sets the price of the stock so that it is never above the market price and no more than 10 percent below the market price for the previous three months. Eligibility is restricted to employees who have had twelve months of continuous service, as of December 30 of any given year. As of January 1, 1922, total company employment was 47,256; total eligible employees was 28,130, and total subscribing employees was 12,981 (46 percent of those eligible). An employee can at any time withdraw the funds deposited with interest of 6 percent per annum, or in the equivalent amount of company common stock. This withdrawal right applies whether employees remain with the company, resign, or are discharged for good cause. (The policy regarding withdrawals for employees terminated for cause is not explicitly discussed, but an accompanying table suggests that such employees are able to withdraw accumulated deposits.)

In the first twenty months of the existence of the plan, total contributions of $8,386,052 were made into the fund. As of September 30, 1922, there were 11,494 active subscribers with an average amount subscribed of $657. The average cost of the 38,364 shares was $152. Over the twenty-month life of the plan, 4,088 employees withdrew their funds. The reasons given were the following (percentage distribution in parentheses): resigned (15.9), dismissed for cause (6.25), laid off permanently (13.1), laid off temporarily (5.85), monetary reasons (55.6), retired under the annuities and benefit plan (1.3), and deceased (2.0).

Housing

The company is only minimally involved in providing employee housing. After the advent of the new industrial relations program in 1918, however, it undertook several initiatives on a local basis. At an eastern refinery the company financed the construction of fifty homes and sold them at cost to employees (at a price of $5,500). It also bought several sections of nearby property and demolished the run-down housing, saloons and stores on it. No construction of new housing had yet begun, however. In a southern state the company owned twenty-eight houses and rented them to employees. In the various producing fields a small number of homes were erected, given the paucity of any other suitable dwellings in these remote areas.

Publications

The company also initiated publication in 1919 of a bimonthly magazine. Distributed to all employees and stockholders, the magazine reports on developments in the company and oil industry. Circulation is 50,000. Individual subsidiaries and refineries also publish magazines or newsletters.

Cafeterias

The company has recently established cafeterias for wage-earners at several eastern refineries. Lunches cost an average of $.25 to $.30. Workers located more than two minutes away from a cafeteria can have a box lunch delivered. None of the cafeterias is self-supporting. At other facilities the company is considering establishing eating facilities for wage-earners, but no action has yet been taken. Most of the facilities do have, however, a dining hall or restaurant for officials, minor executives, and clerical forces.

Company Stores

During the high inflation years of 1918–19 the company opened stores at four refineries. In each case this action was taken upon petition of employee representatives. The purpose was to furnish, at cost prices, food and other necessities needed by employees and their families. When these stores were founded, prices at outside stores were considerably above the prices of the company's stores. The company operated these stores at a loss and closed several when the prices charged at the outside stores came down.

Bands

In four refineries bands have been formed, composed of twenty-five to fifty employees. The instruments are purchased by the company and then paid for on an installment plan by the employees. The bands practice outside of work hours. They play during selected lunch hours, company-sponsored events, and outside charitable functions. The three refinery bands located near the corporate headquarters also play together as a consolidated band at the annual joint conference of the industrial representation plans.

Recreational and Social Activities

Individual refineries sponsor athletic associations that field baseball, basketball, and bowling teams. The company generally provides the facilities and helps employees with the cost of the uniforms and equipment. Social events, such as summertime picnics and athletic contests, are also sponsored. The company has also made financial contributions to support YMCA clubhouses in various communities in which it has facilities.

Case Study Summary

In the space of a two- to three-year period the Top-Grade Oil Company completely transformed its human resource management system. Earlier, the company had used a largely traditional "hired hand" employment system; after World War I it transitioned to a new and pioneering "human resource" employment system. The hallmark of this new system was a more professional, scientific and humane approach to people management that sought to win greater cooperation and productivity through fair treatment, job security, employee voice, and a "win-win" reward system.

Certain findings and lessons stand out from this case study. The first is that the Top-Grade Oil Company was most certainly practicing strategic human resource management. The decision to adopt the new HRM model was made at the highest level of the company, made the HRM function an integral part of company operations, gave the HRM executive high-level access and influence, specifically tailored the new HRM program to align with the company's strategic business plan, and formulated the new HRM program in an integrative and synergistic way.

A second insight is that the new HRM system was indeed a substantial investment in the people management function. In switching to the human resource model, the company added substantial new costs, including the large overhead cost of the new industrial relations department and the large fixed and variable costs of the many new HRM programs and activities, such as the representation plan, medical services, and pensions. The promise of job security also effectively turned employees from a variable cost to a quasi-fixed cost. All together, therefore, the new HRM system both raised cost and made cost less flexible.

A third insight concerns the channels through which the company expected to gain back its investment and generate a positive return on HRM. Part of the rise in cost was to be recouped by direct, tangible savings and productivity gains in operations and labor management. Turnover, for example, was reduced, with savings in hiring, training, and separation cost; similarly, the new medical services and safety program significantly reduced accidents and injuries and consequent missed days from work and insurance payments. The other part of the positive rate of return expected from the new HRM system was more indirect and intangible: by providing job security, voice, higher wages, and fair treatment, the company hoped to raise morale and create a greater alignment of interests, thereby gaining increased cooperation, work performance, good citizenship behavior, and probability of avoiding unions—all of which were to lead to higher productivity and enough cost savings to more than pay for the cost of the new HRM system.

The case study does not provide data sufficient to determine if the new HRM system was indeed a profitable investment. We do know, however, that the Top-Grade Oil Company maintained its new HRM system throughout the 1920s, thus providing at least suggestive evidence that the system was a paying proposition. Other contributing factors, however, cannot be neglected. One is the influence exerted by the principal shareholder; another is the company's accommodative economic environment. With respect to the latter, this company had a dominant position in its industry and steadily rising sale volume throughout the 1920s, both of which helped insulate the HRM program from the full brunt of short-run cost pressure.

9

A High-Road Employer
in a Low-Road Industry

The Great Eastern Coal Company

The second case study from the IRC archives features one of the largest coal companies in the United States. It is an insightful example of the tight constraints that product market conditions can exert on a firm's labor strategy and human resource management program. This firm endeavored to take the high road in labor management, but the cutthroat competition in the coal market and existence of hundreds of low-road competitors in the labor market left it with few good choices and little room for maneuver with its employees.

Background

The Great Eastern Coal Company was one of the largest producers of bituminous coal in the eastern United States, operating ninety-one mines in five states: Maryland, West Virginia, Pennsylvania, Virginia, and Kentucky. In 1923 employment was 10,600. The company earned a profit in every year of operation, including a sum of $3.5 million in 1923. Given that the company's capital assets were valued at $155 million, the rate of return on capital (profits as a percent of capitalized value) was quite low. All measures of profitability had declined considerably since 1917 due to federal price controls during World War I and the downward pressure on coal prices thereafter arising from the marked imbalance between productive capacity in the industry and coal consumption.

In the introduction to the industrial relations program of the company, the IRC report provides the following summary statement:

> It is trite to characterize the bituminous coal industry as over-developed and over-manned. With a potential production far in excess of the capacity of

134

national industry to consume, there exists a ruthless competition among operators for available markets. With labor constituting from sixty to sixty-five per cent of the cost of production, the first point of attack for the reduction of producing costs is ordinarily wages.

Wage reductions of thirty to forty per cent in nonunion fields during a period of depression, such as now exists in the coal industry, are not uncommon. Meanwhile, the scales in union fields remain unchanged as a result of the policy and unparalleled strength of the United Mine Workers.

In the operators' associations, both local and national, dissension and lack of unity prevail. The very existence of some operators compels them to adopt tactics subversive of the best interest of the industry. Others, through ill-advised motives jeopardize the future of the industry through acts which tend to influence public opinion in favor of nationalization of mines or to invite the complete dominance by the union, committed at present, perhaps through force of circumstance, to arbitrary measures.

The Company is probably faced with as complex a labor problem as ever confronted an industrial company, since it operates under both union and nonunion conditions in this over-developed industry, disorganized on the operators' side, and is forced in the present market to meet selling prices based upon reduced wages.

Quite apart from the relations of the company to the national and district labor organizations of the industry, internal personnel or employment management problems of unusual magnitude exist. Chief among these is the development and maintenance of complete industrial communities. Particularly in the southern divisions, literal transformations have been made by the company of mountainous wilderness into modern towns with living conveniences theretofore unknown to native inhabitants.

The construction of railroads, highways, and other means of communication; the erection of power plants; the building of houses; the establishment of local government; the operation of stores; and the provision of facilities for social life of the employees and their families have, therefore, been added to the usual problems of production.

Other phases of the task involve the recruiting of employees, the administration of joint relations with employees as individuals, or by groups, the training of executives, the maintenance of health agencies and sanitary facilities, and the prevention of accidents under hazardous conditions.

Administration of Industrial Relations

The company has no formal department responsible for the conduct of human resource management activities. The vice president of operations is charged with the formulation of the company's labor policies. Under his administration, industrial relations activities are administered largely through the line organization, with the assistance of certain staff specialists. The general manager of each of the six divisions is responsible for the administration of all local employment relations work, except those aspects specifically assigned to staff specialists. The staff specialists include the following:

Director of Employment Relationship Department. This department is responsible for labor recruiting, conduct of the divisional employment offices, collection and tabulation of employment statistics within the company, rec-reational activities and buildings, and publication of the monthly company magazine.

Consulting Engineer. The consulting engineer, working with the director of safety, has responsibility for the safety and accident prevention work in the company.

General Purchasing Agent. The general purchasing agent has responsibility for the supervision and operation of the company's stores.

Architect. The company architect is charged with supervision and maintenance of the company's employee housing.

Expenses in 1922 for the various phases of industrial relations work are shown in table 3. The company stores made a large profit each year; the company housing in two previous years made a profit but in three others (including 1922) registered a loss, yielding an average annual deficit on housing of $28,648.

The IRC report references an additional category of labor expense but does not include it in the table from which these data are drawn. This category, called "labor maintenance," includes expenditures for detectives, guards, undercover men, special employees and "sundry items which tend to secure closer cooperation of labor leaders and political advantage from state government administration." The average annual expenditure for these items for the six years 1918–1923 was over $220,000.

Joint Relations

The situation regarding the governance of joint relations between the company and its employees varied considerably by division and year. Until 1918 the company operated on a nonunion basis. In 1918, the Blairstone

Table 3. Expenses for Industrial Relations Work, 1922

	Total expenditure ($)	Expenditure per employee ($)
Employment relationship department	63,166	8.22
Recreation	21,802	2.84
Education and community work	22,208	2.89
Health	21,042	2.74
Sanitation	55,764	7.25
Safety	13,960	1.82
Civic improvements	37,928	11.45
Stores (profit)	(+)187,642	(+)25.51
Houses	46,949	6.11

field in West Virginia, responsible for 40–50 percent of the company's total output, was organized by the United Mine Workers (UMW). Other fields were subsequently unionized, but as of 1923 only the Blairstone field remained under union contract.

In June 1918, due to wartime conditions and the influence of the United States Fuel Administration (a temporary wartime agency), the company introduced employee representation plans into all divisions but the one in Pennsylvania (due in the latter case to opposition from other operators). The representation plan in the West Virginia and Maryland divisions facilitated union organization and recognition and were thus soon supplanted by the latter. In particular, the representation plans committed the company to a policy of recognizing "the right of their employees to join any union, labor organization, or society that they may choose and agree that they shall not be discriminated against for having joined such organization"—a policy that company officials believed paved the way for organization of the men.

The UMW contract contained the following important provisions:

- All employees, with certain exceptions, must be union members.
- A monthly checking off of union dues and fees up to $5 per month per employee.
- The negotiated wage scale and eight-hour day.
- Noninterference with the company's authority to administer mine operations and hire and fire employees
- The right of employees to a checkweighman.
- Mine committees for the adjustment of disputes, including binding arbitration.
- Fines to be assessed against either party in case of contract violations.

In two other divisions operations were maintained on a nonunion basis and by 1920 the company had let the representation plans disintegrate. A revamped representation plan was introduced in Pennsylvania in 1922 and in the Maryland division in 1923 after the UMW's defeat in a strike. The twin purposes of the representation plans were "to promote and maintain a spirit of cooperation between the operator and the employee," and "to provide means for the adjustment of disputes or grievances and for communication and conference."

Within each nonunion division, the representation plans called for the company to fund the position called the operator's commissioner , and this person was to devote full-time attention to the administration of the agreement. In several divisions this step was never implemented; in the Pennsylvania division the person chosen was a former union official. The employees also had the right to hire a representative (at their expense, estimated to be about $1.00–$1.50 per worker per month) called the employee commissioner who gave his full-time attention to serving their interests. At each mine a committee of three men was elected for one year; the chairman represented his mine on a general committee known as the "chairmen of committees." Mine committees were formed at all the nonunion divisions, but some did not have much vitality. In the Pennsylvania division, the chairmen of committees elected A. W. Bittner, a well-known UMW organizer, as the employee's commissioner.

With respect to the resolution of grievances, the plan required that an employee with a grievance first take the matter up with his foreman, and if this failed to secure an adjustment, present the case to the superintendent. If no agreement could be reached, the mine committee took up the matter with the superintendent. If disagreement still existed, the next step was to seek satisfactory adjustment from a joint decision of the operator's commissioner and employee's commissioner. The final three steps were appeal to the general manager of the division, appeal to a joint board of review (composed of three representatives of the company and employees, respectively), and, finally, appeal to binding arbitration by a neutral umpire.

In one division, fifty-four cases were settled between superintendents and mine committees in 1923, and seven cases were referred to the commissioners. The one grievance case highlighted in the IRC report involved discharge of two committeemen on the grounds they were loading dirty coal. Subsequent investigation by the general manager disclosed, however, that the real reason for discharge was their activity on behalf of the mine committee. They were reinstated and the superintendent was subsequently dismissed.

Employment

Employment at the company varies a good deal depending on the state of the coal market and disruption by strike activity (as in 1922). Numbers of employees in 1920, 1921, and 1922 were, respectively, 9,318, 7,689, and 10,592.

Hiring and Termination

The hiring of new workers is done by the mine superintendents and foremen. Applicants are accepted or rejected based on oral interviews. The company's stated preference is to hire married men with families, but the large majority of newly recruited employees are single or unaccompanied by family members. A severe housing shortage at several divisions was a contributing factor. In only three of six divisions are new hires asked to sign forms relating to certain terms and conditions of employment, the most important being a waiver to accept the terms of the state workers' compensation law. No division requires new employees to sign a "yellow dog" contract.

In some periods an adequate supply of labor is forthcoming through individual applications at the various properties. But the company also operates a labor-recruiting program, particularly to help staff mining properties in remote areas. Labor recruitment is done through a two-pronged approach. One is recruitment of employees directly by the company, primarily through the employment relationship department, located in Blairstone, West Virginia, and two free (no-fee) employment agencies in Pittsburgh, Pennsylvania, and Huntington, West Virginia. The company also solicits labor referrals from several for-profit employment agencies, although the quality of labor so obtained is generally inferior. In times of labor scarcity, the company will pay the transportation cost for employees recruited from outside the local area. In 1922 a total of 1,780 employees were recruited through these various agencies.

The company has recorded the country of origin/ethnicity of all employees. Between 1919 and 1922, 55 percent of employees were American-born whites; 14 percent were Latins; 13 percent were Slavs; 12 percent African Americans; and the remainder were of various nationalities.

Transfers and discharges are also handled by the mine superintendents and foremen. In the unionized properties, discharge is subject to review by the mine committee. When an employee severs his connection with the company, an exit interview is done to determine the reason by the mine clerk at the time of final settlement. Ninety-six percent of separations have been classified as voluntary and only 4 percent arose from discharge. Two-thirds of the people voluntarily leaving the company did not give a specific reason; of those that did "slack work" was the most often cited. Among discharges, one-third of the cases were due to drunkenness and one-third due to inefficient or irregular work.

Length of Service and Turnover

The workforce of the company tends to be relatively young and of short job tenure. These facts are evident from the statistics presented in table 4.

Forty-five percent of the workforce is thirty years of age or less; slightly less than 10 percent is over the age of fifty. The coal industry traditionally utilized a large amount of child labor in this period, but such is apparently not the case with this company. The detailed statistics by age from which the above compilation is drawn begins at age sixteen, suggesting that persons of younger age are not in the company's employ, and employees aged sixteen to seventeen account for only 1.7 percent of total employment. (Three sixteen year olds, however, are reported as having two years of service—out of a total workforce of 11,889—suggesting they were hired at age fourteen or fifteen.)

Regarding length of job tenure, 43 percent of the workforce has been employed for less than two years and over one-third has been on the job less than twelve months. In one division, 24 percent of the workers with less than one year of job tenure had been hired more than once during the course of the year. Only 16.4 percent had been with the company more than ten years. Although these figures indicate that the great majority of employees have little

Table 4. Employees Classified by Age and by Length of Service (%)

	Percent
Age	
Under 21	8.4
21–30	36.8
31–40	28.6
41–50	16.3
51–60	7.5
61–70	2.0
71+	0.2
Not given	0.2
Length of service (years)	
<1	35.1
1	8.2
2–5	25.3
6–10	15.0
11–15	7.4
16–20	4.5
21–25	2.7
26–30	0.9
31+	0.9

prospect for continuity of employment for more than a few years, the company does practice a promote-from-within policy for certain key positions, such as mine foreman, fire boss, mine inspector, local superintendent, and general manger. Length of service is given some weight in determining promotions, but ability is the main criteria.

Not surprising given the data presented above, the labor turnover rate for the company is relatively high. The turnover rate is calculated as the number hired in a year to fill vacancies caused by employees leaving the company, divided by the average number of employees working. For the years 1919, 1920, 1921, 1922, and 1923, respectively, the labor turnover rate was 185, 163, 117, 202, and 201 percent. The figure for 1923 indicates that the company's workforce turned over, on average, twice during the year.

The average turnover rate varies principally with market sales and the availability of railcars. Turnover rates also vary widely across divisions, with some divisions having rates two or three times as high as others. Major workforce characteristics associated with lower turnover are being married and with a family, being a native-born American, and ownership of a home. Isolated mines tend to have a lower proportion of all three characteristics and, correspondingly, higher turnover. This latter fact would seem to operate as a constraint on the (potential) exercise of monopsony power by the employer (i.e., the ability of an employer in a "one company town" to exploit a captive workforce by paying less than market wages.)

The company estimates the cost of labor turnover as roughly $20 per employee, or in the aggregate close to $400,000 in 1923.

Wages, Hours, and Earnings

Wages

According to the IRC report, the wage rates paid by the company are determined by four factors:

- the economic condition of the coal market
- the supply of labor
- the level of wages in the industry as a whole
- the degree of influence of the United Mine Workers in each field

As one reads the report, it becomes apparent, however, that a fifth factor should be listed—namely, government intervention in industrial relations during World War I.

The level of wage rates in the Pennsylvania division for three classes of labor—machine loaders, motormen, and outside labor—for the years 1913–1923 is shown in a chart in the IRC report. Wage rates moved up and down in reaction to market and institutional forces, but only haltingly and in discrete steps. Wage rates remained stable for three years (1913–1915), but then nudged upward in two steps during 1916 as coal orders and the general state of the economy strengthened under the influence of the war in Europe. When the United States entered the war in 1917, the coal industry was placed under the supervision of the United States Fuel Administration. During the life of the agency, wage rates were advanced four times, the fourth and highest rate being reached in August 1920. The remarkable upward advance of wage rates granted by the Fuel Administration—from $.20 per hour at the end of 1916 for outside labor to $.80 in mid-1920—reflected the combined effect of strong labor demand, a rapid increase in the cost of living, the attempt of the government to preserve labor peace in the industry, and a national miner's strike in 1919. Then, in late 1920 the national economy plunged into a short but deep recession/depression and wage rates in the nonunion divisions were sharply reduced, on the order of one-third in the Pennsylvania division. In the heavily organized Maryland and West Virginia divisions, the UMW was able to successfully maintain wage rates at the 1920 level. In August 1922, upon the end of a four-month strike in the industry, the company restored wage rates in the nonunion divisions to the 1920 level.

Three different methods of wage payment are used by the company: piece rates (tonnage, yardage, and deadwork), hourly rates, and monthly rates. Workers directly engaged in the mining of coal are typically paid a piece rate, such as a stipulated price per ton (or car) of coal delivered to the mine head. Different rates are paid depending on the difficulty and danger involved. A "yardage" rate per ton is paid to workers who remove slate and other rock from the coal vein; a "deadwork" rate per ton is paid for removal of rock and debris from the mine. "Inside" and "outside" men—workers performing jobs such as hoisting, loading rail cars, tending pumps—are generally paid on an hourly basis, while the superintendents, mine foremen, engineers, and other such employees holding a management or technical position are paid a monthly salary.

The report offers two brief observations on wage determination that merit mention. The report contrasts the 1917–20 period of government control, when wages were uniformly raised across the divisions in four large steps, and the period of unregulated labor market competition in 1916–17, when under the pressure of a strengthening economy labor bidding led to a series of wage changes that were smaller, more frequent, and nonuniform across divisions. Apparently free-market wage determination in this situation had its drawbacks, per the observation that the uncoordinated labor bidding and wage changes "caused much instability and confusion."

The second observation speaks to the importance of product market conditions in the determination of wages (as opposed to textbook models where wage rates are determined solely through the forces of labor demand and supply). Although the job and working conditions of a pick miner or car loader typically did not differ greatly across the six divisions of the company, rates of pay did. For example, the ton rate for pick miners in January 1916 in a unionized division was $.52, while in a closely located nonunion division it was $.31. Some of this variation could be accounted for by living costs, unionization, nearness to organized towns, and the characteristics of the workers (e.g., nationality). But of great significance were two other factors; first, that coal is largely a standardized commodity and a mine can only continue in operation if it meets the market price; and, second, individual mines differ considerably in the per-ton cost of production due to differences in the thickness of the coal seam, the amount of timbering and deadwork required, and access to a railhead. Hence, the only way higher cost mines could stay in operation was to reduce some other element of production cost. Since labor represents the largest proportion of total cost in coal mining, higher cost mines had to pay lower wage rates if they were to stay in operation. This fact led to the creation of separate "wage contours" for approximately similar labor employed in mines of different profitability. Thus, the IRC report observes, "Due to differences in mining conditions in the six divisions, such as the height of the coal mined, a direct comparison of mining rates is of little value. The levels of mining rates in various divisions have been established through years of competitive conditions in the industry."

Hours

In 1917 the coal industry, under the exigencies of World War I and at the direction of the United States Fuel Administration, went from the ten to eight hour day. The industry also went to a six-day work-week, with Sundays off for all employees but those engaged in essential services.

In the nonunion divisions the only holidays observed are the Fourth of July, Christmas, and New Year's Day. The UMW contract with the company mandates seven holidays (New Year's Day, Decoration Day, Labor Day, Christmas, April 1, the Fourth of July, and Thanksgiving) for organized employees. The report notes that the lack of more holidays in the nonunion divisions is essentially a moot issue because of the considerable number of days not worked each year due to weak demand or car shortages and the fact that the miners take time off whenever they desire to do so.

Most of the company's mines operate on a one-shift basis. The regular starting time is 7:00 or 7:30 A.M., with one-half hour allowed for lunch. In the unionized divisions, once the employees enter the mine the UMW contract requires the company to pay them a minimum of two hours of work.

The IRC report notes, "The number of days worked each year is an item fully as important as wage rates in determining the earnings of the miners." It goes on to note that limited days of work is "one of the greatest problems of the coal industry" and "Much time is lost due to unfavorable market conditions. Frequently a good demand for coal has been accompanied by a car shortage." The average days worked per year for all mines owned by the company for the years 1919–1923 were, respectively, 204, 179, 163, 132, and 190. Assuming available annual workdays are 309 (six days for fifty-two weeks, minus three holidays), the proportion of time worked in these years was 66 percent, 58 percent, 50 percent, 43 percent, and 59 percent, respectively. Coal miners were thus idle approximately 45 percent of potential workdays.

Office employees and managerial/technical employees generally work six-day weeks, averaging between forty-five and fifty-one hours per week. In all but one division they get one hour for lunch. Salaried employees also get two weeks paid vacation. No general policy statement exists concerning necessary length of service before a salaried employee qualifies for vacation days and the matter is left to the discretion of the general manager. The usual practice is six months to one year of service.

Earnings

The chief concern of the mine employees is earnings per year—the product of the wage rate times hours worked. Unfortunately, the section of the IRC report in which the earnings data were to be presented is omitted (a brief note states it will be provided later, but no such section is included or otherwise available). One solution is to substitute similar data from an IRC report done a year earlier for another large coal company in the same general geographic area. Although the exact figures will not be comparable, general patterns should match closely.

In the recession year of 1921, the average annual income of "full-time" workers (a worker with positive earnings in every two-week pay period) was $1,341 for miners and $1,710 for day workers. (Data for part-time workers, representing 51 percent of total employment, are not provided.) It is further reported that in 1920 (a more prosperous year) 85 percent of the total payroll went to 1,790 employees who earned over $1,000 and the average income for this group was $1,864. In 1921, the percentage was 72.3 percent and average income was $1,405. Only 3 percent of employees earned more than $3,000 in 1920, a proportion that shrunk to 1 percent in 1921.

Training

The company has no organized plan or program in place for the training of employees. The general policy is to hire people who have some previous mining experience or, with green hands, to select those who appear capable of quickly mastering the work. In either case, the company places the responsibility for acquiring needed training and job skills upon the employee through observation of workmates and on-the-job experience.

In the five states the company operates in, fire bosses, mine inspectors, and mine foremen are required to pass state examinations. The company encourages its employees to take classes in preparation for these examinations and provides local instructors and classroom space. These classes are held in the evening and are open to all employees.

Health and Sanitation

Health

The company employed twenty-nine doctors in 1923 to take care of the health and injury problems of its employees. Only one division (Maryland) did not have company doctors, as these mines were located near independent towns and the employees could contract for their own medical care. Employees in this division with workmen's compensation injuries, however, were required to use company-designated doctors. The company doctors were responsible for servicing the needs of employees and their families in forty different communities.

Although the details differ modestly across divisions, in those divisions with company doctors a monthly checkoff is made from each employee's pay to cover company-provided medical care. A typical charge is $1.50 per month for married employees and $1.00 for single employees. In some divisions a 5–7 percent commission charge for making the checkoff is also added. In one division the full amount of the checkoff is passed on to the doctors, and the doctors bear the full cost of office expenses, drugs, and supplies. In another division, the doctors receive a salary, the company pays the cost of drugs, supplies, and the like, and any surplus or deficit is the company's. No reason for these differences in policy is given. The doctors are also allowed to carry on a private practice with other patients to the extent their time and interest allows. The amount paid to the doctors varies a good deal, but an annual payment of $4,000–$6,000 is common.

Two divisions with mines in more remote areas also employ dentists. At all other divisions, employees depended on dentists who practice in towns near the mines.

The company does not directly operate any hospital. It does, however, provide modest subsidies ($2,000–$3,000 per year) to several private hospitals in communities close to its mining operations.

The company employs fifteen visiting nurses in five of its divisions. The nurses are field representatives of the employment relationship department, and made over 11,000 home visits in 1922.

The total net cost of medical service to the company in 1922 was $21,043, or $2.74 per average employee.

Sanitation

Mine superintendents are charged with responsibility for maintaining sanitary conditions around the mines and, more particularly, the mining communities. The actual work of sanitary inspection is typically delegated to the company's doctors and nurses, supplemented by occasional inspections by a general manager or similar executive person. The doctors write monthly reports on sanitary conditions based largely on observations accumulated through individual house visits, and include in the reports recommendations for improvement.

Eight areas of sanitation received attention:

1. *Water supply. All mining towns have to be supplied with clean, safe drinking water. A number of alternative sources of water supply are utilized, including open springs, deep wells operated by electrical pumps, shallow wells operated by hand pumps, and from rivers and reservoirs. The doctors are responsible for periodically testing the water for bacteria and mineral content. Filtering and chlorinating plants are installed by the company where necessary. Uncontrolled grazing of livestock, frequent in the more remote mining properties, often contaminates the water from springs and shallow wells, and water shortages are occasionally encountered across nearly all divisions.*
2. *Bathhouses. Three divisions have no bathhouses for the employees; three others have in the last four years started to erect such facilities. Eleven existed as of 1923. Separate rooms are provided for white and black employees. The constraints in building additional bathhouses are*

said to be cost and water availability. Bathhouses are particularly welcomed by the employees for health and convenience reasons (e.g., inside workers often emerge overheated from the mines and, without a bathhouse had to walk some distance home in the cold of winter; home bathing facilities are generally small and primitive).

3. *Garbage. All company homes are provided a large metal garbage can and garbage is collected once a week.*

4. *Outbuildings. In most of the company's towns, outbuildings such as cow barns, chicken coops, and pigpens are not permitted. In several towns community cow barns have been erected.*

5. *Toilets. Most company houses have outdoor toilet facilities (outhouses or "privies"). This situation is recognized as clearly undesirable on health and sanitary grounds (e.g., they attract a great fly population), but greater progress has been slowed by the cost of conversion to indoor facilities. In some cases the "vaults" of the outhouses are not emptied on schedule and effluvia flowed over open ground.*

6. *House screening. The company encourages tenants to screen windows and doors during fly season, but has only had only modest success. In one division, only 18 of 225 houses are screened.*

7. *Yards. The company also encourages tenants to maintain clean yards. In general, considerable success is enjoyed in this task, but only with frequent reminders and occasional inspections by the general manager.*

The average annual cost of sanitation to the company for the five years 1918–1922 was $57,000.

Safety and Accidents

Safety

The safety work of the company is overseen by the consulting engineer, who reports directly to the vice president in charge of operations. Reporting to the consulting engineer is a director of safety and chief mine inspector. A variety of committees are also involved with safety work. At the apex of the company is the central safety committee, composed of general managers and similar-ranked executives from the six divisions, followed by division safety committees and local mine safety committees. At the local level three employees are included as members. Recruiting volunteers among the employees is sometimes difficult. At the meetings of the local committees, inquiries into accident cases are held, dangerous practices by mine workers discussed, and preventive measures recommended. Employees interviewed by IRC investigators have stated very few complaints with the work of the committees.

State mine inspectors visit company properties several times a year in three states but very seldom in three others due to understaffing and "political complications." The mining laws in the former states are substantially more comprehensive than in the latter, but all state laws exhibit notable weaknesses (e.g., no state mandates sealing up abandoned workings containing dangerous gases). Regular inspections for mine gas and unsafe conditions are also made by company inspectors. Much less attention is made to safety conditions outside the mines, reflecting the lower accident rate among outside workers.

In addition to state and company inspectors, the company endeavors to promote greater safety awareness and knowledge among the employees. First-aid teams have been formed at many mines and contests are held among the teams to generate enthusiasm and test their skills, starting at the local level and then ascending to division, company, and national competitions. The company also sponsors safety rallies at the individual properties during which safety films and lectures are given, safety posters and bulletins at mine entrances are put up, and two pages are devoted to safety in each monthly issue of the company magazine.

The company has set up mine rescue stations at several locations to deal with major disasters, such as mine fires and explosions. Rescue teams are equipped with self-contained breathing apparatus and are trained in dealing with underground disasters.

The company also keeps statistical records of annual nonfatal accidents, broken into three categories: Class A, resulting in absence from work of 1–6 days; Class B, resulting in absence from work of 7–35 days; and Class C, resulting in absence from work of more than 35 days. Over the four-year period 1919–22, the average annual number of nonfatal accidents was 959, or a rate of 103 per 1,000 employees and 138 per million tons of coal produced. The average number of Class A accidents was 290; Class B accidents, 510; and Class C accidents, 160. Accidents are far more likely to happen for inside work, comprising 86 percent of the total.

Injured employees and their beneficiaries qualify for payments under the various state workmen's compensation laws. From 1918–23, the company's direct and indirect payments under these laws to injured employees and their beneficiaries amounted to $137,000. In one division, the average total payment received by the families of six deceased miners in 1923 was $3,800 (approximately two year's "normal" earnings), typically paid in weekly installments of $12.

Company Housing

An important part of the company's industrial relations program is provision and maintenance of company-provided housing for employees. In the more geographically isolated or mountainous divisions, all employees live in company housing; in several of the others the proportion of employees in company housing ranged from 20 to 70 percent. Since 1905, the company has built twelve complete communities.

The company's policy is to assign, whenever possible, separate living quarters to families, while single and unattached men are put in boarding houses. At the more remote mining properties, private home ownership is not feasible nor generally desired because the company owns all the surrounding land and employees do not want to settle there. Where mining properties are in more populated and accessible areas, home ownership is more attractive and feasible. The policy of the company is to allow the employee freedom of choice in the matter of owning/renting in the private housing market or renting from the company. Ownership is encouraged, however, as it builds a more stable workforce.

IRC investigators judge the state of the company's housing to be in good condition, although pockets of dilapidated housing have been found (e.g., in some cases families are living in shanties and tool shacks). The large majority of homes have electricity, but relatively few have indoor running water or indoor toilet facilities. Bathtubs are available only in housing for higher-level managerial employees. Coal stoves are used for heating. The most common type of house has three rooms.

The boarding houses for single workers are large frame buildings with numerous rooms that serve as sleeping quarters. Steam heat and showers are typically provided. Workers are generally grouped together by language and race.

Housing rents varied by location and number of rooms. In one division, the rental rate ranges from $5 to $13 a month, with the greatest proportion costing $6.50-$7.50. Typically garbage pickup and cleaning of outhouses is performed at no extra cost.

The leasing contracts used by the company vary from division to division in terms of the rights and obligations of the tenants. While the company is in general "liberal" in its housing policy, several divisions continue to use leases that are relatively invasive of tenants' rights. For example, these leases forbid the tenant from harboring any person deemed objectionable by the company, and give the company the right to at any time come upon the tenant's premises; and the tenant's right to occupy the house ceases immediately upon termination of the employment relationship.

Although the company has the right to evict strikers from its housing property, it endeavors to minimize this practice. During the lengthy strike of 1922, it issued no eviction notices through the first four months, and then only in small number. It also gave striking employees a "rent holiday" during the course of the dispute, recognizing that many had no means to pay for housing. This gesture promoted considerable goodwill among the workforce upon its return to work, although some employees took advantage of the situation by living rent-free until the strike was over and then moving away. The company did bring in replacement workers, however, and they were often quartered in the boarding houses.

Annual gross earnings from housing average roughly $600,000 per year. During the 1914–1917 period, the company realized a profit of around $100,000 per year, but since 1917 an annual deficit of about $5,000 has been incurred.

Company Stores

The company operates forty-two stores scattered among five of the six divisions. Some are housed in large two-story buildings and carry a full line of merchandise, groceries, and meat; others are housed in small single-story buildings and carry only selected items of merchandise. The latter tend to be found in areas where other private stores are relatively accessible. The policy of the store management, according to the report, is "to make as much money as possible."

The degree of competition faced by the company store varies markedly. In developed areas, such as in Pennsylvania and Maryland, the stores are in direct competition with a number of private stores; in more remote areas effective competition is often quite limited. Large numbers of catalogs are received by the mining families from mail order houses, however, and many purchases are made via this medium.

Scrip and store money are issued by the company upon request to those employees who want to draw their pay in advance. The scrip consists of cards of various denominations with a series of different amounts printed thereon. The amount of each purchase is punched, and when the face-value of the card is reached it is taken back by the store manager. The company charges a commission rate of 1 percent on the value of the scrip toward the cost of the service.

A comparison of prices of many standard items sold at company and independent stores shows that prices at the former are somewhat higher in some cases and in others somewhat lower. Prices charged at "chain" stores, however, are considerably lower. Prices for similar items also show frequent variation across company-owned stores, reflecting in part a lack of centralized administrative control.

The annual sales of the company stores typically exceeds $3 million. The average annual profit margin from 1914 to 1922 was a very healthy 37 percent. The profit margin of company stores across each division is inversely related to the degree of competition from independent stores, ranging from a low of 24 percent in a division where competition is high to 97 percent where competitions is quite limited.

For the company as a whole, 31 percent of payroll is received by the stores. This proportion is 20 percent in the "high competition" division and 48 percent in the "low competition" division.

Magazines and Recreation

The company publishes a monthly magazine that is distributed to all employees free of charge. The annual cost to the company is approximately $17,000. A large proportion of the material is devoted to social and personal notes contributed by employee correspondents. Editorials and inspirational articles are included to promote thrift, health, and good habits. Articles on mining, economics, and politics are sometimes included, as are feature stories on special events in particular communities. Occasionally articles are published in a foreign language.

Recreational activities in the mining communities are centered in the company-provided recreational buildings. Twenty-one such buildings are operated by the company. The modern ones contain a theater, auditorium, poolroom, barbershop, refreshment counter, and lodge room. The facilities are segregated by race.

The company also sponsors a full-range of athletic teams and activities.

Community Relations

The extent of company involvement in community relations depends greatly on the degree of isolation of the community. In well-populated areas, the company occupies a place in the community similar to that of a large manufacturing firm. In remote communities, however, the company is heavily involved in all aspects of community life and services. In the latter, the company must provide basic social infrastructure, such as a town hall, constable, post office, school board, churches, roads, and playgrounds. Over the period 1918–22, expenditures for civic improvements totaled over $600,000.

Recommendations and Observations

The last part of the IRC report is devoted to recommendations and observations. It begins by noting that the company has assumed a "role of outstanding leadership" in the industry and that this is "particularly true . . . in its general treatment of labor problems." It goes on to note, "Motivated largely by the reward of financial success rather than by altruism, the company follows the broad policies of providing modern facilities and wholesome living conditions for its employees and of maintaining wages at levels which result in large production and, therefore, tend to yield to employees the highest annual earnings possible under competitive conditions." It concludes the introductory remarks with these observations:

> For some of its liberal provisions for employees and for its adherence to certain wage, housing, and other labor policies, the company has been cordially damned by a substantial group of competing operators. The responsibility placed upon the company officials is, therefore, of the first magnitude, In contrast with notoriously bad labor conditions existing in part of the coal industry, the evidence contained in this report indicates an acceptance of this responsibility and sincere efforts on the part of company officials to secure for the industry a wider application of sound business principles, and the recognition of employment relations as a major problem of management."

Following this introduction are numerous recommendations. Summarized below are the most important ones.

The Director of Industrial Relations

The first recommendation is to create a new executive position, the assistant to the vice president for industrial relations affairs. This person would report directly to the corporate vice president in charge of operations (the person immediately under the president with responsibilities roughly equivalent to a chief operating office in a modern company). The report counsels that a clear distinction be maintained between line and staff, and that the ultimate formulation of labor policy should remain with the executive line management. The responsibility of the director of industrial relations is to provide advice and counsel in the development of policy and to "exercise control in a progressive manner" in the execution of labor policy. The report elaborates on the rationale for this new position, noting, "An administrative assistant to the vice-president of operations is needed to assist him in dealing with a multitude of problems which now require attention but which, under the present organization, must be left unconsidered and uncorrelated. These problems involve the major subjects of this report, many of which are incidental in comparison with the primary problems of mine operation. It is, in our opinion, uneconomical for the division general managers, and ultimately the vice-president in charge of operations, to give these incidental, though vital subjects, the detailed attention required."

The report suggests the following as the principal duties of the new industrial relations director:

- to assist the vice president in charge of operations in all matters pertaining to industrial relations
- to translate labor policies of the company into a cohesive administrative program and direct the staff in the execution of the program
- to supervise the extension and administration of the employee representation agreements
- to coordinate the work of the staff departments with each other and with the problems of line management
- to receive and digest detailed reports from staff and prepare summaries for the executive group

The Industrial Relations Department

The report further recommends the creation of an industrial relations (IR) department that reports directly to the director of industrial relations. The proposed IR department would have seven subdivisions: employee representation, employment relations (e.g., an employment office, the company magazine), training and education, medical services, safety, stores, and housing. A number of these staff positions already exist so to a significant degree the department represents a realignment and centralization of reporting relationships. The exception is a new position created to supervise the (proposed) employee representation plans.

The Employee Representation Plans

The IRC report recommends that the company undertake a new initiative to establish and operate employee representation plans in the non-union divisions. The report is entirely silent on the issue of trade unionism, other than to recount the factual development of unionism in the company and industry. Nor does the report discuss the rationale and need for some form of employee voice, or discuss the relative advantages and shortcomings of representation versus unionism. In this report, the need for and relatively desirability of employee representation is simply a maintained assumption.

Given this, the report begins its recommendation by observing, "Unionism and employee representation have met in direct conflict in the operation of the company. Unfortunately, the stage was set in all cases to mete out disaster to the newer movement." It goes on to say that "notwithstanding the limited favorable experience in the Pennsylvania Division, employee representation as applied in the midst of strong cross-currents in the labor problem in the company has not stood the test; but the test has not been a fair one in any case." Three reasons are cited:

1. *Unilateral implementation. The report states, "Without exception, they have been prepared by the company without the assistance or cooperation of employees.... Self-determination was conspicuously absent [and] the interest which might have resulted from the joint creation of the plan was lost to the employees. Something for which they had not asked was given to them; it was an act which warranted their suspicion."*
2. *Excessive management control. According to the report, management has exercised control too tightly over the operation and activities of the plans. It concludes, "[This] does not augur success for the agreement. A series of healthy arguments is likely to develop a more virile relationship than the dependence of the employees' organizations."*
3. *Instability of employment. The third problem bedeviling the representation plans, according to the report, is the unsettling disturbance given to employer-employee relations by the instability of production and employment. It notes, "The high turnover, with the influx of men who, as a logical result of unfortunately bitter experience, distrust any coal operator and regard him as their enemy, ... has obstructed the operation of the plans."*

In a remarkable passage, the report continues, "it is well to face frankly the charge made by a union organizer of national prominence. The general unsoundness of his political and economic theories does not render less pertinent the following statement of William Z. Foster [communist labor organizer and leader of the 1919 steel strike]. Space precludes full replication of Foster's statement, but an excerpt gives the flavor,

> "They serve to delude the workers into believing they have some semblance of industrial democracy. They consist . . . for the most part of 'hand-picked' bosses and 'company suckers.' . . . The 'lick-spittle' committees are always careful to see that they handle no business unless it relates to 'welfare work' or other comparatively insignificant matters."

After this quotation, the report admonishes management, "If employee representation is to become efficacious in dealings with employees, the company executives must recognize these charges and examine diligently the means for preventing their foundation in fact."

Next comes a passage that is a remarkable harbinger of the arguments used a decade later by the administration of Franklin Delano Roosevelt and supporters to justify passage of the National Industrial Recovery Act (1933) and its provisions encouraging the cartelization of product markets and unionization of labor markets. The report states,

> It is our earnest opinion, formulated after extensive study of the joint relations problem in this company and in other industries, that under existing conditions the shop committee form of employee representation, with its many potentialities, has serious limitations when applied in the eastern and southern fields of the coal industry. . . . These conditions are largely the result of the present chaotic condition of the industry as expressed in over-development, instability of market prices and producing costs, and general disorganization among the operators. Order out of this chaos cannot be expected until a regulating force exists which will correlate production with demand and therefore stabilize prices and costs. This regulating form might take the form of government interference, control through an operator's combination, or a close union shop which would, through the establishment of arbitrary wage rates, stabilize producing costs.

The report notes, however, that "none of these alternatives is an issue at the present time," and thus partially by default the initiative in shaping joint relations falls to the company. What IR strategy should it pursue? The IRC report counsels,

> A "laissez faire" policy is unthinkable. A program of welfare activities is impotent. The one course which to us appears promising is the extension of employee representation agreements into all fields where joint dealings are now unorganized.

But, the report notes, this path also faces obstacles, observing,

> In the extension of employee representation the company will doubtless be hampered as in the past by the slowness with which operating officials as a group abandon the practices of industrial warfare traditional in the coal industry and accept 'open diplomacy' in dealings with employees. The use of company spies and associated tactics is inimical to the interests of joint agreement and is prima facie evidence of insincerity and weak faith. In the practice of industrial representation, those companies which have failed to 'go all the way' have generally spent in vain such time, energy, and money as they have put into this work.

These obstacles notwithstanding, the report concludes that the revitalization of representation plans is the only viable option for the company and it should proceed swiftly to reintroduce them into the nonunion fields. For such a program to have a significant chance for success, however, the IRC report states that the plans in each division must have expert and dedicated leadership by people with considerable experience in joint labor negotiations. It thus recommends that the company create a new staff function in the (proposed) industrial relations department with responsibility for operation of the employee representation plans, and that a person be hired for this position in each division.

Training

Three recommendations are made regarding training. Of highest priority, the company is urged to begin a formal training program for foremen. The report notes that "the demands upon the foreman are so great that few individuals have the innate ability to meet all them without specific training." A second recommendation is to establish within the (proposed) industrial relations department an education and training department. In addition to conducting foreman training, the staff would also offer night classes for nonnative, non-English-speaking employees in English, civics, and subjects related to mining.

Wages

The IRC report states, "Wage rates constitute perhaps the most vital single factor in the coal industry's labor problem." It goes on to note the company is placed in a difficult position. A portion of the company's workforce is organized and the company is committed to paying the UMW wage scale; the other portion is nonunion but after the 1922 coal strike has also been paid at roughly the union scale. In order to preserve labor peace and the goodwill of its employees, the best course of action, states the IRC report, is to maintain wage rates. But doing so places the company is an untenable competitive position, given that many other companies in unorganized parts of the industry are paying wages 30–40 percent below the union scale. The result, according to the report, is that the sales department, in order to meet competition, often takes contracts that are priced below the company's cost of production.

What is the best wage policy in this situation? The IRC report counsels, "When the 'bottom is out of wages,' as it is today, the company is more considerate of its employees if wages are lowered to the point where coal may be sold and work provided than if it maintains high rates and offers little work. In the making of reductions, if such should eventually be deemed necessary, the company should negotiate all changes with employees."

Sanitation and Medical Services

Several recommendations are made: a program to eliminate outside toilets; erection of bathhouses at all mining properties; better coordination of medical services by creation of a medical services director's position; and greater uniformity across properties in medical fees, payments to doctors, and the like.

Company Stores

The report commends the company for operating its stores "above the average found in the coal industry." The report is nonetheless critical of the store management for endeavoring to maximize profit from the operation of the stores. As noted earlier, the return on investment in the stores has been well over 30 percent. The report remarks on this situation, noting, "These profits [are] . . . wholly unjustified. . . . It is difficult to believe that the Company management would consciously resort to exploitation of its employees, . . . as other coal operators who follow unscrupulous practices have frequently done in similar situations." The solution to this problem, according to the report, is to completely separate store revenues and coal revenues and charge store prices that yield roughly a 6 percent rate of return on investment. As part of this effort, the report recommends the stores be spun off to a newly created autonomous subsidiary company that is given responsibility to manage all aspect of store operations.

Pensions

The report notes that the company is already running a de facto small-scale pension program for superannuated employees. Two hundred and forty-seven employees have twenty-five or more years of service—considered then to be a considerable length of service, and over three hundred are over sixty years of age. These employees, according to the report, are kept on the payroll as a reward for good service, even though in a number of cases they are not able to do a full day's work.

The better policy, the report states, is to establish a pension plan and move these employees off the payroll. The benefits include increased efficiency in operations by removing superannuated workers, opening up more promotion opportunities for younger employees, reducing the risk of accident, and reducing turnover and gaining longer length of service. The report recommends a pension system that is contributory, voluntary, has an age of retirement of sixty-five, provides death benefits to family survivors, and has a fixed (flat) payment per month that varies with pay class, perhaps with a modest adjustment factor for years of service.

Costs of the Recommendations

The report ends with brief summary of the costs of implementing the recommendations. It starts with this observation: "It is indeed a serious demand which justifies additional expense under present conditions in the bituminous industry."

For purpose of context, the report notes that from 1918 to 1922 the net cost of all employment work done by the company totaled approximately $700,000. Then, in a one-sentence paragraph, this statement is made, referring apparently to use of undercover men, payments to labor leaders and politicians, and the like: "In the same five years there was spent approximately one million dollars on a different approach to the labor problem, or 1.45 percent of payroll."

In examining the cost implications of the recommendations contained in the report, additional expenditures or reduced revenues are put into three main categories: additional staff, change in organization and personnel of the company stores, and the pension plan. The cost of additional staff is estimated at $40,000—a cost justified on the grounds it will contribute to increased efficiency of operations and serve as "an insurance against possible future labor trouble with attendant losses reaching into the hundreds of thousands of dollars." The change in the company stores is estimated to cost approximately $200,000, while the cost of the pension plan is estimated at 1–2 percent of payroll. Then, adding in all other proposed changes to the company's IR program, the IRC report estimates the combined gross cost at between three and four percent of payroll. Without allowing for any savings or economies in operations, this increase in payroll translates into a profit reduction of 1.13 percent, or a reduction of earnings in 1922 from $3,099,608 to about $2,750,000.

Case Study Summary

This case study illustrates the significant constraints that economic conditions place on a firm's human resource management strategy and program.

The coal industry was caught in the economic vise of overcapacity on the supply side and declining markets on the demand side. The result was relentless downward pressure on prices and profits, forcing coal industry operators to continually pare down costs if they were to survive. Since many costs associated with the mine properties and physical plant were relatively fixed in the short run, the remaining source of significant cost reduction was in the labor area. The outcome was a slow, painful, and cumulatively large process of deflation and liquidation of labor—a process that wreaked misery on both sides of the employment relationship, spawned a militant union and equally militant group of operators, and set the stage for deep hostility and conflict in labor relations. Tragically, this "lose-lose" outcome was to be repeated in many other industries ten years later during the Great Depression.

This case study also provides an insightful counterpart to the case study of the Top-Grade Oil Company in chapter 8. Assume for the sake of discussion that the same principle shareholder of Top-Grade Oil had also owned a majority stake in Great Eastern and was similarly intent on implementing there a high-road human resource employment system. Would such a program have been successful at Great Eastern, and would it have made sense from a profit perspective? The answer to both questions is surely no. Even the most progressive business owner would quickly come face-to-face with the reality that a transformed HRM system would have little chance of success in an environment of razor-thin profit margins, highly unstable and intensely competitive product markets, the presence of hundreds of other firms desperately attempting to survive by cutting and further cutting labor cost, and an industry history and culture of deep-seated labor conflict and adversarialism. Thus, rather than advancing up the high-road to progressive HRM, the best that could be expected of Great Eastern Coal was to try to hold the line on labor standards as long as possible and then slowly retreat back down the low road when survival presented no other option.

Focusing directly on Great Eastern's HRM system, three features deserve brief highlight. The first is that it remained in the 1920s very much in the style of the traditional nineteenth-century supply-and-demand and "hired hand" models of employment. Personnel practices and programs were sparse and rudimentary; responsibility for labor policy and labor management were vested almost entirely in line management; and wages, turnover, and conditions—outside the union sector at least—were strongly driven by the market. The bulk of the coal mining labor force was quite mobile and intermittently moved from company to company as jobs appeared and disappeared, with sometimes extensive periods of unemployment in between. At least this industry was scarcely affected by the advent of professional HRM in the early decades of the 1900s.

A second feature of note is that HRM at Great Eastern was in certain respects far more extensive and broad-based than at other companies, particularly those in urban areas. In order to obtain and keep a work force in the remote sites where the mines were located, Great Eastern had to invest in and operate company housing, company stores, and a wide variety of employee social services, such as schools and churches. Most companies located closer to a population center did not need to perform these parts of the HRM function, as is true of nearly all companies today. Note, however, that it is not a case that these HRM costs disappear (workers always have to have housing, schools, and doctors); it is rather a case of who pays these costs, and how.

And, finally, we get a glimpse in this case study of some factors that frequently inflamed employer-employee relations both in the coal industry and a number of other industries. Although employment practices at Great Eastern were considerably above average, the company nonetheless engaged in certain questionable activities. Great Eastern, for example, selectively used spies and undercover men to infiltrate the workforce and report back on what people said and did; it also spent over a million dollars on lobbying, influencing, and perhaps bribing local politicians, judges, and police. Another long-standing complaint of coal miners was that the coal companies exploited them by paying low wages and then exploited them again by charging high prices for company housing and for provisions at the company store. The fact that the company stores at Great Eastern earned a profit margin of well over 30 percent suggests that workers may well have had a legitimate complaint. Shareholders, however, could counterargue that these high prices were necessary to help offset the exploitation of their sunk capital in a business that was far from returning a competitive rate of return. Evidently, the depressed state of the coal industry gave both sides numerous grounds for complaint and a very infertile environment for progressive application of HRM.

10

The Middle Ground
of HRM in the 1920s

The United Steel and Coal Company

In this chapter is an IRC survey done in 1924 of a large vertically integrated company that operated both a steel mill and accompanying coal and iron ore mines. This company had been traditionally managed up to about 1915; after a long and bitter strike the company decided to change course and upgrade and humanize its approach to employee relations. The centerpiece was a companywide employee representation plan. Although unique in fundamental respects, this company's human resource management system nonetheless represents for the 1920s something of a middle point in terms of formalization and modernity.

Company Background

The company is the largest industrial corporation in its state. It produces steel rails for the railroad industry and a host of other iron and steel products. Its steel mill is located in a small- to medium-size town in a relatively remote geographical area. The company also vertically integrated backward and bought or established a variety of businesses that supply inputs to the steel division. For example, it operates twenty-six coal mines scattered across parts of the state to provide coal and coke; two iron mines; a series of quarries for limestone, feldspar, and other ingredients for steelmaking; several railroads; a timber and lumber company; and a number of other subsidiary businesses. Although two-thirds of the coal produced is sold to outside buyers, the steel business nonetheless provides greater stability to the mining operations than would otherwise exist. In 1924, the total number of employees was 10,200, with the largest groups being in the steel mill operations (4,500) and coal mining (4,100). The company was only marginally profitable, reporting a net profit in 1924 of less than one-half million dollars.

The Organization and Administration of Industrial Relations

The first section of the IRC report is devoted to the organization and administration of industrial relations, and begins with the general observation, "The maintenance of harmonious and helpful relationships through-out the organization ranks in importance with production, distribution, finance, and other major functions of management." It then lists three general principles to be followed in the organization and administration of industrial relations:

"1. *Executive control of industrial relations is an administrative staff function. Therefore it is desirable that the individual entrusted with the management of industrial relations should be directly responsible to the president or some other high officer of the company.*
2. *The several divisions of industrial relations are usually organized and operated coordinately, the activities included in the divisions being necessarily interrelated. For this reason, it is desirable that all the division heads should come under one executive head.*
3. *Where a company has more than one plant at which an industrial relations staff exists, each local staff should be directly responsible to the chief works executive in the local plant.*"

These three principles are emphasized because none are well followed in the company.

In this regard, the IRC report observes, "The industrial relations program of the company is quite decentralized and is administered largely through the regular line organization." The exception to this statement is at the very top level of the company, where the president has personally taken responsibility for supervising and monitoring industrial relations activities. The company does not have an industrial relations department per se. Rather, the administration of companywide industrial relations is primarily in the hands of two people: a vice president in charge of industrial relations and the president's industrial representative.

The vice president personally oversees and administers all aspects of industrial relations, including acting as chair of the joint conferences, conducting all phases of public and community relations, and editing the company magazine. For support he has only one subordinate, whose primary job is to oversee churches, schools, and social activities in outlying coal camps and quarries.

The only other company-level person with significant industrial relations staff responsibility is the president's industrial representative. He attends all meetings of the plan of employee representation, represents management at these meetings (called "conferences"), and investigates and endeavors to adjust grievances in all the departments.

Below these two people are several other mid- to lower-level staff people who report directly to line management and on a "dotted-line" basis to the vice president of industrial relations. Examples are the personnel director of the steel works, the chairman of the service board, director of the medical department, and the safety inspector.

What stands out from the IRC report is that the industrial relations program at the company is heavily oriented toward the industrial representation plan, while most other aspects of industrial relations management are relatively undeveloped or absent altogether.

Joint Relations

The centerpiece of the industrial relations program at United Steel and Coal is the employee representation plan. This plan was a direct outgrowth of a major strike and union organizing campaign before World War I.

Before describing the structure and operation of the representation plan, it is instructive to consider its purpose(s), as seen by the IRC counselors. The report states in this regard,

> The history of labor from the eighteenth century to the present day has made clear . . . that the human element in industry is the factor of greatest importance. Progress depends upon cooperation and in industry cooperation must be based on the acceptance by employers and employees of some practical application of the principle that capital and labor are interdependent. Capital cannot exist without labor, and labor without capital is helpless. . . . Confidence and good-will are the foundation of every successful enterprise, and these can be created only by securing a point of contact between employer and employee. They must seek to understand each other's problems, respect each other's opinions, and maintain that unity of purpose and effort upon which the very existence of the community which they constitute and the whole future of democratic civilization depends."

The report then lists these specific objectives:

> "1. *to provide organization and procedure for collective negotiation regarding hours, wages, working conditions and other terms of the employment contract, particularly affecting the welfare of the workers*
> 2. *to facilitate organization and procedure for the prompt adjustment of individual and group complaints and grievances*
> 3. *to facilitate preparation of subordinates for positions of responsibility*

4. to provide a 'double track' channel of communication
5. to aid employees to appreciate the difficulties of the managerial function"

Initially separate representation plans were established for the coal department, the steel operations, and the office and salaried employees. In late 1921 these plans were consolidated into one, covering all employees except in certain of the timbering, rail, and supply operations.

The features of the representation plan include the following:

- annual election of representatives by secret ballot
- a representative is elected for approximately every 150 employees
- joint quarterly conferences are held in each major district of the company (approximately six in number), and at least one companywide joint conference is held per year
- each joint conference elects employee and management representatives to serve on four committees: the Joint Committee on Cooperation, Conciliation, and Wages; the Joint Committee on Safety and Accidents; the Joint Committee on Sanitation, Health, and Housing; and the Joint Committee on Recreation and Education
- these committees typically meet once a month, with the Committee on Cooperation, Conciliation, and Wages being the most active
- all matters concerning wages, hours, and other terms and conditions of employment are open to consideration
- issues before the committees are decided by majority vote, with the number of management representatives and employee representatives equal in number
- the company has pledged a policy of nondiscrimination on account of membership in a labor organization
- the company retains the right to direct the workforce, including the right to hire and fire
- workers with grievances are to first seek to resolve them with the foreman or superintendent, accompanied by the employee representative where such is desired; if resolution of the grievance is not accomplished, the worker can then appeal to higher-level officials (the president's industrial representative, the general manager, the president), with referral to a neutral umpire and binding arbitration as the last steps (if both parties agree)
- employee representatives are promised nondiscrimination for carrying out their duties and have the same rights of appeal as regular employees.
- all expenses associated with the operation of the plan are borne by the company.
- a written "memorandum of agreement" signed by company executives and employee representatives spells out certain basic terms and conditions of employment agreed to by the company covering employment, living,

and working conditions (e.g., rent on company housing, work hours, wash facilities, wage schedules, semimonthly payment of wages, etc.)

The IRC report does not provide much detail about the operation of the representation plan. It states that no grievance (as of late 1923) had been taken to arbitration, but that four had been appealed to the president. In the steel works, a total of 320 questions were considered by the joint committees in 1923. The largest number of issues concerned working conditions; 56 concerned wages. The report relates that in 1923 a joint conference was called to consider a wage increase at the time the eastern mills went on the eight-hour day, and the joint conference lasted eight hours and adjourned at 4:00 in the morning.

A table in the statistical appendix indicates that the company's expenditures to operate the employee representation plans were in the range of $10,000–$12,000 per year, not counting the salary of the president's industrial representative. By way of comparison, the company spent $60,000 per year for support of the local YMCA clubs, $8,000 on "special employees," and $6,000 for the company magazine. Special employees were several people who represented the company with local peace officers; they also reported to the company executives on labor matters, including union activity. The IRC report says the company discontinued in 1924 all "undercover" men and the special employees were "liaison agents."

Despite the representation plan, the company experienced three strikes between 1918 and 1923. The first, in September 1919, affected the steelworks and arose from the nationwide steel strike called by the National Committee for Organizing Iron and Steel Workers, led by William Z. Foster. The report states that the strike was not aimed at conditions in the company, and early on the employee representatives organized a "back to work" movement (which failed, reportedly because coal supplies were unavailable due to government restrictions). The report also notes that one of the demands of the unions was "right of collective bargaining," and states that the reply of the company was "[t]he right of collective bargaining exists under our Industrial Representation plan." This reply is revealing, since it indicates that the company regarded the representation plan—or at least presented it this way for purposes of public relations—as an alternative method of collective bargaining with employees.

The second strike, a nationwide coal strike, began in November 1919. State troops were called into maintain order and, the report states, when the fear of violence subsided the men returned to work and within two months coal production had largely returned to normal.

The third strike began in September 1921 and was in reaction to a series of three wage reductions at the company's mining operations. One district had not agreed to the wage cuts in joint conference and went on strike when they were instituted. The strike spread to other mines of the company, and martial law was declared at several places to prevent violence. In early 1922 the miners returned to work and, upon termination of the nationwide coal strike of that year, the company restored the wage scales to the level existing before the first round of reductions in 1921.

At the end of the section on joint relations, the IRC report summarizes the investigators' conclusions. The comments are interesting in light of the mixed and sometimes critical assessment reached by other observers at that time of the performance of employee representation plans at this and other companies. The IRC report states (modestly paraphrased):

> Perhaps the result of greatest economic value which is to be had from a well-functioning plan of employee representation is to enlist the best efforts of every employee and officer of the company to attain, through cooperative effort, the greatest possible combined power for the common good of the business.
>
> It seems to us, in view of the fact that the company's plan of employee representation has been long established, that this result has not been attained in the measure that might be expected. The minutes of meetings and our discussions with employees and officials of the company indicate that while the plan has resulted in a especially high morale, there had not been a capitalization of that moral to the extent of bringing forth united efforts on the part of everyone to lower costs. . . .
>
> It must be said to the credit of the management that they have at all times been willing to accept as the scope of subject matter for joint consideration all items of mutual concern to employee and management, and that the joint deliberations have been conducted in a spirit of frankness and directness that has done much to make the plan the conspicuous success which it is.
>
> It has been noted that the joint conference plan met with a more intimate and prideful endorsement by the employees, supervisors, and officials of the coal department than it did by the personnel at the steel works. In fact, it may be said that the plan, as related to the coal department, stands as one of the most conspicuous successes anywhere achieved in employee representation. Probably the largest single factor contributing toward this remarkable success has been the painstaking and efficient devotion to his duty on the part of the President's industrial representative.

Employment

The IRC report leads off the section on employment with a discussion of the activities/services an efficiently operating employment department should provide. These include:

1. *recruitment of labor supply, including detailed analysis of local and "outside" sources of labor (e.g., immigrants, African Americans from the South)*
2. *selection of applicants, including completion of a comprehensive job analysis, list of necessary job qualifications for each occupation, personal interviews with applicants, and physical examinations*
3. *preparation of employment records, including a written summary on a standardized form of each person's personal characteristics and past job*

experience and all subsequent promotions and transfers while in the company's employ

4. *placement of the employee, including a brief orientation talk to explain important facts about the company and its labor policy, followed by escorting the employee to meet the foreman, who introduces the new employee to workmates and instructs him in the job tasks and safety hazards of the work*

5. *transfer and promotion of employees, with the employment department acting as an interdepartmental clearinghouse working in cooperation with the supervisory forces to efficiently allocate labor and minimize exits from employment*

6. *preparation of statistics, including reports on turnover, adequacy of wage scales, accidents, and other such labor data*

7. *review of exits from employment, leading to a centralization of the discharge and layoff function whereby the employment manager personally interviews all employees leaving the services of the company for purposes of retaining desirable employees and relocating them to other jobs and determining causes of voluntary separations, including factors such as poor conditions and grievances (seeking adjustment with the foreman where appropriate).*

The report states that these employment procedures had been in operation for "periods up to fifteen years" in many industries, implying a beginning date for this aspect of personnel work at roughly 1910.

The implementation of the above-cited employment procedures has only been recently and incompletely accomplished at the company. In the steel works, a centralized employment procedure was established in June 1922, while no employment department had yet been set up in for the coal division.

In the steel division, all employees are hired through the central employment office at the main entrance to the plants. The employment department consists of a director (the personnel manager), a chief clerk, a stenographer, and an interpreter.

The employment procedure in use consists of the following: a personal interview by the personnel manager, the chief clerk, or the interpreter; filling out an application card with standard personal data; a physical examination; and a group presentation on the representation plan, pension plan, medical service, and other company policies. New employees are guided to their jobs by a person from the watchmen's department.

No job analysis has yet been done, though exit interviews have been performed for approximately one-half of the persons leaving service. A special census of employees was performed in 1923 to obtain data on nationality, age, and length of service in connection with a study of group life insurance, but such data are not regularly maintained. Standardized records are kept on leaves of absence, and transfers and employee turnover is calculated on a monthly basis. No regular reports are made, however, by the employment department to the manager of the steelworks or the vice president in charge of industrial relations.

The authority for discharge is vested in the foreman and superintendent, but subject to review under the joint representation plan. The usual procedure in cases of discharge is for the foreman to obtain the approval of the superintendent before the discharge becomes effective. The offenses for which discharges may be made are posted throughout the mill and mines In other cases (such as poor work performance), the company has adopted a rule that the employee be notified in writing that a repetition will result in discharge, but these written warnings are not always used in practice.

As a safeguard against favoritism in employment, the company stipulates that no person shall be employed in a department in which a relative has a position of authority. Layoffs are made on the basis of seniority and job performance, but efforts are made to retain employees with dependents. Promotion from the ranks is encouraged.

The IRC report contains a number of statistical tables in an appendix, but provides no discussion or analyses of these data in the text. Summarized below are relevant employment-related data.

Employment Relations Expenses

The company's expenditures in calendar year 1922 for activities related to employment relations were the following (in dollars):

Social and Industrial Betterment: 198,620
Pensions: 69,759
Donations: 17,572
Employment—Steel Works: 5,597
Memberships (Associations): 460
Special Employees: 8,135
Safety: 17,635
Workmen's Compensation Payments: 99,891
Hospital Contributions/Deficit: 114,630
Housing: 150,309
Total: 672,623
Per Employee: 68

Nationality

The company's employees were distributed among the following ten "nationalities" (in percentages):

American: 34.2
Mexican: 20.6
German/Austro-Hungarian: 12.0
Balkan: 2.4

English/Irish: 2.3
European Latin: 20.5
Negro: 3.8
Scandinavian: 1.0
Russian/Slav: 3.6
Asian: 0.6

Length of Service

Employees of the company had the following years of job tenure (in percentages):

0–4: 52.0
5–9: 25.5
10–14: 9.6
15–19: 7.1
20–24: 4.0
25+: 1.8

More disaggregated data were not provided.

Turnover

An indication of the flows into and out of employment at the company are given by the following data for the calendar year 1924 (relative to an annual employment level of approximately 10,200):

Additions to Employment: 5,628
New Employees: 932
Reemployed: 3,069
Transfers: 1,627
Deductions from Employment: 5,344
Quits: 3,648
Discharges: 69
Transfers: 1,627

The monthly turnover rate for the period from April 1923 to August 1924 is reported as 6.6 percent on a monthly basis, or 80 percent per year.

Wages and Hours

The IRC report begins the section on wages with a statement of general principles concerning best practice in compensation management, explaining,

Wages should be related primarily to performance. The requirements of every job should, as far as possible, be stated in advance and the wages paid made dependent on the skill required and the service rendered, as indicated by the quantity and quality of output. Wages should be governed also by competitive and local conditions, with due regard for the maintenance of a reasonable standard of living. This idea is fundamentally opposed to the practice which seeks to group together at a uniform wage large bodies of employees, classed in a trade, regardless of individual performance, and even though scattered in various plants widely scattered. . . . The determination of specific wage rates involves job specification, job standardization and job analysis.

With regard to the practices of the United Steel and Coal Company, the report states,

The wage policy of the company is definitely stated in the Memorandum of Agreement. . . . The essential provisions are:

1. That wage rates shall conform substantially to the wage rates being paid for like work under similar conditions in competitive industries.
2. That all wage changes shall be made in joint conference to be held within thirty days after the change in wages at competitive operations.

Wage History: Steel

The report provides a history of general wages changes in the steel division from 1913 to early 1924. From March 1, 1913, to February 1, 1916, there were no general changes in wages. Over the next five years (to February, 1920) wages were increased eight times (seven times at 10 percent, one time at 15 percent). During 1921 (including January 1, 1922), wages were then reduced three times in two cuts of 15 percent and one cut of 10 percent. In September 1922, wages in steel were raised 20 percent; in 1923 two more increases of 10 percent and 12 percent were made.

From 1913 to 1924 money wages advanced a total of 151 percent, although in 1923 they were still 1.5 cents below the peak reached in 1920. When the rise in consumer prices is subtracted out, real wages in 1924 were 83 percent of those in 1917. Average annual earnings for steelworkers employed full-time in 1923 was $1,426. Two-thirds of the steelworkers were in the earnings range of $1,000–$1,500, with a considerably skewed right-hand tail of the earnings distribution for workers above $1,500.

A variety of methods of wage payment are utilized: hourly; by tonnage; by salary; hourly plus bonus; salary plus bonus; and by salary, bonus, and tonnage. In 1924, 72 percent of the steel division employees were on hourly rates; 18 percent were on tonnage rates; and 5.5 percent on salary.

All general changes in rates, except salary, are made through joint conferences. The wage changes are made in a uniform percentage amount across labor grades. Periodically, a committee of management and employee representatives visits eastern steel mills and reports back on prevailing wages at competitive firms. In effect, the wage of United Steel's mill workers is effectively pegged to the wage paid at eastern mills, particularly at the industry leader, the U.S. Steel Corporation.

Wage History: Coal

The overall pattern of wage changes in the coal division was roughly parallel to that of the steel division, although the percentage changes were frequently larger both up and down. Wage changes in coal were influenced not only by market forces but also by the U.S. Fuel Administration during World War I and the wage agreements negotiated in organized mines by the United Mine Workers Union. Union rates have a significant influence on company wage policy, but in the Depression of 1921 the company, after joint conference with the employees, followed the nonunion segment of the industry and lowered wage rates on an average of 23–34 percent (depending on method of payment). The employees agreed to this reduction as a way to preserve the company's competitive position and the amount of available work. In 1923, average annual earnings of full-time employees in the coal division was $1,820.

Most coal miners are paid on a tonnage rate. The industrial representation plan gives the miners at each operation the opportunity to have a checkweighman. This person's pay is collected from a per-capita deduction from the miners' pay. Employees at only three of the mines elected to have a checkweighman.

Hours

The company adopted an eight-hour day in 1918. Most eastern mills did not make this move until 1924, under considerable government pressure. In the steel works, employees rotate shifts once a week, except in blast furnaces where they rotate every two weeks. A six-day work week is company policy. Many of the operations in the steelworks require continuous operation, so employees rotate in and out of Sunday work.

Safety, Accident, and Medical Activities

The company has no general firm-level safety organization; rather, safety is the responsibility of the general manager of each operating division. The safety program in the steel division is headed up by a safety inspector. He works with joint safety committees of foremen/supervisors and production workers, as provided for in the industrial representation plan. The safety program in the coal division is headed up by the chief mine inspector, who also works in cooperation with the joint safety committee at each of the mines. Monthly prizes are given to the supervisory forces having the lowest time lost record.

In the steel division, the movement to the eight-hour day in 1918 was accompanied by a marked reduction in the accident rate (from 1.12 per hundred employees in 1915–18 to .61 in 1919–23). Since the eight-hour day, the days lost per accident were 16.5. The company's safety program is apparently far less successful than at other steel mills in the vanguard of the safety movement. In 1923, the company's accident frequency per million hours was 31.4, compared to 12.8 for a select group of other mills. As contributing factors, the IRC report notes that the safety work "has shown a decided lack of supervision both on the part of the steelworks management, the industrial relations department, and the safety inspector"; that "the safety inspector has not met with committees as a general practice and frequent inspections of the plant have not been made" and "safety rallies for employees . . . throughout the plant are not held."

In the coal division, by way of contrast, the accident rate per ton of coal produced at the company is significantly below the average of other coal companies in the state. The IRC report attributes this successful safety performance to several factors: "the work has been well correlated through the efforts of the manager;" "the supervision has been of a high order;" and "the proper functioning of the various safety committees."

The company employs full-time doctors, nurses, and other medical staff to take care of health and accident problems among employees. It also owns and operates a company hospital. The dependents of employees are also eligible for health and medical treatment at reduced rates, as are pensioners. The hospital has operated at a net loss of $30,000–$80,000 in recent years.

Training and Education

Education and training activities are also decentralized to the division level of the company.

Apparently vocational training focused specifically on work-related skills in the steel division is minimal at the company, as no general program is described. Only two examples of vocational training are mentioned. The first is that there are forty-one apprentices in various departments. The report goes on to observe, however, that "The employment of apprentices has been principally the result of a demand to take care of the sons of employees." The second exception is organization of a foremen's club, to which about half the eligible foremen and lower-ranking supervisory staff in the steel division belong. It sponsors "social affairs and educational talks." General educational classes are conducted at the steel works' YMCA building. These include courses on English, citizenship, and cooking and sewing. Fees are paid by the company.

Regarding the coal division, the report states, "Under the Smith-Hughes Act [federal legislation enacted in 1917 to encourage vocational education] vocational classes for company employees are held throughout the coal mining districts. . . . The mechanical and electrical arts, together with arithmetic as applied to mining are taught." Classes are also held to prepare employees for the state examinations for fire bosses and mine foremen. The coal division has also organized foremen's clubs at several of the mine districts.

Housing

Housing is a necessary part of an industrial relations program for companies with facilities in rural and sparsely inhabited areas, and the United Steel and Coal Company is no exception. To administer the housing program, it created a rental department that reports directly to the general manager of the company.

When the steel works was erected in the very early 1900s, the company built 250 bungalow homes in the adjacent area. As a medium-size community began to develop around the steel works, however, private housing became increasingly available and no further housing investment was needed. The one exception was the building of fifty new homes in 1921 after a disastrous flood. In 1919 a decision had been made to sell the existing stock of company houses to employees.

Company housing is still needed at the coal camps. The company owns over 1,600 homes across four coal districts. The IRC report states that the quality and maintenance of the company's housing shows a "markedly favorable contrast to those found in most mining communities." Electric lighting is installed at all coal camps except one, 20 percent of houses are equipped with running water, and while few houses have indoor bathrooms the outhouses are kept clean and in good condition. The company makes an effort to design homes with different outside structures and floor plans to avoid the monotony found in many company towns; it keeps the homes painted; and it has regular pick-up of garbage and trash.

Rent at the company's housing is characterized as "low" and "perhaps too liberal." The company's housing is not self-supporting and pays back only about one-half of the investment and operating expense. The rent is based on a monthly fee of $2.00 per room, plus an additional monthly charge for various "conveniences." A bath, for example, costs $3.00 per month, a sink $2.00, a cellar $1.00, and a garage $2.00.

The Company Magazine

The company publishes a company magazine five times a year. This publication supersedes an earlier and claimed-to-be pioneering magazine started a decade or so ago.

The IRC report provides general management advice on employee magazines. It frames the goals as "to stimulate industrial efficiency" and "induce a cheerful morale." It advises companies that better results are obtained if employees are given significant opportunities to participate in all phases of the magazine and that they should avoid effort to mold employee opinion along lines favorable to the company.

The magazine was created under the terms of the representation plan and every issue contains news items about the meetings, agenda, and decisions of the joint conferences. Each issue also focuses on one particular phase of the company's industrial relations program, such as wages and hours, the medical department, the safety program, and so on. Also included are a wide variety of short articles related to company affairs, community events, and matters affecting employees and their families (births, deaths, marriages, etc.), as well as poems, educational articles, and advice on aspects of home economics.

The IRC consultants give the company's magazine a high grade, although they counsel management to "popularize" the contents to a greater degree and give employees more opportunity to contribute material.

The Retirement Plan

In 1917 the company created a retirement plan for all its employees. Before this, the company, like a number of others, followed an informal arrangement where its loyal and well-performing long-serving employees, when too old or infirm to perform their regular jobs, were kept on the payroll and given some form of light-duty work.

Under the new plan, all employees are eligible for a monthly retirement benefit who have attained the age of sixty-five (for women, fifty-five) and have been employed a total of twenty-five years. This group of employees is subject to compulsory retirement unless given special exemption. After thirty years of service, employees may be retired at the age of sixty (for women, fifty). Employees incapacitated in the service of the company may also on a special case-by-case basis be given retirement benefits, as may the widows and orphans of employees.

The payment is calculated as 30 percent of the average pay per month of service during the last ten years of service, with a minimum payment of $20 per month. To preserve the financial solvency of the retirement plan, the company mandated that no one over the age of forty-five (later raised to fifty at the request of employee representatives) could be hired as a new employee. The benefits paid under the plan started at $5,000 in 1917 and increased to $80,000 in 1923. This amounted to approximately one-half of 1 percent of the payroll. The IRC consultants calculated that retirement benefits would grow to as much as 10 percent of the payroll and observed that the company did not have adequate funds earmarked to cover this obligation. The report counsels the company, therefore, to put the retirement plan on a sound actuarial basis.

The Mutual Benefit Association

The company started a mutual benefit association for employees in 1920. The association is a form of industrial insurance whereby employees make monthly contributions to the plan and become eligible for a monthly benefit in case of death, disablement, or prolonged sickness. The plan involves an expense for the company in that it covers the cost of administration and office space; the benefits according to the IRC report are a more stable, responsible, and loyal workforce and less call on the company for special charitable contributions.

The monthly employee contribution is 60 cents; in return an eligible employee receives $7 per week during a disabling sickness or accident and a death benefit of $100. In 1924, 61 percent of the company's employees were plan participants.

Community Relations

The company invests in or contributes to a variety of activities and programs in local communities as an aid to its employees and for purposes of improved community relations and development. The company, for example, helps recruit teachers and provides funds for school betterment in outlying camps; assists in building churches and funding Sunday School programs; operates post offices in outlying areas; funds YMCA clubhouses and camps; and sponsors two social events each year in towns where the company has a substantial presence. The YMCA clubhouses are a focal point for local social activities, such as dances, movies, theatrical presentations, and music groups. Members contribute dues of $6 per year; the company nonetheless incurs a substantial expense.

The report states that the company delegates all matters of law enforcement to county officials and ensures as company policy that all outlying camps and towns are "open to all law abiding persons and no discrimination is made against union officials or outside merchants who are competing with the company stores."

Case Study Summary

This case study depicts a company that largely used a traditional "hired hands" employment model up to the mid-1910s and then over a ten-year period moved part way toward a new "human resource" model. It effectively occupies a middle area in the distribution of HRM programs among American companies of the 1920s, with companies such as the Top-Grade Oil Company (see chapter 8) at the higher end and companies such as Great Eastern Coal (see chapter 9) on the lower end.

As with a number of other companies depicted in this volume, the impetus to change the traditional HRM system came from the outbreak of a long and violent strike and the dreaded prospect of being organized by a trade union. Faced with these unpalatable outcomes, the owners of the company made a strategic decision to try a different approach to HRM. Their goal was to restore labor peace, gain the cooperation and goodwill of their workers, and keep out unions. Rather than practice a hardball style of "union suppression" with heightened firings, intimidation, and spies, the company instead opted for a softer style of "union substitution" through which it sought to displace workers' desire for a union by removing frictions, improving conditions, and providing greater opportunities for voice, joint decision making, and due process in the administration of discipline and discharge.

The centerpiece of the new HRM system was an employee representation plan. Called by its critics a "company union," the representation plan let workers elect representatives who then in periodic meetings with management officials jointly discussed issues of concern to either party, particularly with regard to employment-related matters. The evidence provided in this case study suggests the representation plan was only partly successful. On the "plus" side it provided an improved channel for two-way communication; led to demonstrable improvements in working conditions (including those in housing, social services, etc.); offered greater protection against arbitrary and unfair discipline and discharge; was a forum for employees to press managers for improvements in wages, hours and other basic parts of the employment package; and was responsible for a general increase in morale and peaceful relations. On the "minus" side employees perceived the plan to be relatively powerless to effect more wide-ranging and substantive change (e.g., general wage increases); chafed at the lack of independence from management control; saw many lower-level officials give only lip service or half-hearted support to the plan; and on three occasions still went out on strike. One must judge, therefore, that the employee representation plan went only part way in accomplishing the company's goals and fell significantly short in a number of areas.

The United Steel and Coal Company did not implement most of the other formal parts of the new human resource model. In particular, the company did not create a centralized HRM department to administer and advise on employment policy, nor did it create functional specialty areas to manage specialized HRM programs such as staffing and benefits. In effect, the new HRM system rested on one major pillar—the industrial representation plan, while other parts were quite underdeveloped or nonexistent. A variety of reasons no doubt account for the somewhat stunted and one-dimensional nature of the company's new HRM system, but surely the very low profitability of the company's operations was a significant inhibiting factor—a factor HRM by itself can most likely only improve on the margin.

11

Paternalism Combined with Decentralized and Informal HRM

Mega-Watt Light and Power

Nearly all Industrial Relations Counselors Inc. (IRC) surveys in the 1920s were of firms engaged in manufacturing and natural resource extraction, with the result that sectors outside durable goods production were unrepresented. This chapter's case study features the single exception—an electric utility. This company's human resource management program attained a high level of cooperation and loyalty among the employees, yet did so in a most rudimentary and nonsystematized way. The key was a company culture and management philosophy that gave long-standing emphasis to positive treatment of employees through a highly individualized and personalized system of corporate paternalism and welfarism. The result was a strong bond between workers and company, albeit obtained only with some greater labor expense and threatened by the company's rapid growth through merger and acquisition. This IRC report was completed in late 1927.

Background

The Mega-Watt Light and Power Company (MWLP) was formed in 1925 from a merger of five smaller electric utilities and power generating companies. Several of these companies, in turn, had recently been formed from mergers and acquisitions. As of mid-1927, MWLP was divided into eleven subsidiaries, including two short-haul railroads. The company served eighteen counties in two adjoining states with a population of 2.4 million people. MWLP generated power from both hydroelectric facilities and coal-fired plants and distributed the power over 2,500 miles of high voltage transmission lines. Employment in 1927 was 3,452. The company achieved high profitability, earning a return of 12 percent on invested capital in 1926.

A major management challenge facing the newly formed company was melding the diverse organizations into an effectively coordinated whole. According to the IRC report, considerable progress had been made in several areas, such as operations, finance, and line repair and maintenance. One area remaining badly fragmented and nonintegrated was the labor management function. Immediately after the merger, MWLP formed an employee relations committee to help coordinate and standardize all labor policies and practices of the company. The committee was headed by the chair of the corporation's board of directors and had seven managers and personnel staff from across the subsidiaries. The committee met on a number of occasions, prepared several reports, and made recommendations in areas such as life insurance and pensions. However, divergent interests among the subsidiary divisions and lack of concerted direction from the top of the corporation resulted in no action being taken on any of these matters. As a result, the committee discontinued meeting over most of 1927. One can reasonably conjecture that IRC was brought in partly to break this logjam.

The Organization and Administration of Industrial Relations

The IRC report notes an interesting divergence in the industrial relations situation at MWLP. On one hand, the formal practice of industrial relations is quite skimpy and haphazard. The report observes, for example, that there are only two positions in the entire company that explicitly deal with some phase of industrial relations: those of the safety engineer and the matron of women. The latter is responsible for providing discipline of the female clerical staff and monitoring their absenteeism and tardiness. Further, the only printed policy governing employment in the company concerns the comportment of the female staff. One subsidiary company, however, has a functioning welfare department, although it apparently operates in a largely informal and adjunct manner. With this situation in mind, the IRC report observes,

> There has been informal treatment of personnel problems, a lack of defined labor policy and responsibility and an absence of recorded rules and methods of procedures. What has been everybody's business has been nobody's business, as a result of which ... there are almost as many ideas and practices relative to personnel management as there are responsible supervisors in charge of individual units.

Yet, on the other hand, the IRC consultants found a high tenor of employer-employee relations at MWLP and a general feeling among the employees of cooperation and loyalty. Part of this high tenor of relations is explained by unwritten but widely practiced procedures and traditions on the part of management. One example cited is a well-recognized program of promotion from within; a second is close personal attention to employee mishaps and hardships—for example, a top executive personally delivering death benefits to the families of workers killed on the job. Among the very few formal employee programs at MWLP, nearly half of all money spent is on one program explicitly designed to wed the employees to the company—an employee stock purchase plan.

More important, however, than particular programs or traditions is the positive spirit and philosophy toward employees and their welfare that pervades the company's management at all ranks. At MWLP, it is personal leadership ("personality") that is the driving force in successful HRM rather than practices per se.

The role of personalized leadership is illustrated in these two examples from the IRC report. Speaking of the parent company, the consultants remark on

the very strong influence of the personalities of its organizers and officers on the exceptional spirit of loyalty and good fellowship. In the operating department particularly, the personality of John Smith stands out as having had an incalculable effect upon the men throughout his organization in the interests of harmonious working relationships. . . . There is a resulting background of traditional good will that has made for a firm foundation of the very best sort of personnel management.

Similarly, at a subsidiary the report notes,

At every point of contact the first reason given for employee enthusiasm and company reputation was the personality of Charles Jones. It is evident this his democratic spirit, aggressive leadership and personal interest in employee well-being have done more than any other single influence to weld the organization together and inspire a feeling of mutual respect and confidence.

Although the IRC report does not state it in these words, MWLP has secured the loyalty and cooperation of employees by a well-developed but almost completely informal practice of corporate paternalism and welfarism. Paternalism and welfarism are core values of the company's management that the leadership deliberately practices in a highly visible, personal, and individualized manner. These core management values and behaviors are described as

a well-defined management spirit of sympathetic interest in and consideration for the welfare of employees [and] a desire for good fellowship and resulting close personal contact between company officials and rank and file employees. With this combination of spirit and good motives there has, in general, developed an emphatically expressed feeling of mutual respect and loyalty which has given to each company [subsidiary] a community reputation for being a good place in which to work, and has resulted, therefore, in the building of a personnel of a uniformly high standard, with consequent freedom from so-called labor disturbances, and an unusually large number of long service employees in supervisory positions.

Whether the expenditure of attention and money on employees has contributed to the company's superior profitability or is made possible by it is an interesting but unexplained consideration. Clearly, however, superior employee relations are achieved with minimal accoutrements of formal and professional HRM.

Despite this seemingly positive record, the IRC report concludes that MWLP very much needs to centralize, formalize, and professionalize its HRM activities. "Business as usual" will no longer perform well, IRC concludes, for several reasons. One is the death or retirement of several long-serving and influential top executives; a second is a thinning of the ranks of long-service supervisors steeped in the culture and traditions of the company; a third is the tremendous growth in the size and geographic spread of the company; and a fourth is the large influx of younger workers who lack a well-developed sense of company loyalty.

From these factors arise an increasingly disconnected and jumbled set of personnel policies and practices that lead to inefficient use of the company's human resources and the potential for perceived or real inequities and discrimination. The IRC report notes, for example, that in other large industrial companies $50 to $75 per employee per year covers the cost of a well-rounded industrial relations program, yet MWLP is spending more than $100 without enjoying many of the benefits. It also advises MWLP management that "consistency is of prime importance in the administration of a successful personnel program" and the company's lack of standards and centralized oversight, when coupled with rapid growth and diversification, threaten to undermine the climate of positive employee relations. The IRC consultants thus counsel MWLP to create a position of manager of industrial relations with several subordinates, such as to administer job evaluation, training and medical services. The report does not recommend an employee representation plan, but does counsel management to seek employee participation in devising new HRM policies and programs.

Employment

The handling of hiring, promotion, transfer, termination and record keeping exemplify the highly decentralized and fragmented nature of industrial relations practices at MWLP. On this matter the IRC report states, "The outstanding characteristic of employment practices . . . is the absence of predetermined rules and policies."

All aspects of employment are left to the determination of officials in the different operating divisions of the company. In some divisions hiring, promotion, transfer, and termination are done by the superintendent, in other cases by lower-level supervisors, and yet in others by a chief engineer or other technical person. Practices vary widely. In some divisions department heads have unrestricted authority to terminate employees, while in others termination can only proceed after the employee and supervisor have had a meeting with the superintendent. One division has a strict rule that women must resign upon marriage; another has a formal policy that promotions are based on a combination of quality of work and length of service. The closest thing to a standard employment practice across divisions is the unwritten but widely followed policy of promotion from within. In only one division is there a centralized personnel record keeping function; in the majority of divisions the only written personnel records are for attendance and payroll.

The age distribution of employees is as follows: 45.5 percent are 25 years of age or under, 32.5 percent are between 26 and 45 years, and 22.7 percent are over 45 years of age. With regard to length of service, 19 percent have been with the company less than one year, 40 percent from 1 to 5 years, 22 percent from 5 to 10 years, and 19 percent 10 years of more. Women comprise 15 percent of employees; 65 percent of the men and 18 percent of the women are married. Seventy percent of employees are classified as full-time.

Wages and Hours

The IRC report states that "Differences in wages and hours practices and policies constitute the most serious situation which the Company faces in the field of industrial relations. . . . Widely differing wage rates, based on scales built up at random rather than scientific principles, may lead to serious dissatisfaction on the part of employees [and] may lay the corporation open to a charge of discrimination." A brief review will indicate the basis for this dire conclusion.

Wages

The company's informal and decentralized HRM system is reflected in several dimensions of wages. One is the *methods* and *schedules* of wage payment.

Workers' pay is most often on an hourly basis, but some workers receive various types of incentive rates while others are paid a fixed amount per day, week, month, or year. The report notes that workers within one occupation—meter readers—are paid in four different ways. Likewise, some workers receive their wage payments at the end of each day, while others are paid weekly, biweekly, or monthly. Surprisingly, even deductions from workers' paychecks, such as for the stock purchase plan, exhibit considerable variation—sometimes a single deduction is made per pay period, but other times as many as six deductions are made.

Also almost completely lacking are written or formalized wage schedules. The company has no occupational or job classifications on which to base a wage structure, nor are there any guidelines on minimum or maximum wages for particular jobs. Likewise, some employees receive no extra compensation for working overtime, while others receive time and a half. In this and nearly all other respects, pay determination is left almost entirely to the discretion of lower-level line and operations managers and supervisors.

Not surprisingly, due to these factors another dimension of wages—*per-period pay rates*—also exhibits considerable diversity at MWLP (characterized by IRC as "heterogeneous and haphazard"). Among a workforce of 3,000 employees, IRC finds slightly more than 300 distinct pay rates—or about one pay rate per ten employees. In a particular occupational category, such as lineman, minimum pay for workers on an hourly rate ranges from 45 cents in one part of the company to 60 cents in another, while for those linemen paid on a weekly basis minimum pay range from $27 per week to $54. Commenting on this situation, the IRC report concludes, "Thirty rates for unskilled laborers can hardly be justified by labor market conditions."

Great diversity also applies to wage *changes*. For forty-five job categories for which the IRC could obtain consistent data, between 1915 and 1927, wages in twenty-nine categories have increased faster than the cost of living, but wages increased slower than the cost of living in the remaining sixteen.

Average annual earnings for employees at MWLP are above average for similar workers in the regional labor markets. In 1926, full-time workers received $1,703 per year. Across the eleven subsidiaries, annual earnings varied from a low of $1,594 to a high of $1,906.

Hours

Employees work 5, 5-1/2, 6, and 7 days per week; some work 8 hours a day while others work as many as 12 hours. As a result, weekly work hours for employees in a given job classification show great variation. General utility men worked from 41 to 75 hours, unskilled laborers from 38 to 72, and clerks from 38 to 56.

Another dimension of hours is time off for holidays and vacation days. Because of differences in holiday and vacation policy across subsidiaries, the system of days off is very diverse. Employees in most subsidiaries receive six holidays (New Year's Day, Memorial Day, the Fourth of July, Labor Day, Thanksgiving, and Christmas), but employees in several receive fewer, and one subsidiary gave no holidays at all. Of those employees receiving holidays, only slightly more than one-half get paid for the time off; the others get no pay.

With regard to vacation time, 21 percent of employees receive no vacation, while 30 percent receive ten vacation days and 47 percent receive fourteen days. Like holidays, some workers receive paid vacations while others do not.

Training and Education

The situation with respect to training and education at MWLP is summarized in this observation:

> The general tendency throughout the several companies has been to depend upon the initiative of the individual employee in taking advantage of outside educational opportunities. Training on the job has in general been allowed to take its own course by day to day development through experience in specific tasks.

The principle vehicle for skills training is the promote-from-within system. Lower-level employees that show aptitude and initiative are promoted up a step and receive instruction in their new job from fellow workers or a supervisor or foreman. In terms of a formal in-house training activity, the closest thing found in the company is in the distribution and meter departments of one subsidiary, where on rainy days long-serving employees instruct new linemen on cable-splicing and new meter readers on making accurate reports. Another subsidiary pays the cost of tuition and books for select employees who enroll in an electricity course at a local trade school.

Training and educational programs for foremen and supervisors have been discussed by the employee relations committee but with no action to date.

Accident Prevention and Medical Services

The company has no organization-wide person in charge of safety activities, nor is there any organization-wide set of policy guidelines for safety work or record keeping and reporting system with regard to accidents. The company employs several safety engineers, but they work under the direction of the general manager of individual subsidiaries. In only one of the eleven divisions of MWLP is there a functioning joint safety committee. Several others were started, but then lapsed. Safety announcements and accident reports are posted on bulletin boards, but no employee meetings or rallies are held to promote greater safety awareness and education.

Accident and fatality rates show a marked variation across divisions. For the company as a whole, the accident frequency rate (lost time accidents per one million hours worked) for the previous three years was 24.9; the lowest rate at a subsidiary was 15.4, the highest was 55.4. From January 1, 1925, to September 1927, the company has a total of 52,751 days lost due to accidents.

The medical services of MWLP are limited to provision of first aid and surgical treatment of employees injured while at work. First aid kits are located at various facilities; if further treatment is necessary it is usually given by local doctors who are paid on a fee basis by the insurance carriers. One subsidiary has a two-room dispensary staffed by two nurses.

In 1927, prodded by rising costs of workmen's compensation, the company began to actively consider making a physical examination a requirement of employment. To date, however, this policy is in effect in only one subsidiary.

Life and Disability Insurance and Mutual Benefit Associations

MWLP provides life and disability insurance to employees, with the partial exception of one subsidiary, and hence approximately 84 percent of employees are covered. The rules for eligibility and amount and length of payment vary considerably across divisions, however. For example, one division provides an average of $600 of insurance coverage per employee, while another provides $1,700. The total cost to MWLP of providing group life and disability insurance is $36,000 (relative to an annual payroll of $6.6 million), or approximately $10 per employee.

The company also has a mutual benefit plan for employees, although these are organized at the division level and differ considerably in benefit and eligibility schedules. Under the plans, employees contribute a monthly fee, which is matched by the company, and then become insured against earnings loss from nonwork accidents, sickness, and death. For the company as a whole during 1926, the benefit associations covered 71 percent of the employees; there were 79 disability cases (with an average days loss of 35 per case), six deaths, and a benefit payout of $3,319.

Pension and Stock Purchase Plans

Nine of the company's eleven divisions provide employees with some type of old-age pension plan, although three different plans exist among them. Provisions vary, but one plan stipulates that all employees must retire at age 65 and those with at least ten years of continuous service immediately prior to retirement can qualify for a pension. The annual pension payment was calculated as 1.5 percent of the highest amount of pay within this ten-year period. As of 1927, a total of forty-two employees of MWLP and its subsidiaries were pensioned; the total cost to the company was $68,099 (but with one pensioner accounting for fully $21,000 of this cost). The plans are entirely funded by the company. The IRC calculates that the total pension liability of MWLP is approximately $600,000, while the company has a pension reserve fund of $130,000. Unless the company substantially increases its contributions to the reserve fund, in future years it will need to pay pension obligations out of general operating funds.

Another form of deferred or indirect compensation provided by MWLP is in the form of a stock purchase plan. Like pensions and most other personnel practices, the details of the stock purchase plan vary across subsidiaries. The general approach, however, is to offer employees an opportunity to purchase stock in the company at a modestly reduced rate. The IRC consultants found that 91 percent of employees have purchased one or more shares. This exceedingly high proportion is due to two factors. The first is that company management provides considerable encouragement—sufficiently strong to be described as coercion by some employees—to participate in the stock plan; the second is that until 1927 the stock purchases of employees had greatly appreciated in market value. The IRC report observes, "The plan is proving an exceedingly profitable one to employees and is generally regarded by them as the best thing that the companies have done in their interests."

Employee Services and Activities

MWLP also provides a number of different services or activities for the benefit of its employees. Examples include a company magazine, several cafeterias in the general office and administration buildings of the subsidiaries, various types of company-sponsored athletic teams, a small number of women's study clubs, social events such as dances and picnics, long-term service buttons, sale of coal and gasoline at cost to employees, and Christmas gifts (a turkey, or $5).

Case Study Summary

This company practiced HRM in a largely traditional way in terms of decentralization and lack of formalization. It had no formal human resource management department, nor did it have specialized HRM staff or nearly any type of formal HR program or activity. Direct investment in formal HRM was nil. Yet, at the same time, the company succeeded in obtaining a peaceful and cooperative workforce and many employees expressed considerably loyalty to the company and stayed with it for a considerable time.

The secret was not in specific programs or methods but in a general management approach to employee relations. Mega-Watt won employee cooperation and loyalty by making the company a good place to work, using financial incentives to align interests, and inculcating in all ranks of management a paternalistic ethos in which individual employee treatment and welfare was an explicit concern.

There was, however, a growing downside to Mega-Watt's practice of HRM. The company had grown to over three thousand employees through

numerous mergers and acquisitions. Increasingly, the practice of decentralized management, individual treatment, and lack of formal policy was creating a crazy-quilt pattern of compensation rates and practices, work hours
and schedules, vacation and holiday provisions, and a myriad of other
HRM practices. The company needed, therefore, to introduce more centralization and formalization into its employee management function to improve efficient use of labor and achieve greater uniformity in practices and
treatment. The interesting HRM challenge raised in this case study, therefore, is how to promote greater consistency and formalization in HRM that
goes with a large company without also eroding the small company "we
care about you" culture built on individual treatment and enlightened
paternalism.

12

The "Hired Hand" Model in a Large Manufacturing Firm

New Era Radio

Of the six IRC case studies, this one most closely approximates the "hired hand" or supply-and-demand model of human resource management (HRM). New Era Radio was a rapidly up-and-coming manufacturer of radios and other consumer electrical products and was noted for its leadership in new technology and product development. In the area of labor management, however, it badly lagged behind and had a very haphazard and poorly run HRM program marked by huge swings in hiring and firing. This consulting report was completed in late 1930.

Background

The company was organized shortly after the end of World War I to provide wireless communications service between the United States and Europe. Over the next ten years the scope of its business expanded rapidly, partly through internal growth and diversification and partly through acquisition. The company not only became a dominant player in international, marine, and aircraft radio services but also branched out to become a major manufacturer of radios and other electrical entertainment devices and the owner of a major broadcast radio network. In 1930, average annual employment at New Era Radio (NER) was 23,816. Roughly 60 percent of employees were in the manufacturing subsidiary; the remaining employees were distributed across eight other subsidiaries. The manufacturing part of the company is the focus of this case study.

The Organization and Administration
of Industrial Relations

The company has no centralized industrial relations function. Rather, oversight of industrial relations is subdivided among three vice presidents, in charge of factory operations, engineering, and office services, and they oversee the workforce in their respective areas. The auditor/comptroller is in charge of nonemployment matters, such as insurance, medical issues, and pensions. These executives set general policy; the implementation of labor policy is delegated down the line to division, department and section heads. The IRC report states, "The whole personnel program lacks co-ordination, cohesiveness, and balance."

The company's labor policies have not been specifically defined and codi-fied. The closest to a formal description of labor policies and practices at NER is a set of bulletins periodically issued by the vice president of manu-facturing to superintendents and department heads under his jurisdiction. These bulletins cover such things as hourly rates, work hours, vacation days, and job assignment. No written summary of the company's labor policies and practices is distributed to employees, the partial exception being a copy of the regulations of the beneficial association and a leaflet describing the plan for group life insurance. Without written standards and guidelines, nu-merous examples of waste and inequity appear. The report notes, for ex-ample, "It is not unusual to find employees of more than twenty years of service being laid-off, while newer employees are retained in service." A sec-ond example cited is the lack of definition of what constitutes "continuous service" with regard to preserving life insurance and pension benefits, with the result that some employees who are laid off and then brought back on reemployment are credited with continuous service and others are not.

The executives of the company are preoccupied with the production, sales, and finance sides of the business, partly due to the rapid growth of the company but also because of the rapidity of technical innovation, the high degree of competition in its product markets, and the tremendous instability in sales. The IRC report observes on this matter, "It may be said that major executive attention and emphasis have centered on operating problems to an almost complete exclusion, in some instances, of consideration of the human or personnel aspects of the problem."

One area of industrial relations that has received attention is the threat of unions. The IRC report speaks of "a feeling of . . . possible labor difficulties. Communistic literature has made its appearance [with] pleas to join the Metal Workers Industrial League." In response, the company placed under-cover men in the plants to keep officials informed of employee opinions and actions.

The result of the fragmented and neglected management of industrial re-lations is, in the words of the report, a "decided feeling of unrest and instability" and a failure "to build up that esprit de corps and maintenance of morale that is so essential." The report ends this section with the observation, "The crux of the entire labor situation resolves itself into a lack of personnel-mindedness on the part of several of the company's executives."

Employment

Matters relating to hiring, transfers, promotions, terminations, and employment records at NER are delegated to the vice presidents of manufacturing operations, engineering, and clerical services, as noted above.

The company has a centralized employment office for factory workers. The head of the employment office has the title labor supervisor, indicating a mid- to lower-level position in the management hierarchy. At peak employment times, the labor supervisor has twenty-two staff members reporting to him. They comprise the following personnel: interviewers (3); typists for records; beneficial, insurance, and filing clerks (6); clock number and assignment worker (1), payroll records keeper (1), and messenger (1). The number of personnel are cut back when employment declines. The employment office is a 50 foot by 90 foot space with no rooms or subdivisions, except a small room for physical examinations. Thus, job interviews, complaint handling, and other potentially private matters are conducted at desks set out in the open and within easy earshot of other people. In busy hiring periods the employment office is a scene of long lines snaking out the door, a multitude of people speaking at once, and frequent jostling and pushing.

Consumer purchase of radios exhibits a pronounced seasonal swing. Rather than stabilize production by building for inventory (partly because technological changes have made some parts obsolete in a matter of months), or using other stabilization methods (e.g., adding to the product line goods or services that could take up the slack in production capacity during slow times in radio sales), NER chooses to produce for immediate sale and ratchet employment and production up and down accordingly. Not all parts of the plant move in tandem, however, for the report notes that due to lack of production coordination "a group of operators on one operation in a section might be working overtime while another group on another operation in the same section would be temporarily laid-off."

From today's perspective, the result is a near-unbelievable cycle of hiring and firing. In 1930, for example, in March employment was at its minimum (6,058 workers) while in October (further into the Great Depression) it rose to a high (25,400 workers). The IRC report relates that employee numbers were cut from 13,000 to 5,700 in only three weeks in the fall of 1929 (after peak seasonal demand had passed) and then the following year was ramped up in the summer months of peak seasonal sales from 6,000 to 23,000 in a period of about two and one-half months. Not only was employment dramatically increased; so too were the daily and weekly hours of work. Overtime from one-third to one-half of regular work hours was common in some departments.

The company employed a larger-than-average number of female employees—39 percent in 1930—than most other manufacturing plants, made possible because much of the production work was light, semiskilled assembly. Not unexpectedly, seasonal hirings and layoffs were especially pronounced among this group. Also not surprising is that only 15 percent of the workforce had more than five years of service with the company, while the turnover rate varied from 200 to 500 percent across departments.

The IRC report gives this description of the hiring process during the boom period of summer 1930:

> During the period of increase the employment office was taken by storm, thousands of applicants extending in double lines around the block. Foot, motor and mounted police were necessary to maintain order. The machinery for interview, selection and placement could not function. . . . A hurried interview, as each applicant passed the desk of the interviewer, with the next in line pressing forward—a matter of a few minutes, and the applicant was hired or rejected. The employment office could function only superficially in selection; it was more a matter of simply hiring and "getting their record." . . . [In this situation] some of the "riffraff" of the labor market drifts into the plant.

Further causing problems is the fact that foremen frequently send names to the employment office of people they want approved for employment, with consequent dangers of nepotism and discrimination.

The IRC report only tangentially discusses the impact of this huge bulge in hiring on the production side of the business. At one place it notes that "overcrowding naturally resulted in the manufacturing buildings . . . [and] only seemed to add to the sense of confusion." Also no doubt causing large problems for the production heads was that 6 percent of the workforce was absent on a daily basis. The IRC report estimates that 2 percent of work time was lost due to absences and lateness.

Wages and Hours

Wages

Production workers are paid on an hourly basis, supplemented in most cases by a group bonus tied to section or department production. Production workers also get an overtime bonus of one and one-quarter base earnings and a night shift differential of 10 percent. Managerial, office, and supervisory personnel are generally paid on a salary basis. They qualify for no overtime, but unlike the production workers are paid in cases of missed work for lateness or sickness.

Average hourly and weekly earnings show very large disparity. Hourly rates for production workers range from 36 cents per hour to 96 cents for men and 32 cents to 48 cents for women. Even within a particular occupation or job category rates differed considerably. Hourly rates for males in radio assembly varied from 44 cents to 68 cents and varied from 40 cents to 60 cents for men in the shipping department. Company policy is to pay women at approximately two-thirds the rate of men, even for identical jobs.

Weekly earnings exhibit considerably greater variation, particularly over the course of the year. In metal manufacturing, for example, average weekly earnings for the entire year of 1930 was $20.88, bounded on one end by a minimum weekly earnings of $8.62 in December and a maximum weekly earnings of $28.52 in February. Other departments show similar variation. This variation in weekly earnings arose from a combination of stable hourly rates but large variation in hours worked, overtime pay, and production incentive bonus.

The production incentive bonus is based on the amount that actual output of a work group exceeds a standard level. The standard level is determined by time and motion study using experienced workers. The standard rate, once set, cannot without special exemption be revised downward for six months. Approximately two-thirds of production workers are on the bonus plan, and the size of the bonuses range across departments from 3 percent to 113 percent of the base rate.

The company assesses production workers a penalty for lateness. The deduction is one-quarter hour's pay for lateness of one to fifteen minutes, one-half hour's pay for sixteen to thirty minutes, and so on.

Hours

The normal work schedule for production workers is five days per week and nine and one-half hours per day. When a night shift is necessary to meet production demands, the shift lasts twelve hours. Office workers are on an eight-hour day.

Actual hours worked diverge considerably, however, from the normal level because of the large swings in production. In slack months, part-time work is common; in peak months weekly work hours can be sixty or more. In cabinetmaking, for example, weekly work hours varied from a low of eleven to a high of sixty in 1930.

Office and factory workers on a salary basis qualify for one week's paid vacation after six months of service and two weeks after twelve months of service. Hourly employees do not qualify for paid vacations. All workers get six paid holidays per year (New Year's Day, Memorial Day, the Fourth of July, Labor Day, Thanksgiving, and Christmas).

Training and Education

The only formal training offered at NER is in the engineering department. A small group of graduates specializing in engineering and the physical sciences are recruited from nearby universities and technical schools to work in the engineering department. In the first year they rotate through major operations of the company, spending two months in each to become familiar with the technology and production process; in the second year they choose two operational areas to specialize in and spend six months in each. The engineering department also offers an after-work course in the fundamentals of radio.

No formal training program is given for production workers. In the past, the company offered a soldering course for assembly workers, but this was discontinued. The rationale is that the radio assembly jobs have been so finely subdivided that even "green hands" can learn to do the tasks in a small amount of time. To coordinate the on-the-job training for production workers, the company has designated certain experienced employees to serve as "working group leaders." Each leader supervises ten workers and is responsible for showing them how to proficiently perform their job.

Accident Prevention

The company has no organized safety program and is at best a "one man" effort: the only person with official responsibility to conduct safety work is the safety engineer. The IRC report notes, however, that up to the previous year this person was employed in the accounting department. The creation of a post of safety engineer was partly due to a negative safety evaluation given the company by the state department of labor. This report led NER in the early part of 1930 to assign five men to the job of safety inspector, but so far little organized activity has taken place. In no area of the company are there safety teams, and the only educational or training work in safety is posting of bulletins issues by the National Safety Council.

Over the first nine months of 1930 NER reported 186 lost-time accidents in the production departments, including three deaths and twenty-eight partial permanent disabilities. The days lost totaled 28,961. The accident frequency rate was 12.71 (lost-time accidents per million work hours) and the severity rate was 1.98 (days lost per thousand work hours). The accident frequency rate at the company was more than twice the rate at twenty-nine other electrical appliance and machinery firms, while the severity rate was more than three times as high.

Medical Services

NER maintains a central medical dispensary in the main production facility and three branch dispensaries (first aid rooms) in other more distant buildings. The central facility is open twenty-four hours daily. The medical staff includes three doctors, ten registered nurses, and five clerks. The medical department handles all accidents and injuries sustained in the course of work. It is also responsible for administering physical examinations to all job applicants. Employees who become ill at work are given temporary treatment but then sent home for care by a family physician. Family members of employees do not qualify for medical services from the company. The total expense of the medical service department for the first nine months of 1930 was $13,749, or $.09 per $100 of the payroll and $1.29 per employee.

Group Life Insurance, the Beneficial Association, and Pensions

The company makes available to employees a group life insurance plan that covers both death and permanent disability. Employees with more than six months of continuous service are eligible to participate. Employees pay approximately 60 percent of the cost of the plan and the company pays the remainder. The cost to employees is 40 cents per month per $1,000 of insurance. Although the plan is said to be voluntary, all new employees are effectively required to participate. The average amount of insurance per employee is $1,840.

Employees can also obtain sickness and disability insurance through the company's cooperative beneficial association. Employees with more than one month of service can join, although membership is again de facto compulsory for new employees (they sign the application for membership as part of the employment process). An initial entrance fee of 50 cents is charged, followed by a monthly fee of 35 cents. The company contributes an amount equal to the amount contributed by employees per month. Payment for disability is $2 per day for a maximum of one hundred days; a lump sum death benefit of $250 is provided. Over the first nine months of 1930, the association paid out $31,684 on 473 disability cases ($67 per case) and $5,750 on 25 death cases.

From the date of its incorporation NER has had a pension plan for employees. But to the present time the provisions and administration of this plan have never been put in writing. Hence, considerable uncertainty attaches to the criteria used to determine eligibility (e.g., years of service, age) as well as important matters such as the definition of continuous years of service. Common practice to date has been to take the cases of potentially eligible employees and present them to the company president for decision. As of September 1930, forty-three men and two women receive pensions. The monthly payment is figured as 1.5 percent of the last ten years' average pay times years of service, with a maximum of $50 per month. Only in 1930 did the company lay aside money to fund future pensions.

Employee Services

In addition to the insurance and pension programs, NER provides a small number of other "service" benefits to employees. Food dispensaries serving sandwiches, desserts, and beverages are located in twenty-seven of the production facilities; cafeterias are provides for office employees and several dining rooms are available for higher-level managers and executives. The restaurant service operates at a small loss which the company covers.

Also listed as an employee service is a suggestion-box system. Suggestion boxes have been located at convenient points and employees are encouraged to submit their ideas. In the first ten months of 1930s, 258 suggestions were submitted, of which 31 were accepted. Accepted suggestions get a cash award. Twenty-six received the minimum of $5, three received $10, and one each received $25 and $50. About one-half of the suggestions related to fire and safety.

The company provides no formal or organized social or athletic activities for employees.

Case Study Summary

New Era Radio presents a fascinating paradox. On one hand, the company had within a few years come to be a technological leader in the consumer electronics industry and one of the nation's best known and most respected producers in this fast-growing and leading-edge sector. On the other hand, its human resource management system and practices were extremely backward, haphazard, and even chaotic. Evidently, competitive advantage and firm performance in this case were driven by factors located in the company's product market and production process (e.g., product innovation, new technology) and not from factors related to labor and HRM—at least outside a core group of engineers and scientists.

This case study also highlights certain conundrums concerning the modern definition and conceptualization of *strategic* human resource management. Since the company invested little in HRM and gave the "people" end of the business scant attention, one would be tempted to conclude that here is a classic case of nonstrategic HRM—that is, personnel management practiced in a low-level, tactical, administrative, reactive, and cost-focused manner. But the issue is not so clear cut. That is, perhaps the top executives made a judgment that the financial return on management time and company resources invested in other business areas (e.g., new product development, further acquisitions) far out-weighed the return from allocating the same scarce time and financial resources to improving HRM—even as backward and chaotic as the HRM system evidently was. Hence, from this perspective it could well have been an appropriate strategic decision to practice HRM in what appears to be a nonstrategic way.

The evidence provided in the IRC report does not permit a resolution of this puzzle. What is revealed, however, is an approach to producing products and employing people that to a modern observer is practically impossible to imagine for a company of this size and technological sophistication. The company rode a roller coaster tied to dramatic seasonal and cyclical swings in the demand for its principal product, which led in turn to equally dramatic swings in the demand for labor. As a consequence, employment ramped up and down within a single year by a factor of 300 and 400 percent, leading to crash hiring programs and lines of applicants around the block in some months and then a few months later mass layoffs. Here was a supply-and-demand model of employment in full force. Equally evident are some of the benefits and costs. On the benefit side, the company had little overhead expense for labor or HRM, enjoyed great flexibility in hiring and utilization of labor, avoided the costs of long-term employees (e.g., pensions, health insurance), and could quickly get rid of any poor performers or troublemakers. But this approach also had significant costs—larger hiring, training, and turnover cost; haphazard selection and placement of new employees; poor morale and little employee commitment/loyalty to the company; and a substantial element of arbitrary and unsystematic variation in HRM practices such as hiring, compensation, and discipline and discharge. The HRM challenge in this case study is to find ways to stabilize sales so greater stability, order and efficiency can be introduced into production and the management of labor.

13

HRM in the Industrial Heartland III

High-Beam Steel

This is the last of the six IRC case studies. High-Beam Steel, a medium-size multiplant producer of rolled steel sheeting and tubing, was widely recognized at the time as in the top echelon of companies regarding its HRM program and quality of employer-employee relations. This case study and the one at Top-Grade Oil (see chapter 8) are representative of companies at the top level of the industrial relations movement before the New Deal. This survey was completed at the very end of 1930.

Background

High Beam Steel (HBS) is a steel manufacturer specializing in specialty steel sheet. It is vertically integrated and operates coal mines, coking operations, and blast furnaces for the production of pig iron. HBS was one of the first to build a continuous strip mill for the production of steel sheet and by 1929 had become an industry leader in this segment of the business. It also produces various steel products, such as steel wheels and construction materials.

The company has major mines, mills, and fabrication facilities in seven cities in four contiguous states. Employee numbers in 1929 were approximately 11,000; by March 1930 they had declined to 9,771. HBS was incorporated in 1899 and had experienced steady growth and profits under its longtime (thirty-year) president and chairman of the board.

The Organization and Administration of Industrial Relations

The report provides a modest review of the history of the labor management practices and policies at HBS. It states that organized personnel services dated from 1911 when, on the completion of construction of a major new complex of mills and facilities, a centralized employment bureau and medical department were organized at that site. The employment bureau was reorganized as a department in 1916 and in 1923 it was placed under the newly created personnel service division.

In 1915 the office of the director of safety and labor was created, and safety and "mutual interest work" was centralized under this person's direction. The report notes, however, that the company had for many years been active in safety and accident prevention. The safety program was expanded in 1916 with the hiring of a full-time safety engineer, while in 1917 a new mutual interest department was created and a person hired to serve as director. In 1918 a training department was created in order to coordinate and manage the technical and general education programs, including the "High Beamization" classes first offered in 1916.

Until 1923 the heads of the various personnel service departments had reported directly to the company's general manager. In order to achieve better coordination of activities and delegation of decision making and responsibilities, the position of director of the personnel service division was created. The employment, medical, safety, training, mutual interest, and personnel records departments reported to this new director who, in turn, reported to the general manager.

The personnel service director and staff also serviced the company's other mills and facilities on an "as needed" advisory basis. In 1929, another reorganization was undertaken, the company's mills and facilities were grouped into four divisions, and a new personnel service department was created for each division. The director of personnel services for each division reported to the company director of personnel services.

In March 1930, HBS employed a total of 108 people in the various activities of the personnel services department. The breakdown of employment by function was: administration (9), employment (16), medical (31), safety and training (18), mutual interest (5), publications (3), personnel records (21), and insurance (5). The ratio of personnel staff to employment was approximately one to one hundred.

In 1929 the company spent $556,932 on personnel service programs and activities, or an amount of $49.53 per employee and $2.83 per $100 of payroll. A table shows a break down of personnel expenditures, as a percent of total expenditures, by major expenditure item for 1929. The figures are (in percents):

Personnel Service Administration: 6.6
Employment: 10.2

Medical: 18.1
Safety: 6.0
Training: 6.5
Group life insurance: 5.4
Workmen's compensation: 14.3
Personnel records: 5.2
Employee associations: 12.4
Mutual interest, employee magazines, and all other: 15.3

Of all expenditures, 14.3 percent were required by law (workmen's compensation) and the remainder was initiated voluntarily by the company. HBS also contributed $95,000 for "community affairs" in the various towns and cities it had facilities, but these were not counted as part of personnel services.

The IRC consultants state at the end of the section on organization and administration that HBS is distinguished by a long-running commitment to careful administration of personnel relations in its mills and plants and a general policy of fair dealing with employees. Although no specific written statement is given to employees regarding the company's labor policies and practices, there is a more general written statement entitled "High Beam Steel Policies" that describes the company's commitment to satisfying its customers, shareholders, and workers. The report does not reproduce this policy statement but cites an excerpt that states the company is committed to a "spirit of fairness, a square deal . . . a big broad view of every problem."

Employment

The total employee count at HBS in December 1930 was 10,002. This represents an increase over 1925 of 35 percent (net of one-time additions due to mergers and acquisitions). Employment has a distinct seasonal component, usually reaching a peak in mid- to late spring and a trough in mid- to late fall. The major cause is the seasonal pattern of demand for sheet steel by automobile manufacturers. From the peak month to the trough month, for example, the total payroll declines between 10–15 percent in a normal year. From May to December 1929, the drop was much steeper—41 percent, reflecting the onset of the Depression.

The report provides an age distribution of employees. The percent of total employment represented by employees of different age groups is as follows: 21 and under (8.1%); 21–35 (53.3%), 35–45 (23.9%); 45–60 (12.8%); and 60 and over (1.9%). Examined at a more disaggregated level, the greatest number of employees were in the age group 22–24, accounting for 14.8 of employment or slightly more than one out of seven employees. The work forces at the mines were the oldest (21.3 percent age 46 and over).

Only 3.8 percent of employees were women. All women were in office jobs.

More than two-thirds (69.1%) of employees were married; 28.4 percent were single; 1.6 percent were widowed; and 0.9 percent were divorced.

Employees were predominantly white (86.2%); 4.9 percent were black; and 8.9 percent were foreign-born.

The employees were distributed as follows by years of service with the company: under 1 (17.2%); 1–5 (45.8%); 6–10 (19.0%); 11–20 (15.4%); 21–30 (2.6%). Employees with 5 or fewer years of service were disproportionately employed in the mines. In the two coal mines only 24 percent of employees had more than 5 years of service, compared to 52 percent in the company's largest steel production facility.

In 1929 the company had an average of 11,008 employees. Total accessions were 7,305 (4,579 new hires, 1,450 reemployed, and 1,276 returned with continuous service). Total separations were 8,155 (5,492 voluntarily separated, 716 discharged, 1,341 laid off, 573 on leave of absence, and 33 dead). Roughly two-thirds of all separations were voluntary; in earlier years (1925–28) the figure was three-fourths, reflecting the large layoffs in late 1929. The annual turnover rate for the company was 74.1 percent. From 1925 to 1928 the yearly turnover rates were, respectively, 56.9 percent, 79.1 percent, 67.5 percent, and 59.2 percent. Historically, the turnover rate among the mine employees was substantially higher, but in the most recent years had declined to about the same level as the steel facilities. With regard to length of service, 68.8 percent of separations were for employees with less than one year of service, while only 9.4 percent were for employees with more than five years.

One reason for a high turnover rate is the operation of the company's labor reserve department. It is essentially an inventory supply of labor. The department, according to the IRC report, tends to carry an excess supply of labor to guard against unforeseen contingencies, leading to short-term employment for many of these men and reduced earnings. Even new college graduates are assigned to the labor reserve department, leading to very high turnover among them. The report concludes "the department's operations have clearly been unfair to workers."

Employee transfers between departments are arranged by the employment department. Ordinarily, employees are transferred rather than resort to layoff in one section of the works and hire of outsiders in another. In 1929, 4,555 transfers were made. HBS has a definite policy of filling jobs from within.

To aid in the selection of the right people for promotion, at the company's two largest works the personnel service supervisor keeps an up-to-date "good man" book for employees in supervisory, technical, sales, and other nonproduction positions. The book at the largest facility contained over nine hundred names of employees regarded as having potential for upgrading to a higher position. In addition to each person's name, the book contains information on education, age, length of service, religion, present job, and periodic comments on the person's performance and progress by his immediate superior.

In addition to the "good man" book, the company at the larger facilities also conducted a form of performance appraisal through periodic "labor audits." In these audits, the foreman of each department comes to the employment office and rates each of the employees under his supervision. The ratings are entirely subjective opinion on the part of the foreman and fall into four categories: above average, average, below average, and poor. Also recorded for each person is nationality, age, marital status, years of service, and physical disability. At one facility the audit also contained information on home ownership, number of family members, and related "economic status" factors.

No employment tests are used throughout the company, except in the hiring of apprentices for office employment. The consultants note, "the use of aptitude and ability tests is still in an experimental stage so far as general employment is concerned. However, in the selection of employees to become apprentices in the skilled trades sufficient work on tests has been done in many companies to recommend a thorough study of such tests by some members of the personnel service staff."

Terminations, Discharges, and Layoffs

Separations from the company are handled through the employment department. No written policy or guidelines exist on discharges and layoffs. Typically, the decision to discharge an employee, whether for lack of work, poor performance, or an infraction of company rules, is initiated by the foreman of the department. In the case of layoffs, length of service and job performance are used as criteria for allocating the job cuts among employees.

In the case of voluntary separations, each employee leaving the company must go to the employment department where an exit interview is done to determine the reasons for the separation. Then the employee picks up the last pay voucher. In the case of involuntary separations, the foreman makes the recommendation of whom to discharge but the employment department has the right of review for each case and authority to transfer the employee to another part of the company if deemed appropriate. This right is exercised in only a small number of cases.

Leaves of Absence and Continuous Service

An employee may be given a leave of absence for up to one month. Succeeding furloughs may be obtained at one month intervals at the discretion of the company. An employee disabled by sickness or accident, or laid off because of slack work, maintains an unbroken service record for up to one year. An employee who separates from the company for any reason also maintains an unbroken service record if rehired within one month. Also, the company transfers intact the service record of employees acquired from other companies through mergers and acquisitions. The company's policy prohibits using the granting of continuous service as a disciplinary device.

Employment Records and Reports

A formal system of employment records was started in 1918. This function is now carried out by an employment records section in the personnel services department. Staff members in the department collect and analyze the employment forms, records, and reports. In early 1930, twenty-six staff members were employed in the records section, or one per every 376 employees. The company uses twenty-five separate employment forms; twelve are used in the hiring process and thirteen for transfers, changes of pay, and job performance/history. One reason for the large number of forms is that most are done in three colors: white for white employees, pink for foreign-born employees, and blue for "colored" employees. A red "absence card" is also used—given to any employee absent more than two days, and stating that he must get approval of the medical department before returning to work. In addition to these records, each foreman completes a "force report" each day detailing the authorized number of people employed, the rate of pay for each person, the hours worked, and absences. Any employment above the authorized number must get the approval of the plant superintendent. These reports are collected, tabulated, and worked up into a monthly force report for each facility. To date no annual force report has been prepared. The IRC report characterizes the records' function as well-organized, detailed, cumbersome, overstaffed, and underutilized as an information source by company executives.

Wages and Hours

Wages

The report begins the chapter on wages and hours with a quotation from the "High Beam Steel Policies" statement. It reads,

> It is High Beam Steel's wage policy to pay for every class of service a standard of compensation as high as is current in competitive industries. . . . It is High Beam Steel's ambition to develop an organization of such spirit, loyalty and efficiency that it will be possible for individual members to earn and receive better compensation than if performing a similar service in other fields of effort.

The report next provides a brief overview of past wage policies. It states that prior to 1920 most employees were paid on an hourly basis, although tonnage rates were paid in some departments. In 1920 the issue of wage payment came to the fore when the company considered shifting from a twelve-hour day to an eight-hour day. In consultation with outside engineers, the company set up an Emerson bonus plan on new hourly wage rates. The new wage rates were approximately 20 percent higher than the old rates, with the intention that earnings of employees under the new plan would be at about the same level as under the old system. However, actual earnings began to considerably exceed the anticipated level as new equipment and processes were introduced. The company then discontinued the Emerson plan on most operations and adopted a pay scheme using fixed percentage bonuses, such that the base wage rate plus bonus approximated earnings in competing companies. (The bonus was paid as a fixed percentage rate of the base wage for all hours during which production was actually underway, such as in the operation of the open hearth furnaces.) This system was viewed as a temporary plan, however, and new engineering consultants were hired in 1928 to again revamp the wage system. In early 1930 a Bedaux incentive system was installed in several facilities, with the intention that after further study and adjustment the system would be extended to other plants.

As of March 1930, 56 percent of the employees at the three largest steel plants were paid a bonus or other incentive. The actual form of incentive pay was quite varied, however, including a fixed bonus, Emerson efficiency bonus, tonnage rate, Bedaux incentive rate, piece rates, and "other." Twelve percent of the employees in these plants were on a salary basis, while 32 percent were paid a straight hourly or daily rate.

The report states that as a result of the several revisions to the pay system, the absence of standardized job classifications, the complexity of several of the bonus systems, and lack of centralized company control over compensation, "there is a wide variation between plants as to hourly base rates and bonus systems, even for similar occupational classifications, [thus making] any comparison of rates between jobs or between the same named jobs at the several plants open to question." As an example, at one steel facility, oilers in the open hearth department received an hourly rate of 41 cents but 61 cents in the blooming and bar mill (daily earnings were narrower, however—$5.20 versus $5.61), while rates for millwright helpers in these two departments were 59 cents to 71 cents (with daily earnings of $6.37 and $6.00).

The employees hired for the labor reserve department are required to report for work to the department supervisor forty-five minutes before the change of a shift. Often more workers are available than are needed and the surplus workers are sent home with no compensation for their time spent at the plant. At the largest steel plant, the average number of employees in the labor reserve during 1929 was 210, and of those 25 percent on average did not obtain work. The average daily earnings of these men in the first half of 1929 was approximately $4.00.

This diversity of pay rates also made wage comparisons across companies difficult. The IRC consultants concluded the evidence indicated in general that HBS paid at least the going rates and in some cases was the highest paying. One force promoting wage standardization, albeit imperfectly, was that the company submitted a monthly report on rates per hour, earnings per turn, and other compensation data to the National Association of Sheet and Tin Plate Manufacturers. The association, in turn, through its labor bureau, submitted to reporting member companies a tabulation of rates by plants, showing by occupation the high, low, and average rates of earnings. The IRC report concludes, however, that in the absence of standard nomenclature these records are of doubtful usefulness.

The company did not pay extra compensation for overtime in the form of time and a half or double time. In general, the regular rate of pay was paid for overtime hours. For workers receiving the fixed bonus, the overtime rate of pay could actually be lower than for standard hours if the department's production process (e.g., the open hearth furnace) was not considered up and running with production during those extra hours.

Procedures for compensation of the approximately 1,500 salaried employees were also relatively nonformalized. No policy existed establishing minimum or maximum pay limits for salaried employees, nor was there any established procedure for performance appraisal. As a result, pay rates were largely established by department heads based on their personal assessment of each employee's value, contribution, and other factors. A certain measure of control and standardization was maintained, however, because the company's personnel service department collected and published on a monthly basis a mimeographed booklet containing the earnings and last salary increase of every salaried employee currently with the company. The booklets were supposed to be viewed only by the plant works manager and top company executives, but the IRC report notes that in practice the booklets circulated "quite freely" in the lower ranks of management and thus the salary information was widely known. A brief review of salaried pay rates showed wide variation among individual job classifications. For example, earnings rates varied from $60 to $100 per month for junior female clerks, $60 to $140 for junior male clerks, $90 to $175 per month for stenographers, $200 to $500 per month for sales engineers, $135 to $300 per month for draftsmen, and $125 to $305 per month for foremen.

Another feature of HBS's compensation plan was executive bonuses. The system of bonuses was started in 1906 when the four top executives shared in a percentage of the net annual profits. In subsequent years the plan was periodically revised to include a larger group of employees. As of 1929, 1,355 salaried employees received bonuses. They were divided into groups: the "special partner group" (e.g., superintendents, division and department heads, and their assistants), and all other salaried employees with one or more years of service. The former group (258) received four-fifths of the bonus pool (an average payout of $1,325 in 1929), distributed among individuals based on the determination of the company president and board of directors, while the latter group (1,097) received a payment (an average of $81) that was proportional to their years of service and salary level.

The report states that the average annual earnings of employees with the company in 1929 were $1,751. A break down by occupation is not provided.

Another aspect of compensation covered by the report is separation allowances. In early 1929 the company was faced with the problem of having to lay off approximately one-half of the 1,150 employees at its largest steel facility due to the introduction of a new continuous process of rolling steel sheets. This matter, along with the establishment of a revised wage scale, was discussed with each crew of the finishing mill department. A decision was made to provide a separation payment to all laid-off employees for whom other jobs in the company could not be found. Under the plan, employees with one or more years of service received half pay for as many months as they had years of service, up to a maximum of six months. A total of 515 employees received a separation allowance at an expense of $216,299.

Hours

HBS transitioned from a schedule of two twelve-hour shifts in most steel operations to three eight-hour shifts in early 1920. The general principle laid down by the company management was that the three shift schedule could be phased in only if it did not raise total labor cost. The report does not explicitly state whether this was accomplished, but it does note that over the succeeding several months employment increased 11 percent and production 15 percent.

In early 1930, the distribution of employees by hours worked per day was 8 hours (59%), 9 hours (2%), 10 hours (33%), 11 hours (3%), 12 hours (2%), and 13 hours (1%). The report notes, however, that weekly hours for many employees are still quite long because of extensive use of overtime and the continued prevalence of a seven-day workweek (with a double shift every two weeks as employees rotate from one shift to another). At that time 26 percent of employees worked a seven-day week, while 62 percent worked a six day week. The distribution of employees by weekly hours was: 56 hours (43%), 56–69 hours (48%), and 70+ hours (9%). Consideration was being given to eliminating the seven-day week, but again subject to the constraint that it not raise total labor cost.

All salaried employees qualify for a paid vacation. Employees in this group with six months' continuous service receive one week and those with one or more years of service receive two weeks. The annual bonus (previously described) is distributed prior to the annual vacation. Office employees are also given three paid holidays: Independence Day, Labor Day, and

Christmas. Hourly employees do not qualify for a paid vacation; they may, however, upon approval of the superintendent or foreman be granted a leave of absence of up to one month. The report does not indicate if they receive any paid holidays.

Training

The training chapter begins with another passage quoted from the "High Beam Steel Policies" statement. It commits the company to "build up and maintain a high grade, efficient, loyal, ambitious, aggressive, and successful working organization who thoroughly believe in their company, to whom work is a pleasure and extraordinary accomplishment and all-consuming ambition."

Organized training began at HBS in 1916 when instruction in the English language and in citizenship was provided for foreign-born employees. In 1918 a training department was established and a director of training hired at the company's main production complex. In 1927 training departments were established at the other facilities. That year 1,712 employees were enrolled in the numerous courses offered. In 1928 the company had ten full-time training instructors and more than three-dozen part-time instructors and staff. In 1929 the training department was combined with the safety department. At this time the training mission was also reoriented, with general educational classes downgraded and more emphasis given to a "foreman-manager" course and various courses in job/vocational training.

Prior to 1929 a series of training courses were put on for foremen, organized by a selected group of foremen known as the foremen's cabinet. The exact subjects are not described. A new training initiative started in 1929 was called the "foreman-manager" course. The broad aim of the course was to give the foremen a managerial viewpoint. The first course lasted six months and focused on the topic of prevention of waste. Subjects covered included waste of materials and supplies, waste of machinery and equipment, waste and cost of accidents and illnesses, and so on. Meetings were held once a month and led by the division superintendent. At each meeting the foremen received a 3″ x 5″ card, headed "Things to Check," which covered the discussion points of that meeting and which he was to take back to the department and use as a reminder and checklist. The meetings were held in the evening on the employees' time. The second six-month course focused on checking the foremen's progress in implementing the suggestions for waste prevention.

The other major area of instruction was "job training." In earlier years the company had offered a wide variety of general education courses. Examples include accounting, mathematics, business English, chemistry, economics, public speaking, and commercial law. Also included were the "High Beamization" classes, such as in writing and speaking the English language, and a cooperative arrangement allowing certain company men to take courses at two local colleges.

Particularly with the merger of the training and safety departments in 1929, these general education courses were reduced and more emphasis given to instruction and coursework that boosted worker efficiency and opportunities for advancement and promotion. Such courses had been available at the company for a number of years and, in the case of production workers, had often originated from the company's early safety work. That is, the safety program soon discovered that a major reason for accidents was that employees were unfamiliar with the operation of machines and processes. Examples of job-related courses offered at the company include welding, crane operation, galvanizing and pickling, electricity, open hearth practice, and cold rolling, as well as nonproduction skills such as drafting, stenography, and salesmanship. These courses are usually offered on the workers' time and are often led by the foreman or department supervisor and an experienced operator or technician.

The IRC report states that the training of new employees is considerably less thorough and well worked out. After being hired, the new employee is given a talk on safety and general plant regulations and policies. Once placed in a department, the new employee is usually assigned to an experienced worker whose duty is to teach him or her the new job.

The company also provided job training for certain specially skilled segments of the workforce. For example, it ran a small-scale apprentice training program for the skilled trades, such as for molders, pattern makers, bricklayers, and blacksmiths. The apprentice training period was usually four years. In 1929 only thirty-six apprentice positions were provided in the entire company (approximately one apprentice per trade per plant)—far less than necessary to provide an internal supply of labor for these skilled trades.

Another select area of job training was for salaried employees. Here, too, an apprentice program was in operation, largely for clerical and stenographic positions in the general office. The company offered apprentice positions to promising high school students in commercial or business education several months before graduation. These students would begin apprentice training after school (from 3:00 p.m. to 5:00 p.m. and on Saturday mornings) and then, after graduation, would start full-time work with a half day devoted to training and the other half of the day to practical office chores. During training they received $30 per month, and after successfully completing apprentice training of three to nine months they transitioned to a full-time position at a salary of $60.

A third apprentice training program was run for sales employees. The usual length of the sales apprenticeship was three months. During this period the apprentice was placed in various operating departments to learn the nature of the company's products and how they are made; was given instruction in metallurgy, interviewing, business letter writing, and sales techniques; and sent out to make calls with experienced salesmen.

In addition to all of the various training programs described to this point are several others. Each summer, for example, new supervisory personnel, apprentices, and college graduates attend a series of nine meetings that provide a broad introduction and overview of the history, organization, products, and operations of the company. Another source of training is provided at the weekly and monthly foremen's and superintendent's meetings where operational problems are reviewed and addressed. Also, the company's employee magazine carries articles of an educational and training nature, while pamphlets and notices are distributed to employees or posted on bulletin boards throughout the plants.

Safety

The report states that HBS has been a pioneer in industrial safety. The first formal organization for safety work was started in 1910, but even before this supervisors and plant superintendents were charged with accident prevention. In 1915 the company participated in the founding of the National Safety Council.

In 1910 a central safety committee and individual plant safety committees were formed. In 1915 the office of director of safety and labor was created and in 1917 a safety engineer was employed to coordinate safety work in all its phases. Later, departmental safety committees were created. As earlier mentioned, in 1929 the separate training and safety departments were merged and safety work of the company was directed by the supervisor of safety and training. Safety and training departments were also created at the individual plants and the largest mine.

Workmen's safety committees have been established at each plant and mine. These committees vary in size, membership, frequency of meeting, and other details, as is considered most practical for local conditions. Often they are organized along departmental lines and meet once a month. The committees make periodic inspections, check up on cleanliness and unsafe conditions, and make recommendations for safety improvement. They also investigate accidents and make recommendations for their prevention. The safety committees, according to the report, have on the whole "been active in following through and have, as a result of their activities, been instrumental in creating and sustaining an interest on the part of the entire working force in the safety work of the company."

The safety department and committees engage in a continuing program of safety education. The experience of the company is that the educational work must be varied and changed frequently to maintain and enlist the active interest of the workers. Toward this end, a wide range of activities and programs have been initiated: safety bulletins, safety rallies, interdepartmental and interplant safety contests, illustrated safety lectures to new employees, safety prizes and medals, safety parades, first aid training contests, safety outings and picnics, and the organization of safety clubs. The example cited as of "outstanding interest" is the annual award of the "Iron Man" safety trophy, awarded to the work group with the lowest number in accident frequency. Also noted is the fact that from 75 to 80 percent of the workforce has, as a result of contests and safety programs, received first aid training. One of the company's first aid teams in 1925 won the world first aid championship at the 1925 international meet in Springfield, Illinois.

All major and unusual minor accidents are fully investigated by the safety adviser in cooperation with the superintendent and foreman. A written report with photographs is prepared for plant mangers and foremen and photographs with a brief summary are posted on plant safety bulletin boards.

Safety work and accident prevention are continually covered in the company's employee magazine.

The company has invested capital funds in various forms of accident prevention. Guards are placed on power transmission equipment, machine drives, moving parts, and platforms; warning signals are placed on moving equipment; extra lighting is placed in dangerous areas; and cleanliness and orderliness are maintained.

Monthly accident and safety reports are prepared at all company facilities and circulated to management and safety committees.

The frequency rate of accidents at the company declined from 1925 to 1929, albeit less so for serious accidents. In 1925 there were 271 accidents in the company (5 fatal and 13 permanent partial impairment) for 17,322,702 hours worked; in 1929 there were 228 accidents (5 fatal and 34 permanent partial impairment) for 28,324,969 hours worked. Accident incidence and severity was most serious in the mines, accounting for three times as many accidents relative to man hours worked. Relative to approximately one hundred other steel companies, the accident frequency rate at this company was one-third below average, although the rate for severe accidents was one-third higher.

An indication of the effectiveness of organized safety work is indicated by the experience at one of the steel plants purchased by the company in 1927. In the first year of operation 153 accidents were recorded; two years later, after the company had time to implement its safety program, accidents declined to 20.

HBS also pays benefits to injured employees under the relevant state workmen's compensation law. The company self-insures in some states and participates in the state fund in others. In 1929 the company incurred a workmen's compensation liability of $94,678 and set aside $114,482 in reserve funds to cover these liabilities. The report states that the cost of workmen's compensation had doubled from 1926 to 1929, a function of a spike in 1927–28 in serious injuries and fatalities and the rapidly rising cost of insurance coverage for the mines. In 1929, the cost of workmen's compensation payments and premiums amounted to $6.92 per employee and 40 cents per $100 of the payroll.

Medical Service

The company's activity in the area of medical and health care goes back to 1911, when a full-time physician was hired to treat accident victims. Initially, employees were not treated for other health problems or nonwork accidents. Over time, the medical service offered by HBS was broadened to include treatment of sickness and injuries as long as the employee was actually on the job.

Employees not able to report for work are advised to consult a family physician. Although no home treatment is provided, the company checks up on the condition of the sick or injured person through periodic visits of the absentee recorder, visiting nurse, mutual interest counselor, or other person. An exception to this policy is made at the mines where home visits for family members are made due to lack of alternative medical care in the area.

In early 1930 the company employed thirty-one people in the medical service department, including seven doctors and nineteen nurses. Some of the nurses, to promote the work of the mutual interest department (discussed shortly), conduct home visits less for medical reasons and more to promote home sanitation, hygiene, and healthy diet. A total of 242,824 medical treatments were given in 1929.

The medical staff is also responsible for administering physical examinations for all job applicants. At the company's largest steel facility, 22 percent of applicants in 1929 were rejected on the basis of the physical exam. Physical exams (especially eye exams) are also required on an ongoing periodic basis for certain groups of workers in sensitive occupations (e.g., crane operators), and workers absent due to sickness or injury can only resume work if they first are certified fit by the medical department. To police this rule and keep tighter track of absences, a red card is substituted for an employee's time card in all cases where the worker is absent for more than two days and the employee cannot return to work until completing the medical exam and gaining back the regular time card. If the absence extends beyond a full pay period plus two days, the employee is dropped from the payroll.

On investigation the company determined in 1927 that days lost from sickness were thirty times greater than days lost from accidents. Accordingly, a good-health campaign was launched, including talks and publications for employees on sickness prevention and encouragement to seek periodic health checkups. In the largest steel facility sick days in 1929 (19,713) were nearly one-third lower than in 1927, suggesting a fair degree of success.

In 1929 the cost of medical services per employee was $8.80 and the cost per $100 of payroll was 54 cents.

Group Life Insurance

The company initiated a group life insurance plan for employees in 1917. Through a plan purchased from the Equitable Life Insurance Company, all employees with one or more years of service were covered by death insurance equal to one-half year's wage or salary income but not to exceed $1,000. The plan was noncontributory in that the entire cost was paid by the company. In 1920 the plan was liberalized to cover total and permanent disability before age sixty. In 1925 the plan was again liberalized to increase the death benefit to a minimum of $1,000 and a maximum of $5,000. Also, employees were given the opportunity to buy supplemental life insurance at their expense but at a reduced group rate with a modest company contribution. In 1929 a further revision was made to allow approximately thirty-five of the highest ranking executives and officers of the company to purchase supplemental life insurance up to a maximum of $20,000. Although not formalized as official policy, the company on an informal basis also provided group insurance to superannuated employees on the "idle time" payroll.

From 1917 to 1929 claims were paid on 405 cases composed of 357 benefit payments for death and 48 for permanent disability. The average indemnity paid for these cases was $1,653. In 1929, the net cost of the group insurance to the company was $29,956, or $2.66 per employee and 15 cents per $100 of payroll.

The report notes that while the company's plan is relatively liberal by industry standards it does contain one defect: The company's policy statement claims that the company paid the full cost of the noncontributory part of the group insurance program. In fact, the premiums paid by the employees for the supplemental portion of group insurance (collected by the company) exceeded the cost of the insurance and the surplus revenue was used to offset part of the expense of the noncontributory plan.

The Mutual Benefit Association

One of the first employee activities undertaken by HBS was organization of an employees' mutual benefit association, started in 1903. The association provides various kinds of sickness and death benefits to members. No pension plan for employees is provided either through the Association or directly by the company. (However, the company informally provides modest monthly payments as part of an "Idle Time Payroll" to a small number of superannuated employees—fourteen in number in 1930—who were deemed particularly needy or worthy.)

In 1914 the association merged with the High Beam Steel Social and Athletic Club (started in 1913) and became formally known as the High Beam Steel Association. Since then all of the company's social and athletic activities have been developed and administered through this association. As additional properties and facilities were acquired or built, mutual benefit associations were also established there.

All employees are eligible for membership in the local benefits association. Membership is practically compulsory for new employees, who sign an application form at the time of hire. At one plant African American employees are not allowed to join, but this restriction is absent at other plants and is in the process of being removed at the one. The management of the associations is vested in a board of directors elected by the members, with day-to-day administration done by a full-time or part-time secretary-treasurer.

The initiation fee for members is 1 dollar. Monthly dues range from 50 cents to 1 dollar per month. The company also contributes 50 cents per member per month, devoted to subsidizing the athletic and social portion of the association's program.

Members receive two kinds of benefit payments: for sickness and non-occupational disability and for death. The disability payment varies among local associations, but at the largest is $9 per week for white men and $6 per week for women and colored workers. Benefits are payable after one week of disability for a maximum of twenty-six weeks. Death benefits also vary among the associations, but at the largest local association range from $100 to $150 for women and African American workers (depending on years of service) to $150 to $200 for white men.

As indicated, the association also oversees a wide array of social and athletic activities. The social affairs include dances, card parties, "smokers," dramatic plays, minstrel shows, orchestra concerts, choral society presentations, and Christmas, Halloween, and other parties. Outdoors there have been picnics, safety field days, band concerts, and carnivals.

The outstanding social activities include the High Beam Steel band, the [X] town "Friday Nights," and the "Little Theater." The band gradually grew until in 1929 it included sixty-five people, composed one-half by employees and one-half by professional musicians. It has been rated as among the top three such bands in the nation and plays at a variety of local events and venues throughout the year. The company directly subsidizes one-third of the cost. The "Friday Nights" are events organized in the community of the largest steel facility and feature various amateur theatricals, vaudeville acts, and (increasingly) movies. The "Little Theater" is composed of about 180 active members from employees and their families, directed by a professional actor, who stage fifteen or more plays over the course of a year.

Outdoor and athletic activities include baseball, football, basketball, tennis, track, bowling, pool, boxing, wrestling, and other sports. These activities are participated in by large groups of employees, particularly when organized for interdepartmental or interplant tournaments. All sports are conducted on an amateur basis and limited to company employees, except football and baseball which use semi-professional teams (including college stars).

All of the local associations commingle funds for the benefit programs and social/athletic programs. In recent years the associations have used an increasingly larger share of revenues to finance social and athletic activities, such as the band and baseball teams. This practice has left the funds of the associations inadequate on an actuarial basis to fund future projected disability and death payments. Indeed, three of the local associations ran deficits in 1929.

Employee Savings and Investment

The company since 1918 has had an employee stock ownership plan. For the first decade little effort was made to promote stock purchase among the rank and file. As a result, participation was small (an average of three hundred subscribers) and largely limited to the salaried employees. The stock was offered at slightly below market price and was available to all employees with more than one year's service. Employees leaving HBS forfeited all dividends, capital gains, and company contributions, but received back their initial purchase price plus 6 percent interest.

The stock price showed marked appreciation between 1918 and 1928 (from $23 to $80 a share), giving employee stockholders a very good return on their investment. In 1929 the company decided to launch a campaign to extend stock ownership to a much larger portion of the rank and file. As a result, 1,924 new subscribers bought shares under the stock ownership plan. More than one-half of the new subscribers purchased five or fewer shares per person. With the onset of depression in late 1929, the stock price of the company fell significantly below the purchase price, causing 266 new subscribers to cancel their purchases.

HBS does not have a credit union or company savings plan for employees. It has cooperated with local banks, however, so that they have been able to set up branch offices near the company's main plant sites in order that employees have relatively easy access to financial services.

The report states that a number of employees have difficulty managing their financial affairs, illustrated by the fact that in 1929 at its largest facility 910 garnishments were served upon 492 employees.

Mutual Interest

The company has created a "mutual interest section" in the personnel service department at its two largest production facilities. Mutual interest work at the other plants is carried out by a company nurse or absentee recorder.

According to the consulting report, "The objective of the members of the mutual interest sections as stated in High Beam Steel policies has been to slip 'quietly into the homes and lives of our people in times of trouble [but avoid] all aspects of social uplift, or philanthropy, or of meddlesome intrusion into home life or private affairs." It then quotes the company's policy statement: "Mutual interest is the 'manganese' that binds a group of men and women together in every sort of effort."

One area of activity of the mutual interest section is employees' financial problems. New employees at several of the plants are frequently from the backcountry mountain districts and have little or no experience in the handling of money, with barter having been the previous method of exchange. The report states, "Plant wages seem like fortunes to these people and frequently extravagant purchases are made from local merchants who advance easy credit." It goes on to note, "In this situation the mutual interest section constantly faces the problem of being used as a collection agency by the creditors or of subjecting employees to garnishment." To avoid garnishment, the mutual interest counselors endeavor to work out with the employee a plan of payment, although "[f]requently employees' financial affairs are so involved. . . . That the only agency from which the employee can secure funds is one of the questionable loan companies, which charge exorbitant rates of interest."

Another activity of the mutual interest section is to give legal counsel and assistance to employees. Legal help in purchasing a home is one example.

The mutual interest section also keeps in close contact with personal events and happenings of employees and their families. The report states, "Intimate contact is maintained with the Red Cross visiting nurses and civic and charity organizations and the facilities of these organizations are frequently enlisted for High Beam employees. Contact is made with foremen, superintendents, medical departments and other sources of information both within and without the plant in order to keep closely in touch with employees' happenings. Newspapers are scanned for reports of employees." With this information, the mutual interest counselors visit families in which an employee death has occurred and extend the company's assistance and advice. Friendly calls are made on sick or injured employees; flowers are sent by the company in the case of the death of a family member; help is provided in making funeral arrangements; and group insurance and mutual benefit payments are delivered. Flowers are also sent to mothers of employees at the time of a new birth of a child, while counselors endeavor to resolve marital disputes and difficulties.

The mutual interest section also allocates and supervises the land made available to employees for family gardens. At the largest facility thirty-six acres of land adjacent to the mill are divided into 260 garden plots and plowed and harrowed by the company for employee use.

Each mutual interest section has a nurse that visits employees and their families. This nurse is not affiliated with the medical department and does not report to the company doctors. Her job is to maintain close contact

with local civic, health and charity organizations and render aid and counsel to those employees and families in times of injury, death, or personal
hardship. They also coordinate the company's Christmas donations of
clothing, shoes, and coal to needy employees.

Each facility of the company has a person who serves as the absentee recorder. In one plant the absentee recorder reports to the employment department, but in the others this person is a member of the mutual interest section. Each morning the time cards of all employees who have missed a second
turn are taken from the time card rack and replaced with a "red ticket." The
absentee recorder investigates these cases by making personal visits to the
employee's home and then writes up a report on the cause of the absence to
the foreman and director of the mutual interest section. The observations of
the absentee recorder are included in the employee's personnel record and
are used for follow-up work by the mutual interest counselors, mutual interest nurse, and medical supervisor.

Case Study Summary

Two aspects of this case study stand out. The first is that it provides an
interesting portrait of the evolution of HRM practices at one particular
company over roughly a two-decade period. The history of High Beam
Steel reveals that the HRM function did not suddenly appear one year but
slowly broadened and deepened with incremental additions and expansions.
Thus, the first formal HRM activity—a centralized employment office at
one mill—began in 1911, followed over the years by additions such as a
safety engineer, a training department, a centralized personnel services division, a mutual benefits association, and an employee stock ownership
plan. By the late 1920s all of these additional programs and activities cu-
mulated into one of the leading HRM programs in the steel industry.

The High Beam Steel case, along with that of Top-Grade Oil, illustrates a
second important point regarding the early history of HRM. A popular ste-
reotype is that HRM in this period was a grab bag of low-level administrative functions lacking strategic importance or alignment. While this may be
an accurate representation for many companies of this era, it is not so for
leading organizations such as HBS. According to the IRC report, the top
company executives at HBS gave considerable attention and emphasis to
employees and employee relations. They also "walked the talk" by spending
more than a half million dollars per year (almost $3 of every $100 of the
payroll) in the late 1920s on employee service activities/programs and employed over one hundred HRM managers and staff to administer them.
Further, the HRM department was responsible for an extensive, wide-
ranging set of activities spanning nearly all the traditional personnel sub-
functions (e.g., hiring, training, compensation, safety, benefits, employee re-

lations). HRM at companies such as HBS, therefore, was more significant and broad-based than simply a record-keeping and administrative function whose chief responsibility was getting out the paychecks and organizing company picnics. The importance of HRM should not be overemphasized, but neither should it be overly minimized.

14

The Case Studies

Insights and Lessons Learned

The fifteen case studies presented here provide a particularly detailed and in-depth portrait of how American firms in the pre–New Deal era practiced labor management and employee relations. The detail cannot be repeated here, but in this concluding chapter I think it is useful to draw out what appear to me to be the most important insights and lessons learned.

Work Life and HRM Have Come a Long Way

A person reading these case studies has to walk away sobered by the harsh, dangerous, and insecure work world that tens of millions of Americans lived in a century ago and the primitive and often wasteful and unjust methods of labor management. If we compare the conditions, treatment, and management practices at most companies today with those at the companies examined in this book, nearly all of us will be greatly impressed with how far the work world has progressed and how fortunate we are to live now and not then. Yes, there are still today many dangerous, low-paying, and unpleasant jobs in advanced countries such as the United States, but in most cases the worst jobs in the early twenty-first century are better than the average type of job facing the mass of blue-collar manual workers in the early twentieth century in this nation's factories, mills, and mines. If instead of looking at today's worst jobs we focus on the top end of job opportunities, most likely the pay, benefits, conditions and opportunities are beyond the imagination of even our best-off forebears circa 1900. To better appreciate this leap, I suggest closing your eyes and contemplating for just a few moments what it would be like to swing a hammer all day on a track section gang of the Chicago, Burlington, and Quincy Railroad, to tend a row of looms in Oscar Elsas's hot and lint-filled Fulton Bag and Cotton Mills (and then spending the night in his dilapidated company housing sharing two or three rooms with another family), or to work a twelve-hour shift seven days a week in front of a blast furnace belching flaming molten metal—in each case knowing that this job is yours only for the day and if you get hurt, sick, or fired you and your family are quickly staring destitution in the face. Likewise, one might contemplate these common features of labor management practices back then: hiring people from a milling crowd of job seekers standing outside the factory gates at dawn; allowing foremen to shout and swear at people to get them to work harder, a pay system where people standing next to each other doing the same job get very different rates; a job assignment process in which friends, relatives, and fellow countrymen of the boss get the best work and are the last to be laid off; and a governance system where people are routinely fired for the most petty and arbitrary of reasons. Surely the "old days" were actually not very good for most working people, and equally surely labor management practices at most companies today are vastly better than a century ago.

The HRM Transformation

Another thing that stands out clearly from the history of HRM is that its development over the last 140 years—that is, from the early 1870s when the American economy first began in earnest to shift from an agricultural to an industrial focus—was not a smooth, linear trend. Most certainly a major break in human resource management's evolutionary development occurred in the 1930s when the Great Depression and New Deal ushered in the era of collective bargaining and mass unionization of industry; another major if more drawn-out and less climactic break also occurred in the 1980s and '90s as the New Deal collective bargaining system fragmented and retreated in many former strongholds. At least as I see it, however, neither of these represents the most important and profound change point in HRM history. This honor goes to the short period of time bracketing World War I. Here was a paradigm shift so sharp and fundamental that it qualifies as a true *transformation*.

Before 1915, all of the companies in our case studies, and practically in the entire nation, practiced the *traditional* HRM paradigm. The core features of the traditional paradigm are heavy reliance on the external labor market and supply and demand to recruit, price, motivate, and train labor (particularly labor below the skilled craft or managerial level); lack of a functionalized HRM department; HRM policy formulation and implementation by various levels of line management with substantial decentralization and delegation to foremen and department heads; near complete absence of scientific or professional methods of labor management, including next-to-no written policies or guidelines; a highly autocratic regime of workforce direction, discipline, and discharge, sometimes exercised with paternalism and a veneer of humanity but more often with a heavy and insensitive hand; and a hardball strategy of no accommodation to unions. This model was practiced in its most positive version at the Baldwin Locomotive Works and in its most negative version at the Fulton Bag and Cotton Mills.

During the World War I years a new paradigm of HRM—what might be called the *modern* model—first appeared in a small number of pioneering companies in an integrated and recognizable form. Then, in the 1920s, the modern paradigm spread and further developed, becoming the labor management core of the firms in the welfare capitalism movement. The companies that most clearly represent the modern model in our case studies are the Top-Grade Oil Company and the Western Electric subsidiary of AT&T (briefly described in Hugh Adam's mini case study in chapter 1). Also representative of the modern paradigm in its initial phase are the Ford Motor Company (up to about 1920) and High-Beam Steel. The core features of the modern HRM paradigm are creation of an internal labor market in which employees above the entry level are to some significant degree buffered from the short-run vagaries of the external labor market and forces of demand and supply; replacement of "hire and fire" methods with a measure of job security and internal advancement; establishment of a functionalized HRM department with specialized personnel staff charged with supervising and administering labor management; creation of an explicit corporate labor policy that outlines the company's philosophy and approach to labor management and employee relations; development of a plethora of scientifically guided and expertly designed personnel practices and programs, such as job analysis programs, wage classification systems, performance appraisal instruments; and a "union substitution" approach where organized labor is avoided by eliminating the grievances and dissatisfactions that drive workers to want unions.

Only a distinct minority of companies—albeit containing many of the largest and most visible members of corporate America—put in place during the 1920s a reasonably complete version of the modern HRM model. Many other companies, including relatively large companies such as Mega-Watt Light and Power and New Era Radio, stayed with a version of the traditional model throughout the 1920s. Then, as described in *Managing the Human Factor*, as the Great Depression worsened and deepened in the early 1930s many advanced HRM firms had to severely pare back or even largely abandon the modern model and go back to traditional methods of hire and fire, foremen in control, and driving workers through intimidation and threat of job loss. Following on this debacle was the advent of the New Deal, the mass unionization of industry, and the near demise of welfare capitalism and the 1920s version of advanced nonunion HRM.

Some academic writers portray the modern HRM/welfare capitalism model of the 1920s as a short-lived, unstable, and idiosyncratic movement that owed its existence largely to union avoidance objectives.[1] Others, in a somewhat similar vein, portray the "natural" or "base line" model of American labor management as the collective bargaining model of "joint governance" that arose in the 1930s and dominated the economy until the late 1970s.[2] In their account, the fundamental transformation in HRM only occurred in the 1970s and '80s with the birth of the modern (and largely nonunion) "high performance" workplace.

Neither of these accounts, in my opinion, is an accurate portrayal of historical trends and developments. I call the new HRM paradigm of the 1920s the "modern" model precisely because it looks so similar in broad outline to the way HRM is organized and practiced in medium-large firms of the last twenty to thirty years. In support of this claim, I ask the reader to take the HRM program at Top-Grade Oil circa 1925 and judge whether (and to what degree) it more closely resembles the practice of HRM fifty years earlier (1875) or fifty years later (1975). Surely the resemblance is infinitely closer to the modern period. The same transformation is also evident in other dimensions of production, such as a comparison of how cars were manufactured at Ford before 1915 and after 1920—suggesting that labor management and nearly all other aspects of modern industry passed through a major inflection point at this period coincident with and no doubt due to the advent of modern mass production and scientific management.

It is indisputable, of course, that HRM today is organized and practiced in a number of ways that are substantially different from those of the HRM model of the 1920s—just as is car manufacturing at Ford. Further, under the pressures of globalization, more rapid technological change, and the incessant demand of Wall Street for higher earnings, there is some discernible movement among a number of companies toward a more externalized version of HRM that has clear antecedents in the traditional pre–World War I model.[3] Nonetheless, I assert that in terms of the broad organization and practice of HRM the model Top-Grade Oil and other leading welfare capitalist firms put in place in the 1920s is clearly and unarguably the lineal forebear of the model of HRM that is practiced today in the bulk of medium- to large-size American firms and government/nonprofit organizations.[4]

If accepted, this conclusion implies that the fundamental period of HRM transformation—the paradigm shift point—is indeed around the World War I years. In this interpretation, the mass unionization of the 1930s to 1970s is not the hypothesized "base line" or "natural" model of American industrial relations, as some researchers maintain, but a largely unique and unexpected event caused by a closely joined series of large one-time "shocks" (the Depression, the New Deal, World War II, etc.). These shocks knocked the United States far off the evolutionary trend line of HRM development and only over the course of the following half century did it slowly work back (in academic jargon, a "regression to the mean").[5]

Viewed this way, the advanced nonunion HRM system in the leading edge of "high performance" firms that emerged in the 1970s and proliferated over the next two to three decades is not an entirely new management idea and development, nor did it originate de novo (as frequently portrayed) in post–World War II Japan. Rather, the late-twentieth-century high-performance HRM system is more accurately seen as a return to and take-up of the basic principles and ideas that formed the core of the modern HRM model that emerged in America in the World War I years and then broadened and further developed in the advanced welfare capitalist firms of the 1920s. It was this model that Japanese engineers and businessmen came to witness in operation at Ford and other companies in the 1920s, which they took back to Japan and further developed and refined, and which they then reexported to America in the 1980s as part of Japanese management.[6] As evidence, consider the common principles and ideas that underlie both the welfare capitalist HRM model and the HRM component of the modern high performance work system (HPWS): a human (not commodity) conception of labor, development of a unity of interest employment relationship, viewing workers as a form of long-lasting and productive human capital, the importance of fair wages and job security, a mutual-gain form of rewards, and provision of due process in dispute resolution—all built on a foundation of employee participation and voice, called *employee representation* in the 1920s and *employee involvement* in the 1990s.[7]

Before moving on, another side of the HRM transformation also needs acknowledgment. It is the quantitatively larger if decidedly less glamorous side of the story. For every welfare capitalist firm with a transformed HRM function there were dozens and even hundreds of other companies in the 1920s that largely did labor management with a not-much-changed version of the traditional model. We see this in the case studies, per the examples of New Era Radio, Mega-Watt Light and Power, and Great Eastern Coal. The end of open immigration in the early 1920s, by reducing the supply of low-skilled and foreign-born labor, helped reduce the worst features of the prewar traditional model, including the drive system and twelve-hour days. But over half of the industrial workforce continued to work in firms where employment conditions were heavily exposed to short-run market forces, the HRM function had no semblance of professionalization or formalization, and work direction, discipline, and discharge were still practiced in the old-fashioned way. Not surprisingly, when the wave of union organizing started in 1933 it was in industries such as coal mining, textiles, and apparel where the traditional HRM model still held full sway.

Just as the advanced HRM programs of the welfare capitalist firms of the 1920s are mirrored in the similarly advanced HRM systems of companies in today's Fortune 500, so too are the traditional labor management practices of thousands of firms in the low-end and "secondary" parts of the nation's twenty-first-century economy. Examples include fish and poultry processing plants, low-budget hotels and restaurants, and large segments of the service industry. In terms of fundamental models and principles, therefore, the HRM transformation bracketing the World War I years set the stage for a major paradigm shift that still continues to evolve today—albeit largely for one portion of the economy and workforce. This bifurcation, unfortunately, is not always sufficiently acknowledged in many contemporary accounts of modern HRM, particularly those concerning strategic HRM and the high-performance workplace.

The Firm's Most Important HRM Question: The "Hired Hand" or the "Human Resource" Approach?

I have titled this book *Hired Hands or Human Resources?* because it pinpoints the most fundamental strategic issue in the theory and practice of labor management. All firms featured in the case studies presented here, as well as every firm that has ever operated in a market-based economy, have two things in common—first, production can only go forward if they have workers who provide labor and, second, their survival requires that they utilize the labor in a way that is (relatively) efficient and yields at least the minimum necessary level of profit. As is abundantly clear from these case studies, there is no obvious "one best way" to accomplish these two HRM imperatives; rather, the owners of firms (and their hired executives) both past and present obtain labor and utilize it in many different ways and with numerous permutations—often successfully but sometimes not. It is useful to think about the different patterns of HRM practices at companies, such as Endicott-Johnson, Ford, Great Eastern Coal, and New Era Radio in our case studies, as representing distinct (but often overlapping) *employment systems* (ES). A goal of HRM theory and research is to explain why firms adopt different employment systems.[8] The answers are numerous, but one consideration, I assert, overshadows and dominates all others. This consideration is the degree to which labor is treated as a *short-term commodity input* (the "hired hand" approach) versus a *longer-term human capital asset* (the "human resource" approach).

The distinction between labor as a hired hand and a human resource is necessarily a large generalization since neither ideal type stands alone in the real world; rather, the two ideal types represent opposite ends of a continuum. Further, some firms use both models but for different groups of employees; likewise, the models are implemented in different ways depending on firm size and other characteristics. Nevertheless, the hired hand versus human resource distinction is fundamental to explaining why the ES at, say, Endicott-Johnson or Microsoft is so different from others, such as at Great Eastern Coal or McDonald's. Let's examine this further.

Consider first the hired hand strategy. Here employees are viewed as akin to other short-run production inputs, such as fuel oil or rented warehouse space, and the path to maximum profit is to be an expert buyer of labor (the best quality at the lowest price), to efficiently and fully utilize the labor input, and then cease buying (or switch to another supplier) when the input is no longer economical or needed for production. This approach recognizes that labor comes packaged in a human being, but the human side is less important because (for example) the labor is relatively unskilled, the jobs are routine, many unemployed workers want the jobs, the technology of production allows management to control the pace of work, or social and ethical attitudes are not very advanced.

When it comes to HRM, the hired hand strategy has several common features: considerable exposure to the external labor market and substantial sensitivity to the pressures of demand and supply; a stronger "instrumental" and "contract" orientation where both employer and worker look at their relationship in terms of a largely self-interested "what's in it for me?" and "buy low/sell high" mentality; a package of wages, benefits, work conditions, and treatment from management that range from average to minimal, and a management perspective that regards employees as a tactical (nonstrategic) element in business success and the labor input as a short-run cost to be minimized. As a consequence, the employment relation tends to have greater separation of interests between employer and employee; a work climate with greater apathy, noncooperation, and tension; and greater likelihood of the workers seeking union representation (or court litigation). Similarly, in this model the HRM function plays a largely control, administrative, and union avoidance/containment function; generally lacks much strategic importance or input; is mostly or even completely performed by executives at the policy level and line managers at the implementation level; and tends as a functional activity to have an unexciting "dead end" and "dead wood" feel in the organization. In this model a strategic decision is taken to treat labor and HRM nonstrategically, as doing so promotes more profit than other approaches.

The second approach to managing labor is the *human resource* strategy. Here employees are viewed more as a form of human capital and a long-term investment item that complements the company's investment in physical capital. Similar to expensive machines or new product research, firms devote considerable time and money to their labor input, with the idea that the profit payoff comes much less from holding down the direct short-term money outlay on labor (although this remains important) and much more from obtaining superior long-run returns in productivity from greater work effort, deeper cooperation, higher quality and innovation, and improved organizational citizenship behavior. In this model the human dimension of labor takes on much larger significance since distinctly human performance features, such as work motivation, organizational morale, trust, leadership, and quality and creativity are key ingredients to the superior performance of the human capital. For this reason, it makes sense to create an internal labor market that partially buffers employees from short-run market pressures, provides above-market wages to get the best employees, includes long-term compensation items (e.g., stock purchase plans, profit sharing) to link employee performance to long-run company success, invests in considerable employee training, makes available formal channels for employee participation and voice, and devotes considerable attention to fair treatment and good conditions for employees.

The human resource strategy also has several common HRM features. Since the employment relationship is longer term and has a greater element of mutual gain, the interests of employer and employee tend to be more united, the employees have greater loyalty and commitment to the organization, and the climate of cooperation and mutual gain makes employees much more satisfied with their jobs and considerably less likely to join unions or engage in absenteeism, shirking, or numerous other costly and divisive behaviors. The human resource strategy requires, therefore, considerable management attention to labor administration and employee relations, given the substantial investment of time and resources required to create the feelings of goodwill and esprit d'corps that are the key ingredients to the success of the model—and that can also be so easily and quickly damaged by ill-considered or poorly executed management decisions. Since labor is an important source of competitive advantage, firms are naturally led to take a strategic focus toward labor and carefully think about how labor links up with the other parts of their business strategy. Similarly, although a human resource strategy can be successfully performed without a functionalized HRM department—and even without formalized personnel policies or written guidelines of any kind (e.g., that of the Baldwin Locomotive Works), the company's large investment in labor and labor's strategic importance to profitability means that employees are treated well to the point of being akin to "junior partners" in the enterprise. Particularly in large, modern companies the careful formulation and practice of labor management is supervised and implemented through a highly developed and professionally staffed HRM department.

The fifteen case studies featured in this book represent a number of distinct employment systems; in fact, at a detailed level of analysis each one is unique to itself. The question posed earlier now returns—that is, amid this diversity can we nonetheless identify distinct ES forms and explain why firms chose to adopt one rather than another? The answer, I think, is yes to both parts of this question. As we think about a spectrum of employment systems, we have now identified the two end points. One end point is the pure *external labor market* (ELM) model—called here the "hired hand" approach; the other end point is the pure *internal labor market* (ILM) model—identified here as the "human resource" approach. My claim is that firms most closely following the ELM (hired hand) model will have an ES with all of the distinctive component parts and characteristics described above, while firms most closely following the ILM (human resource) model will have an ES with the diametrically opposite component parts and features, as also described above. Among these fifteen case studies, firms such as New Era Radio, Great Eastern Coal, Pullman Palace Car, and Fulton Bag and Cotton Mills appear to most closely approximate the ELM endpoint, while Top-Grade Oil, Baldwin, Endicott-Johnson, and Filene's most closely approximate the ILM model. The companies near the ELM pole, in turn, had adversarial employee relations, very high employee turnover, stunted HRM functions, and very skimpy wages, benefits, and conditions; the companies near the ILM pole had the opposite. And then, of course, there are firms interspersed between the two poles, such as U.S. Steel, Mega-Watt Light and Power, and United Steel and Coal, that combined parts of the ELM (hired hand) and ILM (human resource) models.

The modern management literature recognizes a distinction akin to the hired hand versus human resource models made here. Typically, the labels attached to the two models are, in the former case, *personnel management* and *industrial relations* and, in the latter case, human resource management and strategic human resource management (SHRM).[9] PIR is presented as the "old" model of labor management (e.g., pre-1970s) and HRM/SHRM are presented as the "new" or "modern" models (post-1970). An insight of these historical case studies is that this typology is highly inaccurate. Companies (and academic thinkers) did not suddenly wake up in the 1970s and realize that a human resource strategy can in some situations be a successful path to profits and competitive advantage, as this insight was both articulated and practiced a century ago—albeit in a sometimes different idiom and method than is common today. The examples of Baldwin, Filene's, Endicott-Johnson and Top-Grade Oil surely prove this point, as does John Commons's book *Industrial Goodwill* (1919) and the consulting reports of Industrial Relations Counselors, Inc.[10] Further, the term *industrial relations* was explicitly chosen by companies such as Top-Grade Oil to connote the idea that they were following a strategic human resource model.

The modern literature also errs in one other crucial respect. A common theme of the last two decades among academic HRM writers is that some version of the human resource model—often along the lines of a "high performance" or "high involvement" work system—is universally the best route to high profits and competitive advantage.[11] This universalistic model of HRM is also a dangerously flawed construct—particularly if one is a corporate shareholder! On normative grounds, most people will no doubt agree that a human resource/ILM model is the preferable approach since it embodies many positive features, such as high cooperation, above average wages and benefits, employee voice, and job security. However, most firms do not (and cannot in the long run) choose an ES on normative ("sentimental") grounds of what they would *like* to do but choose instead based on objective and dispassionate business grounds of what they *must* do to survive and earn a profit. No doubt Oscar Elsas at Fulton Bag and Cotton Mills could have earned more profit if he practiced the hired hand model in a less oppressive and punitive manner, just as New Era Radio might have earned greater returns for stockholders if it had a functionalized HRM department and gave greater training and job security to employees. It is an entirely different and far less evident conjecture, on the other hand, that both companies would have made greater profit and shareholder returns if they had swung far to the other end and put in place an advanced version of the human resource model, such as was done at Top-Grade Oil.

Most certainly, the universalistic "high performance" hypothesis could be correct, but I think it is also highly implausible on grounds of both logic and common sense. Parenthetically, it also implies that the executives at these companies committed not small or even moderate acts of HRM mismanagement but massive and very costly errors of judgment. I suspect the consultants at IRC, as well as Commons in *Industrial Goodwill*, came closer to the truth when they introduced important elements of what today is called a *contingency* model of best-practice HRM.[12] They took a universalistic perspective in one respect—more cooperation always boosts performance—but they also recognized there are many alternative methods to get cooperation, some positive and some negative, and that in some cases economic conditions mandate "dog eat dog." Thus, IRC and Commons observed that "best practices" in a market economy have to center on one metric: profit (or return on capital invested). Profit is the variable that determines life and death for a company and the ES that yields most profit is greatly contingent on a host of factors external and internal to the organization. The constellation of these external and internal factors that confronted companies such as Fulton Bag and Cotton Mills and New Era Radio (e.g., highly competitive and volatile product markets, low-skilled and highly transient employees, easy monitoring of work performance) largely preordained that for them some version of the hired hand model would outperform the human resource model. Thus, we see in significant parts of the modern HRM literature the proposition that all (or nearly all) firms would benefit from adoption of formal employee involvement and other high performance HRM practices, while eight decades ago IRC and Commons took the position that these advanced practices are appropriate in some companies but in others much the opposite types of HRM practices (e.g., drive methods, sweatshop conditions) are sure to be more profitable. Although ultimately an empirical issue to be decided by the facts, I place my bet on the contingency position.

Was Early HRM Strategic?

The consensus of opinion in modern management is that early (pre–World War II) personnel management and industrial relations were implemented and practiced in a nonstrategic manner. I know of no study in the modern academic HRM literature that makes a case for the opposite point of view.

We must first ask, What does *nonstrategic* mean? A popular definition of strategic HRM, per the discussion in chapter 7, is "the pattern of planned human resource deployments and activities intended to enable an organization to achieve its goals."[13] This idea, as described there, is then broken into two complementary parts. The first characteristic of strategic HRM is *vertical fit*—that is, conscious effort to design the HRM strategy so it optimally aligns and supports the firm's business strategy. The second characteristic is *horizontal fit*—configuration of the different parts of the HRM program so they fit together and interact in a way that yields maximum synergy and accomplishment of the HRM strategy.[14] A third condition is often implicit and sometimes explicit: that the HRM executive and/or HRM department is a player in the development of the HRM strategy.

Knowing what is strategic HRM, we can then look at the opposite side of the coin and determine the characteristics that define nonstrategic. Essentially, *nonstrategic* means the employees and labor management practices of the firm are largely omitted or neglected variables in the firm's business strategy plan; the employees and HRM function operate largely below the "line of sight" of top executives; the firm may not have a functionalized HRM department and, if it does, the department is largely a low-level administrative and transactional operation that takes care of PIR matters such as hiring, payroll, record keeping, benefits administration, union negotiations, and grievance handling; and these individual PIR activities and programs operate in a "silo" mode in which they exist and operate largely in isolation of each other. In other words, nonstrategic HRM has little link to or bearing on establishing and maintaining competitive advantage.

Armed with these definitions and concepts, what verdict do the case studies yield about the strategic versus nonstrategic nature of early HRM? It seems clear-cut that nearly every company featured here—indeed, I would say all of them—practiced strategic HRM. To claim otherwise is to propose (per the SHRM definition above) that the executives at one or more of these companies ran the business without giving deliberative top-level consideration to how their employees, labor policies, and labor practices impact the company's future profitability and growth. Surely this defies credulity. That is, labor cost at all of these firms was undoubtedly the single largest part of total cost of production, so one can confidently infer that the labor variable was included in the executives/owners strategic business calculations. Further, every firm in this sample made union avoidance a high-priority goal and this fact surely imparted strategic importance to labor and labor management.

Inference aside, the evidence contained in the case studies directly contradicts the nonstrategic claim. We see, for example, that as early as the 1880s the executives in charge of the Burlington Railroad were engaged in a debate about the pros and cons of staying with their "hired hand" model or transitioning to a rudimentary "human resource" approach. Likewise, George Pullman clearly engaged in strategic HRM when he deliberated on the pros and cons of building his new model community for his employees or when he chose to take a strike rather than agree to a wage restoration. Similarly, the Filenes surely had strategic HRM goals in mind when they created the

Filene Cooperative Association, as did Henry Ford when he decided on the five-dollar day, and as did Elbert Gary when he chose to maintain the twelve-hour day at U.S. Steel despite the possibility this would result in the unionization of the mills. The same type of evidence comes from the IRC case studies of the 1920s. The new industrial relations program adopted at Top-Grade Oil in 1918 is a paragon of strategic HRM, as it entailed a paradigm shift in the organization and operation of the company's HRM program and was adopted only after extensive deliberation at the highest executive level. Further, this case study reveals a clear effort to build a composite/integrated HRM program that supported and complemented the program's core strategic element—the employee representation plan. Even at a company such as New Era Radio, where formal HRM policies and practices were minimal and "hire and fire" was the order of the day, they would not have brought in Industrial Relations Counselors to do an A-to-Z labor audit if the executives were not strategically thinking about the link between labor and profit.

The problem in the modern-day HRM literature regarding this matter is that it takes an overly functional and formal view of what constitutes strategic HRM. Implicitly or explicitly, most SHRM writers equate "strategic" with a large and influential HRM department, a human resource/ILM high-performance system, and significant involvement of the HRM department in some kind of high-level planning process. None of these need be true. As exhibit A, look back at the first case study on the Burlington Railroad. The company had no HRM department, spent next to nothing on labor management, and used a hired hand/ELM employment system. But the executives nonetheless extensively debated and considered the business pros and cons of alternative types of HRM systems, which is surely the sine qua non of SHRM. It is also a confusion of the concept to look at a particular company—say, High-Beam Steel—and observe that the personnel department is largely engaged in functional activities such as hiring, training, and benefits administration and conclude from this that HRM at the company is nonstrategic. The HRM department may well be a largely tactical and transactional operation (a strategic business decision?) yet the company may, nonetheless, have a strategically crafted top-tier labor management and employee relations program. How? Because the corporate leadership makes the strategic labor decisions, while the implementation and administration is delegated to the PIR department.

Unions and Laws: How Important Were They?

Long-running debate also continues on another aspect of early human resource management. One view is that the HRM transformation during the World War I period and subsequent rise of the welfare capitalism movement of the 1920s occurred primarily because companies were "pushed" to improve labor management by unions and government enacted laws (a negative "threat" motive).[15] The second view argues that the more important impetus is that companies were "pulled" toward improved labor management by the prospect of greater profit and labor peace made possible by new management ideas (scientific management, industrial psychology, etc.), new technologies (e.g., mass production), a more stable and full employment economy, and a higher sense of social responsibility on the part of a new generation of corporate leaders (a positive "gain" motive).[16]

I perceive that the evidence from these case studies is mixed on the matter. On one hand, we find clear indication that companies were attune to the threat of unions and to some degree shaped their labor policies and practices to ward off this threat. Companies also copied certain union programs, such as mutual insurance schemes, unemployment insurance benefits, and mechanisms for collective voice (e.g., works councils, employee representation plans). In the Burlington case study, for example, the railroads decided to forgo wage reductions in the depression of the early 1890s as a way to avoid further strikes and union organization. Likewise, the United States Steel Corporation adopted its advanced safety and industrial welfare programs partly out of union avoidance motives. In the IRC surveys, there is no question but that the threat of unions and strikes provided the original impetus to the HRM reforms at Top-Grade Oil and United Steel and Coal, and that Great Eastern Coal maintained higher wages and conditions that it would have without the threat of organization by the United Mine Workers. And, of course, the employee representation plans at Top-Grade Oil and United Steel and Coal were not called by critics "company unions" for nothing.

It is difficult to find an independent effect of labor laws on HRM in part 1 of the case studies because for the most part no such laws existed. The first labor laws of consequence for private sector industry were the state-level workmen's compensation statutes enacted in the 1910s. Their influence is discernible in the steel industry case study of part 1 but most clearly shows up, albeit in a delimited way, in the IRC surveys of the 1920s. Every IRC report had a chapter devoted to safety and some had a separate chapter on workmen's compensation. It is evident from the reports that the laws, by imposing an accident and injury tax on the companies and making this tax rise in proportion to their recorded rates of accident and injury (the "experience rating" feature), were quite successful in focusing employers' attention on safety and creating a newfound "safety spirit" in corporate America. Most medium- to large-size companies created a position of safety engineer and a number formed joint safety committees in the plants and, in a number of cases (e.g., Mega-Watt Light and Power, New Era Radio) these preceded the creation of personnel departments or were the nucleus for such. The other effect of the workmen's compensation statutes was to increase company investment in the hiring and training functions in order to prevent accidents and injuries through more selective employee hiring and improved job skills and safety awareness. I come to the conclusion that the safety movement is probably the most under-recognized part of the "big picture" when it comes to the early development of the personnel/HRM function.

Now for the evidence on the other side. As already indicated, the effect of labor laws is necessarily limited because they were quite few in number, not enacted until the 1910s and afterwards, and often were not well enforced. The effect of labor law does not really become a big part of the HRM story until the 1930s and then again in the 1960s and afterward.

Unions also had a limited presence throughout the entire time frame of this book, except for three union "spikes." The first occurred in the 1870s with the meteoric rise (and fall) of the Knights of Labor; the second was during 1898–1904 when the membership of the craft unions affiliated with the American Federation of Labor more than doubled (only to greatly erode for the next ten years); and the third was the World War I years when union density doubled to nearly 20 percent (then eroding to half that much by 1929). One can make an argument that the development of early HRM had some (positive) relationship to these ups and downs of unionism, but the correlation appears modest. As described in more detail in *Managing the Human Factor*, the advent of both industrial welfare and safety movements in the early to middle part of the first decade of the 1900s undoubtedly owes something to the increasing encroachment of unions, and the same applies to the mushroom growth of personnel departments and employee representation plans during World War I. But there is also abundant evidence that suggests much of the development of HRM gained its impetus from other factors of a more forward-looking and profit-oriented nature.

One must start off noting that the unions of this period were either uninterested in or strongly opposed to important parts of the new HRM movement, so in this regard they acted more as a restraining or inhibiting factor. Programs such as profit sharing, gain sharing, and welfare activities, for example, were condemned by unions because they tended to bond the workers to the company. Similarly, unions opposed individual incentive pay systems because they fragmented worker solidarity, while new hiring methods, such as selection tests and personal interviews, were also resisted because they threatened to weed out workers with union backgrounds or proclivities. Probably most excoriated were the employer-created works councils and employee representation bodies, which from the employer perspective were (in part) vehicles for employee involvement and participative management. Tellingly, the unions successfully lobbied the U.S. Congress to write in language in the National Labor Relations Act that, when enacted in 1935, declared these HRM bodies illegal.[17]

Looking more directly at our case studies, we find many examples of new HRM programs or practices adopted for reasons that have much more to do with improved management and productivity than union avoidance. The Burlington, for example, started in the 1880s a promotion-from-within program for skilled and white-collar workers in order to expand the supply of scarce talent and reduce hiring and turnover costs, while at the same time George Pullman built a world-class company town in order to recruit and retain a higher-quality workforce. George Johnson at Endicott-Johnson provided workers with superior wages and job security as a way to create employee loyalty and esprit-d'corps; the Filenes created the Filene Cooperative Association as a method for democratic workforce governance and employee involvement, the U.S. Steel Corporation kept its safety program going in part because it substantially reduced accident costs, and the Ford Motor Company raised wages to five dollars a day to reduce turnover and attract a better class of worker. In the IRC surveys, we are told that Top-Grade Oil stayed with its advanced HRM program because at the end of the day it added to profit by transforming an adversarial relationship to a cooperative one, while High-Beam Steel spent tens of thousands of dollars on employee services and social programs because it reduced turnover, increased morale, and created a tighter bond between company and worker.

My impression, after all the evidence is weighed and sifted, is that unions and laws were a significant impetus and pressure upon management to improve and innovate in labor management and employee relations, but that they were less than half the story in the time period we are examining. Stronger and more important were a group of other considerations: the pressures of market competition to become more efficient, the prospect that new and improved HRM methods would increase profit, the development of new technologies and ideas in people management, and an expanded sense of social responsibility and corporate ethics. Most certainly, companies would have been slower to adopt and innovate in HRM without these outside institutional pressures, but it appears to me that the trend line in HRM would have been substantially upward sloping nonetheless.

The Human Factor

Here is the end point of this chapter, and also the end point of a research project on early HRM that spanned several years and filled two books. If I had to boil everything down and say what is the single greatest insight and lesson learned, it would be this obvious but profoundly important observation: *labor is human, and not a commodity.* This insight is what provides the fundamental reason for being of the twin fields of human resource management and industrial (employment) relations; it is also the reason there is no mechanical, deterministic "one best way" to achieving efficiency and justice in industry as envisioned in either scientific management or the Walrasian (competitive) core of neoclassical economics.

If labor is a commodity, it can be traded in a market like coal or wheat and demand and supply determine its price, quantity, and allocation. If the market is competitive, neoclassical theory demonstrates that the outcome is the most efficient possible, per the First Fundamental Welfare theorem.[18] In such a world, there are no labor problems and thus no need for unions or protective labor laws. Further, production of goods and utilization of labor is efficiently worked out by competitive pressures and price signals "as if by an invisible hand," so while real life managers and entrepreneurs exist in principle they have no active role to play. The upshot is that since the market optimally coordinates production and labor utilization there is no need for a labor management (HRM) function. The PIR fields can disappear.

Much the same result emerges if we approach it from the engineering perspective of scientific management. When late-nineteenth-century economists looked at the work world, they telescoped it into a model of a frictionless market; when engineers such as Frederick Taylor looked at the same thing they telescoped it into a model of a frictionless machine. In Taylor's eyes, there is always one best way to accomplish a given end and the engineer's task is to use the scientific laws and technological arts to discover and build it.[19] Taylor became famous for applying this principle to the design of organizations and work systems. Taylor's greatest challenge was to turn the employment relationship from the highly adversarial and inefficient system he encountered in American industry to a high performing model built on thoroughgoing science, cooperation, and justice (i.e., "zero friction"). To do so he needed the labor parts of the machine to smoothly operate and work at top speed. His solution was to also model workers as commodities, although more like "dumb animal" commodities (e.g., mules). In his experience, workers were inherently inclined to sit down on the job and thus the task of labor management to him boiled down to devising the optimal package of carrots and sticks to motivate the "human mules" to work hard, complemented by thoroughly researched and rigidly enforced rules as to how the work was to be done. If successfully implemented, Taylor claims the end result is elimination of labor problems and realization of maximum prosperity and justice for both employers and employees.

Thus, just as the frictionless market of the economists makes the two fields of HRM and industrial relations unnecessary, so too does the frictionless organization and production process of Taylor and scientific management. They are at a theory level opposite sides of the same coin; that is, one uses perfect markets and the other uses perfect managers and organizations to achieve efficiency and justice. The result of either is that HRM and IR become empty spaces and are absorbed on one side into economics and on the other into engineering and operations management.

These models were put into practice in the late nineteenth and early twentieth centuries, starting first and most thoroughly with the economists' model and later and more selectively with Taylor's. The result, particularly in the case of the economic model, was the development of a large and increasingly ferocious Labor Problem that threatened the capitalist system with massive inefficiency, strikes, radical unions and political parties, and the potential of socialist revolution. Taylor's scientific management did not quell the Labor Problem but, in the beginning, only heightened it.

Why did both the economic and scientific management models of HRM predict optimal efficiency and justice and yet deliver a world-class Labor Problem? The answer hinges on a common assumption in both models—the assumption that people can be treated as if they are commodities (or dumb animals) and that doing so leads in science to good theoretical predictions and in industry to good management principles. For analysis of a number of specific workplace methods and issues, the "labor as a commodity" assumption yields useful insights; when applied to the general conduct of people management and employee relations, however, the concept is not just a little wrong but greatly—and dangerously—wrong.

The twin fields of human resource management and industrial relations were born out of a slow, groping, and experimental effort to solve the Labor Problem through a "middle way" approach.[20] This approach did not reject either competitive economics or scientific management; what it did do is insist that both theories become "humanistic"—that is, take seriously the fact that labor is embodied in human beings and is not a commodity. Of course, when this was done neoclassical labor economics and scientific management changed greatly; in fact so greatly that there opened up intellectual room for a new field of study and vocational room for a new management specialty area. A century ago these were called, alternatively, personnel management and industrial relations; today they have become human resource management and employment relations. While their names and characteristics may differ, all are united by a commitment to the fundamental importance—in science, practice, and ethics—that labor is a uniquely human factor.

The first volume, *Managing the Human Factor*, and this one are in effect a very large travelogue that describes the journey American thought and practice made from the 1880s, when the commodity theory of labor ruled the land, to the end of the 1920s, when the human theory had made substantial inroads, particularly among the top tier of American employers. During this period even the most committed PIR academic or practitioner realized that labor inevitably takes on characteristics of a commodity, animal, and machine—and more so in some industries than others—but they equally insisted that the human aspect of labor is not a "detail" or minor "friction" but is fundamental to sound theory, practice, and policy. This insight remains at the core of human resource management and employment relations today and provides their fundamental raison d'être and intellectual compass. For this insight, in turn, we in the early twenty-first century owe a debt of thanks and acknowledgement to the PIR pioneers of the late nineteenth and early twentieth centuries—people such as Henry Town, John Patterson, Louis Brandeis, John D. Rockefeller Jr., Ordway Tead, Mary Gilson, Henry Ford, Lillian Gilbreth, Meyer Bloomfield, Walter Dill Scott, John R. Commons, and Clarence Hicks.

Notes

Preface

1. Bruce Kaufman, *Managing the Human Factor: The Early Years of Human Resource Management in American Industry* (Ithaca, NY: Cornell University Press, ILR Press, 2008).

1. Early Human Resource Management: Context and History

1. Bruce Kaufman, *Managing the Human Factor: The Early Years of Human Resource Management in American Industry* (Ithaca, NY: Cornell University Press, ILR Press, 2008).
2. The story told here is exclusively of U.S. developments. Up to World War I, Britain, France, and Germany led the United States in certain specific areas of HRM innovation, such as hiring departments, employee welfare programs, works councils, protective labor laws, and social insurance programs. See, for example, Daniel Rodgers, *Atlantic Crossings: Social Politics in a Progressive Age* (Cambridge, MA: Harvard University Press, 1998). After World War I, however, the United States took the lead in the science and practice of personnel management and industrial relations, particularly with respect to crafting an integrated and strategic program suited for mass production industry. Englishman Harold Butler, deputy director of the International Labor Organization, stated in 1927 that "the American literature on the subject [PIR] during the last ten years probably exceeds that of the rest of the world put together." See Harold Butler, *Industrial Relations in the United States*, series A, no. 27 (Geneva: International Labor Organization, 1927), 107. Additional perspectives on early international developments in HRM are provided in Bruce Kaufman, "The Development of Human Resource Management in Historical and International Context," in *Oxford Handbook of Human Resource Management*, ed. Peter Boxall, John Purcell, and Patrick Wright (Oxford: Oxford University Press, 2007), 19–47; Bruce Kaufman, *The Global Evolution of Industrial Relations* (Geneva: International Labor Organization, 2004); Howard Gospel, *Markets, Firms, and the Management of Labour in Modern Britain* (New York: Cambridge University Press, 1992); and Sanford Jacoby, "Pacific Ties: Industrial Relations and Employment Systems in Japan and the United States," in *Industrial Democracy in America: The Ambiguous Promise*, ed. H. Harris and N. Lichtenstein (New York: Cambridge University Press, 1991), 206–48.
3. The terms "traditional" and "modern" are used to mark off chronological periods of development in HRM and in this sense are neutral with respect to normative evaluations (e.g.,

that traditional is "bad" and modern is "good"). That said, it is probably true that by most people's value system the modern HRM system is also the more appealing from an ethical and social perspective. Most certainly, however, it is incorrect to equate "modern" with "best practice" HRM if "best practice" is taken to mean the HRM system that yields greatest profit. A traditional HRM system may in many circumstances be the most profitable in any time period, including the twenty-first century.

4. Walter Licht, *Getting Work: Philadelphia, 1840–1950* (Cambridge, MA: Harvard University Press, 1992).

5. Sanford Jacoby, *Modern Manors: Welfare Capitalism since the New Deal* (Princeton, NJ: Princeton University Press, 1997).

6. See, for example, David Brody, *Butcher Workmen: A Study of Unionization* (Cambridge, MA: Harvard University Press, 1964); and Daniel Nelson, *American Rubber Workers and Organized Labor, 1900–1941* (Princeton, NJ: Princeton University Press, 1985).

7. The events and developments described in this narrative are discussed in Kaufman, *Managing the Human Factor*, as well as in Daniel Nelson, *Managers and Workers: Origins of the Twentieth-Century Factory System in the United States, 1880–1920*, 2nd ed. (Madison: University of Wisconsin Press, 1995); and Sanford Jacoby, *Employing Bureaucracy: Managers, Unions and the Transformation of Work in the 20th Century*, rev. ed. (Mahwah, NJ: Lawrence Erlbaum, 2004).

8. See Bruce Kaufman, *The Origins and Evolution of the Field of Industrial Relations in the United States* (Ithaca, NY: Cornell University Press, ILR Press, 1993); and Kaufman, *The Global Evolution of Industrial Relations*.

9. Kaufman, *Managing the Human Factor*, table 5.1.

10. Ibid., chap. 4.

11. See Irving Bernstein, *Lean Years: A History of the American Worker, 1920–1933* (Boston: Houghton-Mifflin, 1960); and Lizabeth Cohen, *Making a New Deal: Industrial Workers in Chicago, 1919–1933* (Cambridge, MA: Cambridge University Press, 1990).

12. See Clarence Hicks, *My Life in Industrial Relations: Fifty Years in the Growth of a Profession* (New York: Harper and Brothers, 1941).

13. Alfred Chandler Jr., *The Visible Hand: The Managerial Revolution in American Business* (Cambridge, MA: Belknap Press of Harvard University Press, 1977). See also Kaufman, *Managing the Human Factor*, fig. 1.1.

14. Frederick Taylor, *Principles of Scientific Management* (New York: W. W. Norton, 1947).

2. HRM at the Beginning: The Chicago, Burlington, and Quincy Railroad

1. Alfred Chandler Jr., *The Visible Hand: The Managerial Revolution in American Business* (Cambridge, MA: Harvard University Press, 1977).

2. All information concerning the Burlington in this case study, unless noted otherwise, is from Paul Black, "The Development of Management Personnel Policies on the Burlington Railroad, 1860–1900," PhD diss., University of Wisconsin, 1972.

3. Chandler, *The Invisible Hand*, 87.

4. Walter Licht, *Working for the Railroad: The Organization of Work in the Nineteenth Century* (Princeton, NJ: Princeton University Press, 1983).

5. Chandler, *The Invisible Hand*, 179–80; Black, "The Development of Management Personnel Policies," chap. 3. A detailed case study of the development and structure of the management hierarchy at the Burlington in the 1880–1900 period is provided in Oliver Zunz, *Making America Corporate 1870–1920* (Chicago: University of Chicago Press, 1990), 40–66.

6. Black, "The Development of Management Personnel Policies," 72.

7. Licht, *Working for the Railroad*, chap. 3.

8. Black, "The Development of Management Personnel Policies," chap. 7.

9. Licht, *Working for the Railroad*, 51.

10. Ibid., 156. Bribing the foreman to get and keep a job was common throughout industry prior to World War I. See "Job Selling in Industrial Establishments in Ohio," *Monthly Labor Review*, October 1916, 411–15.

11. Black, "The Development of Management Personnel Policy," 268.

12. Ibid., chap. 7; David Lightner, *Labor on the Illinois Central Railroad, 1852–1900* (New York: Arno Press, 1977), chap. 3.

13. Lightner, *Labor on the Illinois Central Railroad*, 150.

14. Licht, *Working for the Railroad*, 73.

15. Lightner, *Labor on the Illinois Central Railroad*, 89.

16. Quoted in Licht, *Working on the Railroad*, 148–49.

17. Quoted in Black, "The Development of Management Personnel Policies," 192; emphasis in the original.

18. George Perkins, quoted in Licht, *Working for the Railroad*, 149.

19. Quoted in Black, "The Development of Management Personnel Policies," 192.

20. Black, "The Development of Management Personnel Policies," 207.

21. *Ibid.*, chap. 6; Licht, *Working for the Railroad*, chap. 2.

22. Black, "The Development of Management Personnel Practices," 179.

23. Licht, *Working on the Railroad*, 160.

24. Black, "The Development of Management Personnel Policies," 168.

25. Ibid., chap. 7.

26. Quoted in Lightner, *Labor on the Illinois Central*, 257.

27. George Perkins, quoted in Black, "The Development of Management Personnel Policies," 265.

28. George Perkins, quoted in Thomas Cochran, *Railroad Leaders 1845–1890* (Cambridge, MA: Harvard University Press, 1953), 173–74.

29. Perkins, quoted in Black, "The Development of Management Personnel Policies," 349.

30. Quoted in Black, "The Development of Management Personnel Policies," 279–80.

31. George Perkins, quoted in Black, "The Development of Management Personnel Policies," 508.

32. Ibid., 363.

33. Ibid., 333; emphasis in the original.

34. Charles Adams Jr., quoted in Black, *The Development of Management Personnel Policies*, 331; emphasis in the original.

35. Sidney Webster, quoted in Lightner, *Labor on the Illinois Central*, 257.

36. Robert Harris, quoted in Cochran, *Railroad Leaders 1845–1890*, 179.

37. Quoted in Black, "The Development of Management Personnel Policies," 272.

38. Quoted in Lightner, *Labor on the Illinois Central*, 257.

39. Robert Harris, quoted in Black, "The Development of Management Personnel Policies," 335, 336.

40. John R. Commons et al., History of Labor in the United States, vol. 2 (New York: Macmillan, 1918), 185–91.

41. Almont Lindsey, *The Pullman Strike: The Story of a Unique Experiment and of a Great Labor Upheaval* (Chicago: University of Chicago Press, 1964), 8.

42. Joseph Rayback, *A History of American Labor* (New York: Free Press, 1966), 135; anonymous, quoted in Lightner, *Labor on the Illinois Central*, 254.

43. Quoted in Lightner, *Labor on the Illinois Central*, 316.

44. Lightner, *Labor on the Illinois Central*, 204.

45. Quoted in Lightner, *Labor on the Illinois Central*, 317.

46. Licht, *Working on the Railroad*, chap. 2

47. Ibid., 123; Lightner, *Labor on the Illinois Central*, 251.

48. Lightner, *Labor on the Illinois Central*, 347.

49. Quoted in Ibid., 255–56.

50. Quoted in Ibid., 261.

51. Black, "The Development of Management Personnel Policies," 294.

52. Licht, *Working for the Railroad*, 195. A contemporary writer of that period states that in 1901 one railroad trainman in every 137 was killed and one in 11 was injured.

53. Charles Russell, "Gravity Yard and Other Shambles," *Independent* 64 (1908): 235.

54. Black, "The Development of Management Personnel Policies," 305–10.

55. Quoted in Black, "The Development of Management Personnel Policies," 217–18.

3. Contrasting HRM Strategies: Pullman and Baldwin

1. E. Bingham, "The Labor Situation at Baldwin," *Iron Trade Review*, February 12, 1903, 40–41; John Brown, *The Baldwin Locomotive Works 1831–1915* (Baltimore: Johns Hopkins Press, 1995), 127.

2. Almont Lindsey, *The Pullman Strike: The Story of a Unique Experiment and of a Great Labor Upheaval* (Chicago: University of Chicago Press, 1964), chap. 2; Stanley Buder, *Pullman: An Experiment in Industrial Order and Community Planning 1880–1930* (New York: Oxford University Press, 1967), chaps. 1–2.

3. Buder, *Pullman: An Experiment in Industrial Order and Community Planning*.

4. Lindsey, *The Pullman Strike*, 49.

5. Ibid., chap. 5.

6. Many employers routinely stated that they had an "open door" and welcomed workers to come in and air their problems and grievances. Frequently, however, the employees who used the open door were fired or quietly eased out, as was the case at Pullman. Another example is at Bethlehem Steel in 1910, where a delegation of three skilled workers presented a list of grievances to the plant superintendent and were all promptly fired. The result was a 108-day strike. See Robert Hessen, "The Bethlehem Steel Strike of 1910," *Labor History* 15 (1974): 3–18.

7. Buder, *Pullman: An Experiment in Industrial Order and Community Planning*, chap. 12.

8. U.S. Strike Commission, *Report on the Chicago Strike of June–July, 1894* (Washington, DC: Government Printing Office, 1895), 557, 609. Unless otherwise indicated, all subsequent quotes in this section are from this report, and page numbers are given parenthetically in the text.

9. Wickes rejected the efficiency wage idea, but other people at the time gave it credence. For example, it is stated in U.S. Industrial Commission, *Final Report*, vol. 19 (Washington, DC: Government Printing Office, 1902), 808–09, that "as wages go up, employers find that it does not pay them to keep any but the most efficient men . . . the pick of the men by this process of selection, quicken their pace. They are led to do it partly by a sense of satisfied ambition in the wages they are getting; and partly by the fear that they may find themselves among the rejected."

10. Richard Ely, "Pullman: A Social Study," *Harper's New Monthly Magazine*, February 1885, 452–66; Sarah Lyons Watts, *Order against Chaos: Business Culture and Labor Ideology in America 1880–1915* (Westport, CT: Greenwood Press, 1991), chap. 2.

11. Richard Ely, "Pullman: A Social Study," *Harper's Monthly* 70 (1885), 452–66.

12. Quoted in Lindsey, *The Pullman Strike*, 91.

13. "Mr. Pullman's Statement, *New York Tribune*, July 14, 1894, reprinted in *The Pullman Strike*, ed. Leon Stein (New York: Arno Press, 1969), 37

14. Daniel Nelson, *Managers and Workers*, 2nd ed. (Madison: University of Wisconsin Press, 1995), 7–8.

15. Brown, *The Baldwin Locomotive Works*, 129, 203.

16. Ibid., 150.

17. Bingham, "The Labor Situation at the Baldwin Works," 40.

18. Horace Arnold, "Production up to the Power Limit," *Engineering Magazine*, August 1895, 916–24; John Converse, "Progressive Non-Union Labour," *Cassier's Magazine*, March 1903, 656–66; Brown, *The Baldwin Locomotive Works*.

19. Brown, *The Baldwin Locomotive Works*, 207.

20. Payroll clerks and timekeepers were frequently attached to the accounting department, as shown in C. Knoeppel, "Maximum Production through Organization and Supervision," *Engineering Magazine*, April 1908, 89. The development of personnel management was in part an elaboration and functionalization of the portion of the cost accounting system devoted to employees.

21. Koeppel, "Maximum Production," 95.

22. Brown, *The Baldwin Locomotive Works*, 207.

23. Bingham, "The Labor Situation at the Baldwin Works," 40.

24. Converse, "Progressive Non-Union Labour," 666; emphasis in original.

25. Ibid., 666.

26. Arnold, "Production up to the Power Limit;" Brown, *The Baldwin Locomotive Works*, chaps. 5, 7.

27. Brown, *The Baldwin Locomotive Works*, 123–26.

28. Ernest Englander, "The Inside Contract System of Production and Organization: A Neglected Aspect of the History of the Firm," *Labor History* 28 (1987): 429–46. Nelson, *Managers and Workers*, 36–39.

29. Arnold, "Production up to the Power Limit," 922.

30. Ibid., 923.

31. Brown, *The Baldwin Locomotive Works*, 152.

32. Ibid., 217–23.

4. HRM and Alternative Systems of Workforce Governance

1. This section is drawn from Gary Fink, *The Fulton Bag and Cotton Mills Strike of 1914–1915* (Ithaca, NY: Cornell University Press, ILR Press, 1993).

2. Fink, *The Fulton Bag and Cotton Mills Strike*, 28.

3. Douglas McGregor, *The Human Side of Enterprise* (New York: McGraw-Hill, 1960).

4. Fink, *The Fulton Bag and Cotton Mills Strike*, 25.

5. Ibid., 25, 29.

6. Recent statistical research finds evidence that a two-tier workforce, with a relatively large segment of workers with frequent turnover and short job tenure and a smaller segment of workers with low turnover and long job tenure, was characteristic of wider American industry in the pre–World War I years. See Susan Carter and Elizabeth Savoca, "Labor Mobility and Lengthy Jobs in Nineteenth-Century America," *Journal of Economic History* 50 (1990): 1–16; and Sanford Jacoby and Sunil Sharma, "Employment Duration and Industrial Labor Mobility in the United States 1880–1980," *Journal of Economic History* 52 (1992): 161–79. Jacoby and Sharma find that roughly one-fourth of workers had a job tenure of twenty years or more.

7. Oscar Elsas, quoted in Fink, *The Fulton Bag and Cotton Mills Strike,* 46.

8. Quoted in Ibid., 50.

9. Elsas, quoted in Ibid., 48.

10. Ibid., 42.

11. Elsas, quoted in Ibid., 64.

12. This section is drawn from Gerald Zahavi, *Workers, Managers, and Welfare Capitalism: The Shoeworkers and Tanners of Endicott-Johnson, 1890–1950* (Urbana: University of Illinois Press, 1988); hereafter in this section, page numbers will be cited parenthetically in the text. See also William Inglis, *George F. Johnson and His Industrial Democracy* (New York: Huntington, 1935).

13. David Brody, *Workers in Industrial America* (New York: Oxford University Press, 1980), 61; quoted in Zahavi, *Workers, Managers, and Welfare Capitalism*, 38.

14. Mary La Dame, *The Filene Store: A Study of Employee's Relation to Management in a Retail Store* (New York: Russell Sage Foundation, 1930); hereafter in this section, page numbers will be cited parenthetically in the text.

15. U.S. Industrial Commission, *Final Report of the Industrial Commission*, vol. 19 (Washington, DC: Government Printing Office, 1902), 734.

16. U.S. Anthracite Coal Strike Commission, *Report to the President on the Anthracite Coal Strike* (Washington, DC: Government Printing Office, 1903).

17. Morton Baratz, *The Union and the Coal Industry* (New Haven, CT: Yale University Press, 1955); Price Fishback, *Soft Coal, Hard Choices: The Economic Welfare of Bituminous Coal Miners, 1890–1930* (New York: Oxford University Press, 1992).

18. Fishback, *Soft Coal, Hard Choices*; Keith Dix, *Work Relations in the Coal Industry: The Hand-Loading Era, 1880–1930* (Morgantown: Institute for Labor Studies, West Virginia University, 1977).

19. Dix, *Work Relations in the Coal Industry*, 39, 44; Frank Warne, "Miner and Operator," *Outlook* 82 (1906): 643–56.

20. Dix, *Work Relations in the Coal Industry*, 8–20, 48–59; Ian Taplin, "Miners, Coal Operators and the State: An Examination of Strikes and Work Relations in the U.S. Coal Industry," PhD diss., Brown University, 1986, chap. 3.

21. Sidney Lens, *The Labor Wars* (New York: Doubleday, 1973).

22. Robert Cornell, *The Anthracite Coal Strike of 1902* (Washington, DC: Catholic University of America Press, 1957); Perry Blatz, *Democratic Miners: Work and Labor Relations in the Anthracite Coal Industry, 1875–1925* (Albany: State University of New York Press, 1994).

23. "A Miner's Story," *Independent* 54 (1902), 1407–10.

24. U.S. Industrial Commission, *Final Report*, 734.

25. John Brophy, *A Miner's Life* (Madison: University of Wisconsin Press, 1964).

26. Dix, *Work Relations in the Coal Industry*; A. F. Hinrichs, *The United Mine Workers of America, and the Non-Union Coal Fields* (New York: Columbia University Press, 1923).

27. Fishback, *Soft Coal, Hard Choices*, chaps. 8–9; Warne, "Miner and Operator," 650–51. One coal miner relates this anecdote: "'When I went to the office for my first pay the 'super' met me and asked me if I didn't know his wife's brother George kept a store . . . the next day I got a quiet tip that my breast was to be abandoned. This set me to thinking. I went to the boss and, after a few words, told him my wife had found brother-in-law George's store and that she liked it. . . . I have had work at that colliery ever since. I know my living costs me from 10 to 15 per cent extra. But I kept my job, which meant a good deal." See "A Miner's Story," 1409.

28. Curtis Seltzer, *Fire in the Hole: Miners and Managers in the American Coal Industry* (Lexington: University Press of Kentucky, 1985), 37.

29. William Graebner, "The Coal-Mine Operator and Safety: A Study of Business Reform in the Progressive Era," *Labor History* 14 (1973): 483–505.

30. John Mitchell, *Organized Labor* (Philadelphia: American Book and Bible House, 1903); Clarence Wunderlin, *Visions of a New Industrial Order: Social Science and Labor Theory in America's Progressive Era* (New York: Columbia University Press, 1992).

31. Anonymous, quoted in William Boal and John Pencavel, "The Effects of Labor Unions on Employment, Wages, and Days of Operation: Coal Mining in West Virginia," *Quarterly Journal of Economics* 109 (1994): 286.

32. Reinhard Bendix, *Work and Authority in Industry: Ideologies of Management in the Course of Industrialization* (New York: John Wiley, 1956).

33. George Baer, quoted in John R. Commons, *Labor and Administration* (New York: Macmillan, 1919), 63.

34. U.S. Anthracite Coal Strike Commission, *Report to the President*, 96–160.

35. Quoted in U.S. Anthracite Coal Strike Commission, *Report to the President*, 97.

36. Quoted in U.S. Anthracite Coal Strike Commission, *Report to the President*, 100–101.

37. Quoted in U.S. Anthracite Coal Strike Commission, *Report to the President*, 113.

38. U.S. Anthracite Coal Strike Commission, *Report to the President*, 80–83; Cornell, *The Anthracite Coal Strike of 1902*, chap. 9.

39. Stanley Vittoz, *New Deal Labor Policy and the American Industrial Economy* (Chapel Hill: University of North Carolina Press, 1987.

40. Bruno Ramirez, *When Workers Fight: The Politics of Industrial Relations in the Progressive Era, 1898–1916* (Westport, CT: Greenwood Press, 1978); Mitchell, *Organized Labor*; Andrew Arnold, "Ordering Coal: Labor, Law and Business in Central Pennsylvania, 1870–1900," PhD diss., University of North Carolina, 2001, chap. 8; John R. Commons, "American Shoemakers 1648–1895," *Quarterly Journal of Economics* 24 (1909): 39–98.

41. Baratz, *The Union and the Coal Industry*; F. Berquist and Associates, *Economic Survey of the Bituminous Coal Industry under Free Competition and Code Regulation* (Washington, DC: National Recovery Administration, 1936).

42. John R. Commons, *History of Labor in the United States*, vol. 2 (New York: Macmillan, 1918), 524–25.

43. Winthrop Lane, *Civil War in West Virginia* (New York: Arno Press, 1969).

44. U.S. Anthracite Coal Strike Commission, *Report to the President*, 37.

5. The Birth of HRM in the Industrial Heartland I: The United States Steel Corporation

1. Charles Gulick, *Labor Policy of the United States Steel Corporation* (New York: Columbia University Press, 1924), 20; Kenneth Warren, *Big Steel: The First Century of the United States Steel Corporation 1901–2001* (Pittsburgh: University of Pittsburgh Press, 2001), chap. 1.

2. Jonathan Rees, *Managing the Mills: Labor Policy in the American Steel Industry during the Nonunion Era* (New York: University Press of America, 2004), 16.

3. John Fitch, *The Steel Workers* (New York: Russell Sage Foundation, 1911), 33.

4. David Montgomery, *The Fall of the House of Labor* (New York: Cambridge University Press, 1987), 17–18.

5. Rees, *Managing the Mills*, chap. 1. Carnegie took pride in being a friend of the working-man and created something of a sensation in a published article, "An Employer's View of the Labor Question" (reprinted in Joseph Wall, *The Carnegie Reader* [Pittsburgh: University of Pittsburgh Press, 1992], 91–101), in which he took a decidedly liberal view on the collective bargaining right of workers.

6. Rees, *Managing the Mills*, chap. 1; John Ingham, *Making Iron and Steel: Independent Mills in Pittsburgh, 1820–1920* (Columbus: Ohio State University Press, 1991), chap. 5.

7. Sidney Lens, *The Labor Wars* (New York: Doubleday, 1973), chap. 5.

8. Fitch, *The Steel Workers*, chaps. 13–14.

9. Quoted in David Brody, *Steelworkers in America: The Nonunion Era* (Cambridge, MA: Harvard University Press, 1960), 28.

10. Carroll Daugherty, Melvin de Chazeau, and Samuel Stratton, *The Economics of the Iron and Steel Industry*, vol. I (New York: McGraw-Hill, 1937), 187.

11. Brody, *Steelworkers in America*, chaps. 1–2.

12. Quoted in Brody, *Steelworkers in America*, 32.

13. Daniel Nelson, *Managers and Workers*, 2nd ed. (Madison: University of Wisconsin Press, 1995), 44, notes that the drive system was most prevalent in highly mechanized industries using unskilled or semiskilled labor where the foreman's principal responsibility was to ensure that workers' effort was maintained at the level necessary to fully exploit the productivity of the machines.

14. Quoted in Ray Stannard Baker, *The New Industrial Unrest: Reasons and Remedies* (New York: Doubleday, Page, 1920), 31.

15. Sumner Slichter, *The Turnover of Factory Labor* (New York: Appleton, 1919), 202–3.

16. See Daniel Wren, *White Collar Hobo: The Travels of Whiting Williams* (Ames: Iowa State University Press, 1987).

17. Whiting Williams, *What's on the Worker's Mind* (New York: Scribner's, 1920), 18, 20.

18. Baker, *The New Industrial Unrest*; John Fitch, *The Causes of Industrial Unrest* (New York: Harper and Brothers, 1924).

19. Charles Hill, "Fighting the Twelve Hour Day in the American Steel Industry," *Labor History* 15 (1974): 19–35.

20. Fitch, *The Steel Workers*, chaps. 7, 13.

21. Rees, Managing the Mills, 143–56; Gerald Eggert, *Steelmasters and Labor Reform, 1886–1923* (Pittsburgh: University of Pittsburgh Press, 1981), chap. 4.

22. Rees, *Managing the Mills*, 84.

23. Gulick, *Labor Policy of the United States Steel Corporation*, chap. 2.

24. Rees, *Managing the Mills*, 7. Steel mills were mostly in the eastern United States, and thus hired European immigrants. Mention should be made that the labor force of the western United States had a large number of Chinese and Japanese immigrants, although they mostly came in the 1860s–80s. They were subjected to intense discrimination and segregation, only modestly less so than workers of African origin. Frenchman Emile Levasseur traveled through the U.S. in the 1890s and reported in (*The American Workman* (New York: Arno Press, 1977), 289, that in western mining operations Chinese workers "did as much work as the whites . . . [but] received just half-pay." More generally, see Martin Brown and Peter Philips, "Competition, Racism, and Hiring Practices among California Manufacturers, 1860–1882," *Industrial and Labor Relations Review* 40 (1986): 61–74; and Ira Cross, *A History of the Labor Movement in California* (Berkeley and Los Angeles: University of California Press, 1935).

25. Don Lescohier, "Big Industry and Labor, 1890–1930," in *History of Labor, 1896–1932*, vol. 3, ed. John Commons (New York: Macmillan, 1935), 293–315; Daniel Rodgers, *The Work Ethic in America 1850–1920* (Chicago: University of Chicago Press, 1974).

26. Fitch, *The Steel Workers*, 148.

27. Dennis Dickerson, *Out of the Crucible: Black Steelworkers in Western Pennsylvania, 1875–1980* (Albany: State University of New York Press, 1986); Walter Licht, *Getting Work: Philadelphia, 1840–1950* (Cambridge, MA: Harvard University Press, 1992), 44–50.

28. Nelson, *Managers and Workers*, chap. 3.

29. In their defense, the steel companies assembled worker witnesses who attested to the reality of the "open door." One said, "'Any grievance he may want to make, he can make it to the foreman and if the foreman won't take it up, he can just simply open the door of the main office and walk right in to the Superintendent'"; quoted in Marshall Olds, *Analysis of the Interchurch World Movement Report on the Steel Strike* (New York: Putnam, 1923), 167. On the other side, Fitch, *The Steel Workers*, 233, quotes a worker who said, "'The galling thing about it is the necessity of accepting in silence any treatment that the Corporation may see fit to give. We have no right to independent action, and when we are wronged there is no redress.'"

30. Daugherty et al., *Economics of the Iron and Steel Industry*, 145. The steel industry's wage structure was notoriously tangled and complex, but this was more a matter of degree than kind. Cyrus Ching, *The Reminiscences of Cyrus Ching* (New York: Oral History Research Office, Columbia University, 1973), 41, has said of the rubber industry that "salary inequities were so outstanding that it would make you shudder."

31. John Garraty, "The United States Steel Corporation versus Labor: The Early Years," *Labor History* 1 (1960): 3–38.

32. Promote-from-within policies, albeit of a relatively nonbureaucratized nature, were frequently found in American industry prior to World War I, particularly for white-collar workers and workers above the unskilled level. See William Sundstrom, "Internal Labor Markets before World War I: On-the-Job Training and Employee Promotion," *Explorations in Economic History* 25 (1998): 424–45.

33. Charles Hook, quoted in Katherine Stone, "The Origins of Job Structures in the Steel Industry," *Review of Radical Economics* 6, no. 2 (1974): 113–73.

34. Fitch, *The Steel Workers*, 148–49.

35. A review of the welfare activities at the USSC by the director of the program is given in Charles Close, *Welfare Work in the Steel Industry*, address to the American Iron and Steel Institute (New York: n.p., 1920); see also Gulick, *Labor Policy of the United States Steel Corporation*, chap. 5,; Rees, *Managing the Mills*, chap. 4. The company estimated it spent $158,000,000 on welfare programs between 1911 and 1925; Harvey Levenstein, "The Labor Policy of the United States Steel Corporation 1920–1927," M.A. thesis, University of Wisconsin, 1962, 95.

36. Elbert Gary, quoted in Stone, "The Origins of Job Structures in the Steel Industry," 141.

37. Stone, "The Origins of Job Structures in the Steel Industry," 137.

38. George Perkins, quoted in Rees, *Managing the Mills*, 118.

39. Rees, *Managing the Mills*, 113.

40. Don Lescohier, "The Campaign for Health and Safety in Industry," in *History of Labor in the United States 1896–1932*, vol. 3, ed. John Commons (New York: Macmillan, 1935), 359–70; Mark Aldrich, *Safety First: Technology, Labor, and Business in the Building of American Work Safety 1870–1939* (Baltimore: Johns Hopkins University Press, 1997), 91–93, chap. 4; Brody, *Steel Workers in America*, 167–68.

41. Horace David, *Labor and Steel* (New York: International, 1931), 31.

42. Elbert Gary, quoted in Rees, *Managing the Mills*, 122.

43. John Fitch, "Illinois: Boosting for Safety," *Survey*, November 4, 1911, 1148–57.

44. Aldrich, *Safety First*, 310–11.

45. Ibid., 93–104.

46. Gulick, *Labor Policy of the United States Steel Corporation*, 141. According to Harold Faulkner, *The Decline of Laissez Faire* (New York: Reinhart, 1951), 270–72, the first pension in the United States was set up 1875 by the American Express Company but the real beginning of the pension movement was after 1910. Faulkner dates the beginning of employee stock ownership to 1893 on the Illinois Central Railroad.

47. A general critique of early pension plans is provided in John Fitch, "For Value Received: A Discussion of Industrial Pensions," *Survey*, May 25, 1918, 221–24.

48. Rees, *Managing the Mills*, 120.

49. Gulick, *Labor Policy of the United States Steel Corporation*, chap. 6.

50. Fitch, *The Steel Workers*, chap. 1.

51. Ibid., chap. 16; Gulick, *Labor Policy of the United States Steel Corporation*, chap. 4

52. See S. Adele Shaw, "Closed Towns," *Survey*, November 8, 1919, 58–64, 87–93.

53. William Ghent, *Our Benevolent Feudalism* (New York: Macmillan, 1902); William Hard, "Labor in the Chicago Stockyards," *Outlook* 83 (1906): 366–73.

54. Fitch, *The Steel Workers*, 214.

55. Ibid., 216.

56. Brody, *Steel Workers in America*, chap. 6; Rees, *Managing the Mills*, chap. 3.

57. In times of threat and crisis, industry executives united around Gary's strategic approach to labor, but in other periods a minority of executives counseled a more humane and participative approach. See Eggert, *Steelmasters and Labor Reform*.

58 Daugherty et al., *Economics of the Iron and Steel Industry*, 187, 1077.

59. Close, *Welfare Work in the Steel Industry*, 5; Industrial Relations Counselors, Inc., *Report on Industrial Relations in [Steel Company "X"]* (name omitted to preserve anonymity) (New York: IRC, 1930).

60. Partial exceptions are one-page articles on the employment department at the Cincinnati Milling Machine Company (a tool producer rather than a steel firm) and Fore River Shipbuilding Company. See "Employment and Service," *Iron Age*, November 16, 1916, 1123; and "Improving the Personnel," *Iron Age*, May 18, 1916, 1198.

61. "An Efficient Labor Bureau," *Iron Age*, September 22, 1910, 671; and "Labor Bureaus as Shop Employment Offices," *Iron Age*, July 28, 1910, 183. Also see Howell Harris, *Bloodless Victories: The Rise and Fall of the Open Shop in the Philadelphia Metal Trades, 1890–1940* (Cambridge: Cambridge University Press, 2000), 103–12, 184–87.

62. See Gulick, *Labor Policy of the United States Steel Corporation*, 144.

63. Williams, *What's on the Worker's Mind*, 11–12.

64. Daniel Nelson, "The Company Union Movement 1900–1937: A Reexamination," *Business History Review* 54 (1982): 335–57; Bruce Kaufman, "Accomplishments and Shortcomings of Nonunion Employee Representation in the Pre–Wagner Act Years: A Reassessment," in *Nonunion Employee Representation: History, Contemporary Practice and Policy*, ed. Bruce Kaufman and Daphne Taras (Armonk, NY: M. E. Sharpe, 2000), 21–60.

65. Rees, *Managing the Mills*, 161–72; Eggert, *Steelmasters and Labor Reform*, chap. 5; Melvin Urofsky, *Big Steel and the Wilson Administration* (Columbus: Ohio University Press, 1969), chap. 7.

66. "Larkin Elected I.R.A.A. President," *Personnel* 2 (1920): 1. Bethlehem had earlier established an employment department that supervised safety and welfare. See "Five Years of Employee Representation under 'The Bethlehem Plan,'" *Iron Age*, June 14, 1923, 1689–92.

67. Stephen Scheinberg, *The Development of Corporation Labor Policy, 1900–1940* (New York: Garland, 1986); Sanford Jacoby, *Employing Bureaucracy*, rev. ed. (Mahwah, NJ: Lawrence Erlbaum, 2004), 135–36; "Larkin Elected I.R.A.A. President."

68. David Brody, *Labor in Crisis: The Steel Strike of 1919* (New York: Lippincott, 1965).

69. Brody, *Steel Workers in America*, chap. 12; Rees, *Managing the Mills*, chaps. 6–8.

6. HRM in the Industrial Heartland II: The Ford Motor Company

1. Joyce Shaw Peterson, *American Automobile Workers 1900–1933* (Albany: State University of New York Press, 1987).

2. Allan Nevins, *Ford: The Times, the Man, the Company* (New York: Scribner's, 1954), 568.

3. David Lewis, *The Public Image of Henry Ford: An American Folk Hero and His Company* (Detroit: Wayne State University Press, 1976); Mary Nolan, *Visions of Modernity: American Business and the Modernization of Germany* (New York: Oxford University Press, 1994).

4. David Hounshell, *From the American System to Mass Production 1800–1932* (Baltimore: Johns Hopkins University Press, 1984), chap. 6.

5. Nevins, *Ford: The Times, the Man, the Company*, 541.

6. Stephen Meyer III, *The Five Dollar Day: Labor Management and Social Control in the Ford Motor Company, 1908–1921* (Albany: State University of New York Press, 1981), chap. 2; David Gartman, *Auto Slavery: The Labor Process in the American Automobile Industry, 1897–1950* (New Brunswick, NJ: Rutgers University Press, 1986), chap. 2.

7. Meyer, *The Five Dollar Day*, 19–21; Clarence Hooker, *Life in the Shadows of the Crystal Palace, 1910–1927: Ford Workers in the Model T Era* (Bowling Green, OH: Bowling Green State University Popular Press, 1997), 20–21.

8. Nevins, *Ford: The Times, the Man, the Company*, 583.

9. Meyer, *The Five Dollar Day*, 16.

10. John Fitch and others, quoted in Ibid., 38–39, 41.

11. Quoted in Ibid., 71.

12. Samuel Levin, "Ford Profit Sharing, 1914–1920, I. The Growth of the Plan," *Personnel Journal* 6, no. 2 (1927): 75.

13. Quoted in Meyer, *The Five Dollar Day*, 103.

14. Quoted in Ibid., 103.

15. Hooker, *Life in the Shadows of the Crystal Palace*, 110.

16. Ibid., 84.

17. Ibid., 81; Levin, "Ford Profit Sharing," 76.

18. John R. Commons, *Labor and Administration* (New York: Macmillan, 1913), 365.

19. Quoted in Meyer, *The Five Dollar Day*, 89.

20. Nevins, *Ford: The Times, the Man, the Company*, 526–32; Hooker, *Life in the Shadows of the Crystal Palace*, 110–11.

21. Meyers, *The Five Dollar Day*, 101.

22. Frederick Taylor, *Shop Management* (New York: Harper and Brothers, 1903), 118–119.

23. George Bundy, "Work of the Employment Department of the Ford Motor Company," in *Proceedings of the Employment Managers' Conference*, U.S. Bureau of Labor Statistics Bulletin 196 (Washington: Government Printing Office, 1916), 63–71.

24. Horace Arnold and Fay Faurote, *Ford Methods and the Ford Shops* (New York: Arno Press, 1969), 43.

25. Ibid., 43–58.

26. O. Abell, "Labor Classified on a Skill-Wage Basis," *Iron Age* (January 1914), 48–51.

27. Gartner, *Auto Slavery*, 237.

28. John R. Lee, quoted in Meyer, *The Five Dollar Day*, 101.

29. William Chalmers, "Labor in the Automobile Industry: A Study of Personnel Policies, Workers' Attitudes and Attempts at Unionization," PhD diss., University of Wisconsin, 1932, 67–68; Levin, "Ford Profit Sharing," 84.

30. Hooker, *Life in the Shadow of the Crystal Palace*, chap. 6.

31. Nevins, *Ford: The Times, the Man, the Company*, 528.

32. Ibid., 560.

33. Peterson, *American Automobile Workers*, 26–28.

34. Levin, "Ford Profit Sharing," 85.

35. Meyer, *The Five Dollar Day*, 105.

36. Ibid., 106; John R. Commons, "Faith in People," in *Industrial Government*, ed. John R. Commons (New York: Macmillan, 1921), 25.

37. Meyer, *The Five Dollar Day*, 83; Bundy, "Work of the Employment Department of the Ford Motor Company," 72. According to Levin, "Ford Profit Sharing," 83, Ford also instituted a unique form of progressive discipline regarding tardiness. A person late to work three times in a year without a good excuse had a hearing before a panel of three impartial people and if found guilty was assessed $10–$25, which was given to charity and had to be personally delivered by the employee, who was driven there in a company car.

38. Nevins, *Ford: The Times, the Man, the Company*, 537–41; Meyer, *The Five Dollar Day*, 109.

39. Daniel M. G. Raff, "Ford Welfare Capitalism in Its Economic Context," in *From Masters to Managers*, ed. Sanford Jacoby (New York: Columbia University Press, 1991), 90–105.

40. Edward Rumely, "Ford's Plan to Share Profits," *World's Work* 27 (1914): 665.

41. Meyer, *The Five Dollar Day*, 118.

42. Ibid., 120; Nevins, *Ford: The Times, the Man, the Company*, 548.

43. Fitch, "Making the Job Worthwhile," *Survey* 40 (April 27, 1914): 88.

44. Meyer, *The Five Dollar Day*, 109.

45. Lewis, *The Public Image of Henry Ford*, 70–71; Upton Sinclair, *The Flivver King: A Story of Ford-America* (Pasadena, CA: Upton Sinclair, 1937), 28.

46. Quoted in John Fitch, "Ford of Detroit," *Survey*, February 7, 1914, 549.

47. Meyer, *The Five Dollar Day*, 118; Nevins, *Ford: The Man, the Times, the Company*, 550

48. Meyer, *The Five Dollar Day*, 116.

49. Ibid., 110.

50. Ibid., 114–17; Samuel Marquis, *Henry Ford: An Interpretation* (Boston: Houghton-Mifflin, 1923), 148.

51. Hooker, *Living in the Shadow of the Crystal Palace*, 111.

52. Ibid., 111–12.

53. Meyers, *The Five Dollar Day*, 119.

54. Nevins, *Ford: The Times, the Man, the Company*, 556.

55. Ibid., 557.

56. Ida Tarbell, quoted in Meyer, *The Five Dollar Day*, 164.

57. Marquis, *Henry Ford: An Interpretation*; Meyer, *The Five Dollar Day*, chap. 8.

58. Gerd Korman, "Americanization at the Factory Gates," *Industrial and Labor Relations Review* 18 (1965): 396–419; Meyer, *The Five Dollar Day*, 149–61.

59. Meyer, *The Five Dollar Day*, 167–68.

60. Quoted in Ibid., 196.

61. Quoted in Ibid., 172.

62. Ibid., 41.

63. Ibid., 176.

64. Lewis, *The Public Image of Henry Ford*, 138, 248.

65. Meyer, *The Five Dollar Day*, 195–202; Murray Godwin, "The Case Against Ford," *American Mercury*, July 1931, 257–66.

7. Industrial Relations Counselors, Inc.

1. Bruce Kaufman, Richard Beaumont, and Roy Helfgott, eds., *Industrial Relations to Human Resources and Beyond: The Evolving Process of Employee Relations Management* (Armonk, NY: M. E. Sharpe, 2003); Richard Beaumont, ed., *People, Progress, and Employee Relations: Proceedings of the Fiftieth Anniversary Conference of Industrial Relations Counselors, Inc.* (Charlottesville: University Press of Virginia, 1976).

2. Henry Kendall, "The First Industrial Counselor—Robert C. Valentine, 1871–1916," *Survey*, November 25, 1916, 189–90.

3. Ordway Tead, *The Labor Audit* (Washington, DC: Federal Board for Vocational Education, 1920).

4. Bruce Kaufman, "Industrial Relations Counselors, Inc.: Its History and Significance." In Kaufman, Beaumont, and Helfgott, eds., *Industrial Relations to Human Resources and Beyond*, 31–114; Howard Gittleman, *The Legacy of the Ludlow Massacre: A Chapter in American Industrial Relations* (Philadelphia, University of Pennsylvania Press, 1988).

5. See John D. Rockefeller Jr., *The Personal Relation in Industry* (New York: Boni and Liverwright, 1923); see also William Lyon Mackenzie King, *Industry and Humanity* (Toronto: University of Toronto Press, 1918).

6. Clarence Hicks, *My Life in Industrial Relations: Fifty Years in the Growth of a Profession* (New York: Harper and Brothers, 1941).

7. George Sweet Gibb and Evelyn H. Knowlton, *History of Standard Oil Company*, vol. 2, *The Resurgent Years, 1911–1927* (New York: Harper and Brothers, 1956), 578.

8. Irving Bernstein, *Lean Years: History of the American Worker, 1920–1933* (Boston: Houghton-Mifflin), 166.

9. Kaufman, "Industrial Relations Counselors," 83–86; Sanford Jacoby, *Employing Bureaucracy: Managers, Unions and the Transformation of Work in the Twentieth Century*, rev. ed. (Mahwah, NJ: Lawrence Erlbaum, 2004).

10. See F. A. McGregor, *The Fall and Rise of Mackenzie King: 1911–1919* (Toronto: University of Toronto Press, 1962).

11. Hicks, *My Life in Industrial Relations*, 140–52; Bruce Kaufman, *The Origins and Evolution of the Field of Industrial Relations in the United States* (Ithaca, NY: Cornell University Press, ILR Press, 1993), 46.

12. Kaufman, "Industrial Relations Counselors," 60–67.

13. Bruce Kaufman, *Managing the Human Factor: The Early Development of Human Resource Management in American Industry* (Ithaca, NY: Cornell University Press, ILR Press, 2008).

14. Hicks, *My Life in Industrial Relations*, x.

15. Edward Cowdrick, "The Expanding Field of Industrial Relations," *American Management Review*, December, 1924, 3–4.

16. Kaufman, "Industrial Relations Counselors," 80.

17. Kaufman, *The Origins and Evolution of the Field of Industrial Relations in the United States*, 57.

18. John R. Commons, *Myself: The Autobiography of John R. Commons* (Madison: University of Wisconsin Press, 1934), 200.

19. Kaufman, "Industrial Relations Counselors," 89.

20. After the early 1930s the IRC reports start to shorten in length and become more focused on particular features or problem areas in the client company's IR program, thus making them less useful and informative for the type of case study portraits done here. In part this arises because for the first decade IRC received a large financial subsidy from Rockefeller and could thus engage in more in-depth research work for these reports; after the mid-1930s his support ended and IRC had to become more "bottom-line" conscious, which meant a shorter and more focused type of consulting report. The last large-scale IR survey with a more or less comprehensive review of the company's entire IR program was done in the very early 1950s. A large-scale survey was repeated over a span of years at only two oil companies, thus providing very limited opportunity to track the evolution of personnel practices over time within individual companies.

21. Kaufman, "Industrial Relations Counselors."

22. Patrick Wright and Gary McMahan, "Theoretical Perspectives for Human Resource Management," *Journal of Management* 27, no. 6 (1992), 295–320.

23. See Canby Balderston, *Executive Guidance of Industrial Relations* (Philadelphia, PA: University of Pennsylvania Press, 1935).

24. John Delery and D. Harold Doty, "Modes of Theorizing in Strategic Human Resource Management: Tests of Universalistic, Contingency, and Configurational Performance Predictions," *Academy of Management Journal* 39, no. 4 (1996): 802–35.

25. See Kaufman, "Industrial Relations Counselors"; Rockefeller, *The Personal Relation in Industry*; Hicks, *My Life in Industrial Relations*; Bruce Kaufman, "The Quest for Cooperation and Unity of Interest in Industry," in Kaufman, Beaumont, and Helfgott, eds., *Industrial Relations to Human Resources and Beyond*, 115–46; and J. Douglas Brown, "Employee Relations: A Historical Perspective." In Beaumont, ed., *People, Progress, and Employee Relations*, 19–23.

14. The Case Studies: Insights and Lessons Learned

1. See, for example, Irving Bernstein, *The Lean Years* (Boston: Houghton-Mifflin, 1960); Howard Gittelman, "Welfare Capitalism Reconsidered," *Labor History* 33 (1992): 5–31.

2. Thomas Kochan, Harry Katz, and Robert McKersie, *The Transformation of American Industrial Relations* (New York: Basic Books, 1986).

3. Peter Cappelli, et al., eds., *Change at Work* (New York: Oxford University Press, 1997).

4. The opposite point of view is presented in Leo Troy, *Beyond Unions and Collective Bargaining* (Armonk, NY: M. E. Sharpe, 1999).

5. I have developed this thesis in more detail elsewhere. See, for example, Bruce Kaufman, "The Future of U.S. Private Sector Unionism: Did George Barnett Get It Right after All?," in *The Future of Private Sector Unionism in the United States*, ed James Bennett and Bruce Kaufman (Armonk, NY: M. E. Sharpe, 2002), 330–58.

6. Bruce Kaufman, *The Global Evolution of Industrial Relations* (Geneva, Switzerland: International Labor Organization, 2004), 500–514; Sanford Jacoby, "Pacific Ties: Industrial Relations and Employment Systems in Japan and the United States," in *Industrial Democracy in America*, ed. Howell Harris and Nelson Lichtenstein (New York: Cambridge University Press, 1991), 206–48.

7. Bruce Kaufman, "The Case for the Company Union," *Labor History* 41, no. 3 (2000): 321–50; Daphne Taras, "Voice in the North American Workplace: From Employee Representation to Employee Involvement," In *Industrial Relations to Human Resources and Beyond*, ed. Bruce Kaufman, Richard Beaumont, and Ray Helfgott (Armonk, NY: M. E. Sharpe, 2003), 293–329.

8. See, for example, James Begin, *Strategic Employment Policy* (Englewood Cliffs, NJ: Prentice-Hall, 1991); and David Marsden, *A Theory of Employment Systems* (Oxford: Oxford University Press, 1999).

9. See, for example, James Duhlebon, Gerald Ferris, and James Stodd, "The History and Evolution of Human Resource Management," in *Handbook of Human Resource Management*, eds., Gerald Ferris, Sherman Rosen, and Donald Barnum (Cambridge, MA: Blackwell, 1995), 19–41.

10. John R. Commons, *Industrial Goodwill* (New York: McGraw-Hill, 1919).

11. Mick Marchington and Stefan Zagelmeyer, "Forward: Linking HRM and Performance—A Never-Ending Search? *Human Resource Management Journal*, 15, no. 4 (2006): 4, observes, for example, "While it is rare to state this explicitly, most studies looking at the HRM-performance linkage use some variant of the high-performance model"; while Brian Becker and Mark Huselid, "Strategic Human Resource Management: Where Do We Go From Here?" *Journal of Management*, 32, no. 6 (2006): 903, states that "these approaches are all variations on the best practice story." See also Jeffrey Pfeffer, *The Human Equation* (Boston: Harvard Business School Press, 1998).

12. Peter Boxall and John Purcell, *Strategy and Human Resource Management* (Basingstoke, England: Palgrave Macmillan, 2003).

13. Patrick Wright and Gary McMahan, "Theoretical Perspectives for Human Resource Management," *Journal of Management* 18, no. 2 (1992): 295–320.

14. Matthew Allen and Patrick Wright, "Strategic Management and HRM," in *Oxford Handbook of Human Resource Management*, ed. Peter Boxall, John Purcell, and Patrick Wright (Oxford: Oxford University Press, 2007), 88–107.

15. Bernstein, *The Lean Years*; Gittelman, "Welfare Capitalism Reconsidered."

16. Daniel Wren, *The History of Management Thought*, 5th ed. (Hoboken, NJ: John Wiley, 2005).

17. Kaufman, "The Case for the Company Union."

18. Hal Varian, *Intermediate Microeconomics*, 5th ed. (New York: W. W. Norton, 1999).

19. Frederick Taylor, *The Principles of Scientific Management* (New York: Harper, 1911).

20. Kaufman, *The Global Evolution of Industrial Relations.*

Photo Credits

1.   Haines Photo Co., Conneaut, Ohio, 1910, Library of Congress no. LC-USZ62-128840.

2.   From the William J. Gaughan Collection, Archives Service Center, University of Pittsburgh.

3–4.   Charles L. Close, *Welfare Work in the Steel Industry.* An address by Close, manager of the Bureau of Safety, Sanitation, and Welfare, United States Steel Corporation, at the annual meeting of the American Iron and Steel Institute, The Commodore Hotel, New York City, May 28, 1920.

5–6.   *Pittsburgh Survey*, vol. 6, *Wage Earning Pittsburgh,* ed. Paul U. Kellogg (New York: Russell Sage Foundation Publications, 1914).

7–10.   From the collections of The Henry Ford.

11.   George F. Johnson Memorial Library, Endicott, New York.

12.   The George Meany Memorial Archives.

13.   Bessemer Historical Society, CF&I Archives, Pueblo, Colorado. Employee Relations Group, INR-ERP-0001.

14.   Abraham Lincoln Historical Digitization Project, Chicago Historical Society (accessed at http://en.wikipedia.org/wiki/File:Pullman_strikers_outside_Arcade_Building.jpg).

15–18.   Western Reserve Historical Society.

19, 21, 22.   From the collection of David Johnson.

20.   Underwood & Underwood, New York, 1913, Library of Congress no. LC-USZ62-10107.

Index

Page numbers in *italics* refer to figures and tables.